Collins Gem

French

Phrase Book

D0773828

CONSULTANT
Josiane Nicolas

GEM PHRASE BOOKS

DUTCH

FRENCH

GERMAN

GREEK

ITALIAN

PORTUGUESE

SPANISH

*Also available Gem Phrase
Book CD Packs*

First published 1993
This edition published 2003
Copyright © HarperCollins Publishers
Reprint 10 9 8 7 6 5 4 3 2
Printed in Italy by Amadeus S.p.A

www.collins.co.uk

ISBN 0-00-714174-2

Your *Collins Gem Phrase Book* is designed to help you locate the exact phrase you need in any situation, whether for holiday or business. If you want to adapt the phrases, we have made sure that you can easily see where to substitute your own words (you can find them in the dictionary section), and the clear, two-colour layout gives you direct access to the different topics.

The *Gem Phrase Book* includes:

■ Over 70 topics arranged thematically. Each phrase is accompanied by a simple pronunciation guide which ensures that there's no problem over pronouncing the foreign words.

■ Practical hints and useful vocabulary highlighted in boxes. Where no article (**le/la/un/une**) is given you will generally see the word written down on signs. We give the pronunciation for all words.

WORDS APPEARING IN BLACK ARE ENGLISH WORDS	WORDS APPEARING IN BLUE ARE FRENCH WORDS

■ Possible phrases you may hear in reply to your questions. The foreign phrases appear in blue.

■ A clearly laid-out 5000-word dictionary: English words appear in black and French words appear in blue.

■ A basic grammar section which will enable you to build on your phrases.

It's worth spending time before you embark on your travels just looking through the topics to see what is covered and becoming familiar with what might be said to you.

Whatever the situation, your *Gem Phrase Book* is sure to help!

CONTENTS

PRONOUNCING FRENCH

In this book we have used a simple system to help you pronounce the phrases. We have designed the book so that as you read the pronunciation of the phrases you can follow the French. This will help you to recognize the different sounds and enable you to read French without relying on the guide. Here are a few rules you should know:

FRENCH	SOUNDS LIKE	EXAMPLE	PRONUNCIATION
■ é	ay	été	aytay
■ È	eh	très	treh
■ c (+ a, o, u)	ka, ko, ku	cas, col, cure	ka, kol, koor
■ c (+ e, i), ç	s	ceci, leçon	suhsee, luhsoñ
■ ch	sh	chat	sha
■ eu	uh	neuf	nuhf
■ eau	oh	beau	boh
■ u	oo	sur	soor
■ g (+ e, i)	zhe, zhee	gel, gîte	zhel, zheet
■ gn	ny	saignant	say-nyoñ
■ oi	wa	roi	rwa
■ ui	wee	huit	weet

e is sometimes weak and sounds like uh. This happens either in very short words (je zhuh, le luh, se suh, etc.), or when the e falls at the end of a syllable:
retard ruhtar, **demain** duhmañ.

h is not pronounced: **hôtel** ohtel, **homard** omar.

There are nasal vowels in French (represented by **ñ**):
un uñ, **fin** fañ, **on** oñ, **dans** doñ, **bain** bañ, **en** oñ.

Final consonants are often silent: **Paris** pa-ree, **Londres** loñdr. However, sometimes the ending is pronounced if it is followed by a word which begins with a vowel:
avez-vous avay voo **but vous avez** vooz avay.

You will find the French quite formal in their greetings, shaking hands both on meeting and parting. **Bonjour, madame** or **bonjour, monsieur** are the politest ways to greet someone. **Mademoiselle** is becoming less frequently used. **Salut** is more informal than **bonjour** If someone offers you something, perhaps an extra serving of food, and you simply reply **merci**, they would take this to mean 'no'. You must say **oui, merci** otherwise you will go hungry!

Please	**Thanks (very much)**	**You're welcome!**
S'il vous plaît	Merci (beaucoup)	De rien!
seel voo pleh	*mehrsee (bohkoo)*	*duh ryañ*

Yes	**No**	**Yes, please**	**No, thanks**	**OK!**
Oui	Non	Oui, merci	Non, merci	D'accord!
wee	*noñ*	*wee mehrsee*	*noñ merhsee*	*dakor*

Sir / Mr	**Madam / Mrs / Ms**	**Miss**
Monsieur / M.	Madame / Mme	Mademoiselle / Mlle
muhsyuh	*madam*	*mad-mwa-zel*

Hello / Hi	**Goodbye / Bye**	**Bye for now**
Bonjour / Salut	Au revoir / Salut	À bientôt
boñ-zhoor/saloo	*oh ruhvwahr/saloo*	*a byañtoh*

Good evening	**Goodnight**	**See you tomorrow**
Bonsoir	Bonne nuit	À demain
boñswar	*bon nwee*	*a duhmañ*

Excuse me! *(to catch attention)*	**Sorry!**	**I'm sorry**
Pardon, monsieur / madame!	Pardon!	je suis désolé(e)
pardoñ muhsyuh / madam	*pardoñ*	*zhuh swee dayzolay*

How are you?	**Fine, thanks**	**And you?**
Comment allez-vous?	Très bien, merci	Et vous?
komoñ talay voo	*tray byañ mehrsee*	*ay voo*

I don't understand	**I speak very little French**
Je ne comprends pas	Je parle très peu le français
zhuh nuh koñproñ pa	*zhuh parl treh puh luh froñsay*

You don't need to say complicated things to get what you want. Often simply naming the thing and adding s'il vous plaît, will do the trick. Even when asking for directions.

the (masculine)
le
luh

(feminine)
la
la

(plural)
les
lay

the museum
le musée
luh moo-zay

the station
la gare
la gar

the shops
les magasins
lay maga-zañ

a/one (masculine)
un
uñ

(feminine)
une
oon

a ticket / one stamp
un billet / un timbre
uñ bee-yay / uñ tañbr

a room / one bottle
une chambre / une bouteille
oon shoñbr / oon bootay-yuh

some (masculine)
du
doo

(feminine)
de la
duh la

(plural)
des
day

some wine
du vin
doo vañ

some jam
de la confiture
duh la koñfeetoor

some chips
des frites
day freet

Do you have...?
Est-ce que vous avez...? or
es kuh vooz avay...

Do you have...?
Vous avez...?
vooz avay...

Do you have a room?
Est-ce que vous avez une chambre?
es kuh vooz avay oon shoñbr

Do you have some milk?
Vous avez du lait?
vooz avay doo leh

I'd like...
je voudrais...
zhuh voodray...

We'd like...
Nous voudrions...
noo voodree-oñ...

I'd like an ice cream
je voudrais une glace
zhuh voodray oon glas

We'd like to visit Paris
Nous voudrions visiter Paris
noo voodree-oñ veezeetay pa-ree

Some more...
Encore du/de la/des...
oñkor doo/duh la/day...

Another...
Un/Une autre...
uñ/oon ohtr...

Some more bread
Encore du pain
oñkor doo pañ

Some more soup
Encore de la soupe
oñkor duh la soop

Some more glasses
Encore des verres
oñkor day vehr

Another coffee
Un autre café
uñ ohtr kafay

Another beer
Une autre bière
oon ohtr byer

How much is it?
C'est combien?
say koñbyañ

How much is the room?
C'est combien la chambre?
say koñbyañ la shonbr

large/small
grand/petit
groñ/puhtee

with/without
avec/sans
avek/soñ

Where is/are...?
Où est/sont...?
oo eh/soñ...

the nearest
le/la plus proche
luh/la ploo prosh

How do I get...?
Pour aller...?
poor alay...

to the museum
au musée
oh muzay

to the station
à la gare
a la gar

to Brioude
à Brioude
a Brioude

There is/are...
Il y a...
eel ya...

There isn't/aren't any...
Il n'y a pas de...
eel nee a pah duh...

When...?
Quand...?
koñ...

At what time...?
À quelle heure...?
a kel uhr...

today
aujourd'hui
oh-zhoor-dwee

tomorrow
demain
duhmañ

Can I...?
Est-ce que je peux...?
es kuh zhuh puh...

smoke
fumer
foomay

taste it
l'essayer
les-say-yay

How does this work?
Comment ça marche?
komoñ sa marsh

What does this mean?
Qu'est-ce que ça veut dire?
kes kuh sa vuh deer

9

Entrée entrance	**Sortie** exit
Ouvert open	**Fermé** closed

chaud hot	froid cold

TIREZ pull	**POUSSEZ** push

à droite right	à gauche left

Eau Potable
drinking water

Dégustation de vin
wine tasting

Prière de...
please...

à emporter
take-away

libre
free, vacant

occupé
engaged

libre-service
self-service

DAMES ladies	HOMMES gents
	MESSIEURS

Hors service
out of order

CAISSE
cash desk

Baignade Interdite
no bathing

à louer — for hire / to rent

à vendre — for sale

soldes — sale

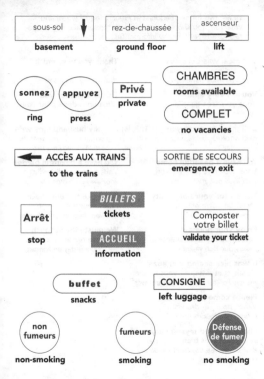

sous-sol ↓	rez-de-chaussée	ascenseur →
basement	**ground floor**	**lift**

sonnez **appuyez** **Privé**

ring **press** **private**

CHAMBRES
rooms available

COMPLET
no vacancies

← **ACCÈS AUX TRAINS**
to the trains

SORTIE DE SECOURS
emergency exit

BILLETS
tickets

Arrêt
stop

Composter
votre billet
validate your ticket

ACCUEIL
information

buffet
snacks

CONSIGNE
left luggage

non
fumeurs
non-smoking

fumeurs
smoking

Défense
de fumer
no smoking

11

There are two forms of address in French, formal (vous) and informal (tu). You should always stick to the formal until you are invited to tutoyer (use the informal tu).

The meal was delicious
Le repas était délicieux
luh ruhpa aytay dayleesyuh

Vou are very kind
Vous êtes très gentil(le)
vooz et tray zhoñtee(-yuh)

Delighted to meet you
Enchanté(e)
oñshoñtay

You have a beautiful home
Vous avez une jolie maison
vooz avay oon zholee mayzoñ

Thanks for your hospitality
Merci de votre accueil
mehrsee duh votr akuy

Enjoy your holiday!
Passez de bonnes vacances!
passay duh bon va-koñs

It was nice seeing you again
J'étais content(e) de vous revoir
zhaytay koñ-toñ(te) duh voo ruh-vwar

Please come and visit us
Venez nous rendre visite
vuhnay noo roñdr veezeet

I have enjoyed myself very much
Je me suis très bien amusé(e)
zhuh muh swee tray byañ a-moo-zay

Thank you very much
Je vous remercie
zhuh voo ruh-mehrsee

This is a gift for you
C'est un cadeau pour vous
say uñ kadoh poor voo

This is... **my husband / my wife**
Voici... mon mari / ma femme
vwasee... moñ maree / ma fam

You have a beautiful garden
Vous avez un joli jardin
vooz avay uñ zholee zhar-dañ

We'd like to come back
Nous voudrions revenir
noo voo-dree-oñ ruh-vuh-neer

We must stay in touch
Il faudra rester en contact
eel fohdra restay oñ koñtakt

see also **EXCHANGE VISITORS**

Christmas celebrations revolve more around food than presents. They start on Christmas Eve (réveillon de Noël) with a lavish meal (often seafood) and lasting many hours. The main course for the actual Christmas lunch is usually goose or turkey followed by the traditional desert, a bûche de Noël (Christmas log). Families start the celebrations with an apéritif before the meal with elaborate nibbles. Champagne sometimes replaces the usual apéritif drinks.

I'd like to wish you a...
Je vous souhaite un/une...
zhuh voo soo-ayt uñ/oon...

Merry Christmas!
Joyeux Noël!
zhwa-yuh noel

Happy New Year!
Bonne Année!
bon anay

Happy Easter!
Joyeuses Pâques!
zhwa-yuz pak

Happy (Saint's) Name Day!
Bonne Fête!
bon feht

Happy birthday!
Bon anniversaire!
bon anee-vehrsehr

Congratulations!
Félicitations!
faylee-seeta-syoñ

Have a good trip!
Bon voyage!
bon vwa-yazh

Welcome!
Bienvenue!
byañ-vuhnoo

Best wishes!
Meilleurs vœux!
may-yur vuh

Good luck!
Bonne chance!
bon shoñs

Enjoy your meal!
Bon appétit!
bon apaytee

Thanks, and the same to you!
Merci, à vous aussi!
mehrsee a vooz ohsee

Cheers!
À votre santé! / À la vôtre!
a votr soñtay / a la votr

see also **MAKING FRIENDS** ☐ **LETTERS**

13

*In this section we have used the familiar form **tu** for the questions.*

What's your name?
Comment tu t'appelles?
komoñ too tapel

My name is...
Je m'appelle...
zhuh mapel...

How old are you?
Quel âge as-tu?
kel azh a too

I'm ... years old
J'ai ... ans
zhay ... oñ

Are you French?
Tu es français(e)?
too eh froñseh(z)

I'm English / Scottish / American
Je suis anglais(e) / écossais(e) / américain(e)
zhuh swee oñgleh(-z) / aykoseh(z) / amayreekañ(ken)

Where do you live?
Où est-ce que tu habites?
oo es kuh too abeet

Where do you live? *(plural)*
Où est-ce que vous habitez?
oo es kuh vooz abeetay

I live in London
J'habite à Londres
zhabeet a loñdruh

We live in Glasgow
Nous habitons à Glasgow
nooz abeetoñ a glasgow

I'm still at school
Je suis encore à l'école
zhuh swee oñkor a laykol

I work
Je travaille
zhuh travye

I'm retired
Je suis à la retraite
zhuh sweez a la ruhtret

I'm...	single	married	divorced
Je suis...	célibataire	marié(e)	divorcé(e)
zhuh swee...	*sayleeba-tehr*	*maryay*	*deevor-say*

I have...	a boyfriend	a girlfriend
J'ai...	un petit ami	une petite amie
zhay...	*uñ puhteet amee*	*oon puhteet amee*

I have a partner *(male/female)*
J'ai un compagnon / une compagne
zhay uñ kompahn-yoñ / oon kompahn-yuh

I'm here on holiday / on business / for the weekend
Je suis ici en vacances / en voyage d'affaires / en week-end
zhuh sweez eesee oñ vakoñs / oñ vwayazh dafehr / oñ weekend

see also **WORK** ☐ **LEISURE/INTERESTS** ☐ **SPORT**

What work do you do?
Qu'est-ce que vous faites comme travail?
kes kuh voo feht kom tra-vye

Do you enjoy it?
Ça vous plaît?
sa voo pleh

I'm... | **a doctor** | **a manager** | **a secretary**
Je suis... | médecin | directeur | secrétaire
zhuh swee... | *maydsañ* | *deerek-tur* | *suhkray-tehr*

I work in... | **a shop** | **a factory** | **the City**
Je travaille dans... | un magasin | une usine | les affaires
zhuh tra-vye doñ... | *uñ maga-zañ* | *oon oozeen* | *layz afehr*

I work from home
Je travaille à domicile
zhuh tra-vye a domee-seel

I'm self-employed
Je travaille à mon compte
zhuh tra-vye a moñ koñt

I have been unemployed for... | **months** | **years**
Je suis au chômage depuis... | mois | ans
zhuh swee oh shohmazh duhpwee... | *mwa* | *oñ*

It's very difficult to get a job at the moment
C'est très difficile de trouver un emploi en ce moment
say treh deefee-seel duh troovay uñ oñplwa oñ suh momoñ

What are your hours?
quelles heures faites-vous?
kel zur feht voo

I work from 9 to 5
Je travaille de 9 heures à 5 heures
zhuh tra-vye duh nuhf ur a sañk ur

from Monday to Friday
du lundi au vendredi
doo luñdee oh voñdruh-dee

How much holiday do you get?
Vous avez combien de vacances?
vooz avay koñ-byañ duh vakoñs

What do you want to be when you grow up?
Qu'est-ce que tu vas faire quand tu seras plus grand(e)?
kes kuh too va fehr koñ too suh-ra ploo groñ(d)

see also **MAKING FRIENDS** ☐ **BUSINESS**

WEATHER

TEMPS VARIABLE *toñ varee-abl*	CHANGEABLE WEATHER
BEAU *boh*	FINE
TEMPS ORAGEUX *toñ orazhuh*	THUNDERY WEATHER
COUVERT *koovehr*	CLOUDY

It's sunny
Il y a du soleil
eel ya doo solay-yuh

It's raining
Il pleut
eel pluh

It's snowing
Il neige
eel nezh

It's windy
Il y a du vent
eel ya doo voñ

What a lovely day!
Quelle belle journée!
kel bel zhoornay

What awful weather!
Quel mauvais temps!
kel moveh toñ

What do you think the weather will be like tomorrow?
Quel temps croyez-vous qu'il fera demain?
kel toñ krwa-yay voo keel fuh-ra duhmañ

Do you think it's going to rain?
Vous croyez qu'il va pleuvoir?
voo krwa-yay keel va pluhvwar

Do I need an umbrella?
J'ai besoin d'un parapluie?
zhay buhzwañ duñ para-plwee

When will it stop raining?
Quand va-t-il arrêter de pleuvoir?
koñ vat-eel areh-tay duh pluhvwar

It's very hot / cold
Il fait très chaud / froid
eel feh treh shoh / frwa

What is the temperature?
Quelle température fait-il?
kel toñpay-ratoor feh-teel

Do you think it will snow?
Vous pensez qu'il va neiger?
voo poñsay keel va neh-zhay

Do you think there will be a storm?
Vous croyez qu'il va y avoir un orage?
voo krwa-yay keel va ee avwar uñ orazh

see also **MAKING FRIENDS**

EN FACE DE *oñ fas duh*	**OPPOSITE**
À CÔTÉ DE *a kotay duh*	**NEXT TO**
PRÈS DE *preh duh*	**NEAR TO**
LES FEUX *lay fuh*	**TRAFFIC LIGHTS**
LE CARREFOUR *luh karfoor*	**CROSSROAD**
LE ROND-POINT *luh roñ-pwañ*	**ROUNDABOUT**

Excuse me, sir / madam!
Pardon, monsieur / madame!
pardoñ muhsyuh / madam

How do I get to...?
Pour aller à/au (etc.)...?
poor alay a/oh...

to the station
à la gare
a la gar

to the Louvre
au Louvre
oh loovr

Is it far?
C'est loin?
say lwañ

We're looking for...
Nous cherchons...
noo shehrshoñ...

Can we walk there?
On peut y aller à pied?
oñ puh ee alay a pyay

We're lost
Nous nous sommes perdus
noo noo som perdoo

Is this the right way to...?
C'est la bonne direction pour...?
say la bon deerek-syoñ poor...

How do I get onto the motorway?
Pour rejoindre l'autoroute, s'il vous plaît?
poor ruhzhwañdr lohto-root seel voo pleh

Can you show me on the map?
Pouvez-vous me montrer sur la carte?
poovay voo me moñtray soor la kart

■ **YOU MAY HEAR**

Tournez à gauche / à droite
toornay a gohsh / a drwat
Turn left / right

Continuez tout droit
konteenoo-ay too drwa
Keep straight on

C'est indiqué
say añdee-kay
It's signposted

C'est au coin de la rue
say oh kwañ duh la roo
It's on the corner of the street

see also **MAPS & GUIDES**

UN TICKET DE BUS *uñ teekay duh boos*	**A BUS TICKET**
UN CARNET DE TICKETS *uñ karnay duh teekay*	**A BOOK OF TICKETS**
LA GARE ROUTIÈRE *la gar rootyehr*	**BUS STATION**

Is there a bus to...?
Est-ce qu'il y a un bus pour...?
es keel ya uñ boos poor...

Which route is it?
C'est quelle ligne?
say kel lee-nyuh

Where do I catch the bus to go to...?
Où est-ce qu'on prend le bus pour aller à/au *(etc.)*...?
oo es koñ proñ luh boos poor alay a/oh...

Where can I buy bus tickets?
Où est-ce que je peux acheter des tickets de bus?
oo es kuh zhuh puh ashtay day teekay d-boos

How much is it to...?
C'est combien pour aller à/au *(etc.)*...?
say koñ-byañ poor alay a/oh...

to the centre
au centre
oh soñtr

to the beach
à la plage
a la plazh

to the shops
aux magasins
oh maga-zañ

to Montmartre
à Montmartre
a moñmartr

How often are the buses to...?
Les bus pour ... passent tous les combien?
lay boos poor ... pass too lay koñ-byañ

When is the first / the last bus to...?
À quelle heure part le premier / le dernier bus pour...?
a kel ur par luh pruhm-yay / luh dehr-nyay boos poor...

Could you tell me when to get off?
Pourriez-vous me dire quand descendre?
pooree-ay-voo muh deer koñ dessoñdr

Please let me off
Arrêtez, s'il vous plaît
areh-tay seel voo pleh

This is my stop
C'est mon arrêt
say moñ areh

18   see also **METRO** ☐ **TAXI** ☐ **LUGGAGE**

*In Paris ticket options include **un carnet de dix tickets** (a book of 10 tickets) which can be used on metro, bus and RER (suburban lines) or **un billet de tourisme** which covers 7 days' travel.*

ENTRÉE *oñtray*	**ENTRANCE**
SORTIE *sortee*	**WAY OUT/EXIT**
LA LIGNE DE MÉTRO *la lee-nyuh duh maytro*	**METRO LINE**
EN DIRECTION DE... *oñ deerek-syoñ duh...*	**IN THE DIRECTION OF...**
CORRESPONDANCE *korespoñdoñs*	**CONNECTING LINE**

Where is the nearest metro?
Où est la station de métro la plus proche?
oo eh la sta-syoñ duh maytro la ploo prosh

I'm going to...
Je vais à...
zhuh veh a...

How does the ticket machine work?
Comment-est-ce que marche le guichet automatique?
komoñ es kuh marsh luh ghee-sheh ohto-mateek

Do you have a map of the metro?
Vous avez un plan du métro?
vooz avay uñ ploñ doo maytro

How do I get to...?
Pour aller à/au *(etc.)*...?
poor alay a/oh...

Do I have to change?
Est-ce qu'il faut changer?
es keel foh shoñ-zhay

Which line is it for...?
C'est quelle ligne pour...?
say kel lee-nyuh poor...

In which direction?
Dans quelle direction?
doñ kel deerek-syoñ

What is the next stop?
Quel est le prochain arrêt?
kel eh luh proshañ areh

Excuse me! This is my stop
Pardon! C'est mon arrêt
pardoñ say moñ areh

I want to get off
Je voudrais descendre ici
zhuh voodray dessoñdr eesee

see also **BUS & COACH** ☐ **TAXI** ☐ **LUGGAGE**

Before you catch your train, you must validate your ticket in the machines situated on the platforms and which carry the warning **n'oubliez pas de composter votre billet**. *Failing to do so could result in a fine that is more than the cost of the ticket. You can book tickets on the French railways website* **www.sncf.com**.

HORAIRE *ohrehr*	TIMETABLE
CIRCULER *seerkoolay*	TO OPERATE
TOUS LES JOURS *too lay zhoor*	DAILY
SAUF *sohf*	EXCEPT FOR
À PARTIR DE *a parteer duh*	FROM
JUSQU'AU *zhuskoh*	UNTIL
DIMANCHES ET FÊTES *deemoñsh eh feht*	SUNDAYS AND HOLIDAYS
ACCÈS AUX QUAIS *aksay oh kay*	TO THE PLATFORMS

When is the next train to...?
Quand part le prochain train pour...?
koñ par luh proshañ trañ poor...

Two return tickets to...
Deux allers-retours pour...
duhz alay-ruhtoor poor...

A single to...
Un aller simple pour...
uñ alay sañpl poor...

First class / Second class
Première classe / Deuxième classe
pruhm-yehr klas / duh-zyem klas

Smoking / Non smoking
Fumeur / Non fumeur
foo-mur / noñ foo-mur

Is there a supplement to pay?
Y a-t-il un supplément à payer?
ee a-teel uñ sooplay-moñ a pay-yay

I want to book a seat on the TGV to Nîmes
Je voudrais réserver une place dans le TGV pour Nîmes
zhuh voodray rayzehr-vay oon plas doñ luh tay zhay vay poor neem

When is the train to...?
Le train pour ... est à quelle heure?
luh trañ poor ... eh ta kel ur

the first / the last
le premier / le dernier
luh pruhm-yay / luh dehr-nyay

When does it arrive in...?
À quelle heure arrive-t-il à...?
a kel ur a-reev-teel a...

Do I have to change?
Est-ce qu'il faut changer?
es keel foh shoñ-zhay

How long do I have to catch the connection?
Combien de temps est-ce que j'ai pour ma correspondance?
koñ-byañ duh toñ es kuh zhay poor ma kores-poñdoñs

Which platform does it leave from?
Il part de quel quai?
eel par duh kel kay

Is this the right platform for the train to Paris?
C'est le bon quai pour le train de Paris?
say luh boñ kay poor luh trañ duh paree

Is this the train for...?
C'est le train pour...?
say luh trañ poor...

When does it leave?
Il part à quelle heure?
eel par a kel ur

Why is the train delayed?
Pourquoi est-ce que le train a du retard?
poor-kwa es kuh luh trañ a doo ruhtar

Does the train stop at...?
Est-ce que le train s'arrête à...?
es kuh luh trañ sareht a...

Where do I change for...?
Où dois-je changer pour...?
oo dwa-zhuh shoñ-zhay poor...

Please tell me when we get to...
S'il vous plaît, prévenez-moi quand nous serons à...
seel voo pleh pray-vnay mwa koñ noo suh-roñs a...

Where do I collect prepaid tickets from?
Où est-ce que je peux récupérer mes billets achetés d'avance?
oo es kuh zhuh puh raykoopayray may beeyay ash-tay davoñs

Is this seat free?
Cette place est-elle libre?
set plas eh-tel leebr

Excuse me
Excusez-moi
ekskoozay-mwa

Sorry!
Pardon!
pardoñ

see also **LUGGAGE** ☐ **TAXI**

TAXI

LA STATION DE TAXIS *la sta-syoñ duh taksee*   TAXI RANK

I want a taxi
Je voudrais un taxi
zhuh voodray uñ taksee

Where can I get a taxi?
Où est-ce que je peux prendre un taxi?
oo es kuh zhuh puh proñdr uñ taksee

Please order me a taxi
Pouvez-vous m'appeler un taxi?
poovay voo ma-play uñ taksee

straight away
tout de suite
too d-sweet

for *(time)*
pour...
poor...

How much is it going to cost to go to...?
Combien ça va coûter pour aller à/au *(etc.)*...?
koñ-byañ sa va kootay poor alay a/oh...

to the centre
au centre-ville
oh soñtr veel

to the station
à la gare
a la gar

to the airport
à l'aéroport
a la-ayro-por

to this address
à cette adresse
a set adress

How much is it?
C'est combien?
say koñ-byañ

Why is it so much?
Pourquoi c'est si cher?
poor-kwa say see shehr

It's more than on the meter
C'est plus qu'au compteur
say ploos koh koñ-tur

Keep the change
Gardez la monnaie
garday la monay

Sorry, I don't have any change
Je suis désolé(e), je n'ai pas de monnaie
zhuh swee dayzo-lay zhuh nay pa d-monay

I'm in a hurry
Je suis pressé(e)
zhuh swee pressay

Is it far?
C'est loin?
say lwañ

Can you go a little faster?
Pourriez-vous aller un peu plus vite?
pooree-ay voo alay uñ puh ploo veet

I have to catch...
Je dois prendre...
zhuh dwa proñdr...

     see also LUGGAGE ◻ BUS ◻ METRO

When is the next boat / seacat to...?
À quelle heure part le prochain bateau / seacat pour...?
a kel ur par luh proshañ batoh / seacat poor...

Have you a timetable?
Vous avez un horaire?
vooz avay uñ orehr

Is there a car ferry to...?
Est-ce qu'il y a un car ferry pour...?
es keel ya uñ car ferry poor...

How much is...?
C'est combien...?
seh koñ-byañ...?

a single
un aller simple
uñ alay sañpl

a return
un aller-retour
uñ alay-ruhtoor

A tourist ticket
Un billet touristique
uñ bee-yay toorees-teek

How much is it for a car and ... people?
C'est combien pour une voiture et ... personnes?
say koñ-byañ poor oon vwatoor ay ... pehr-son

How long is the crossing?
La traversée dure combien de temps?
la travehrsay door koñ-byañ duh toñ

Where does the boat leave from?
D'où part le bateau?
doo par luh batoh

When is the first / last boat?
Le premier / dernier bateau part quand?
luh pruhm-yay / dehr-nyay batoh par koñ

What time do we get to...?
On arrive à quelle heure à...?
oñ a-reev a kel ur a...

Is there somewhere to eat on the boat?
Est-ce qu'on peut manger sur le bateau?
es koñ puh moñ-zhay soor luh batoh

see also **LUGGAGE**

23

How do I get to the airport?
Comment fait-on pour aller à l'aéroport?
komoñ fay toñ poor alay a la-ayro-por

How long does it take to get to the airport?
On met combien de temps pour aller à l'aéroport?
oñ meh koñ-byañ duh toñ poor alay a la-ayro-por

How much is the taxi fare...? **into town** **to the hotel**
C'est combien le taxi pour aller...? en ville à l'hôtel
say koñ-byañ luh taxi poor alay... *oñ veel* *a lohtel*

Is there an airport bus to the city centre?
Est-ce qu'il y a une navette pour aller au centre-ville?
es keel ya oon navet poor alay oh soñtr veel

Where do I check in for...(airline)**?**
Où est-ce qu'il faut enregistrer pour...?
oo es keel foh oñruh-zheestray poor...

Where is the luggage for the flight from...?
Où sont les bagages du vol en provenance de...?
oo soñ lay bagazh doo vol oñ provnoñs duh...

Which is the departure gate for the flight to...?
Quelle est la porte d'embarquement pour le vol à destination de...?
kel eh la port doñbahrk-moñ poor luh vol a desteena-syoñ duh...

■ YOU MAY HEAR

L'embarquement aura lieu porte numéro...
loñbark-moñ ohra lyuh port noomayro...
Boarding will take place at gate number...

Présentez-vous immédiatement porte numéro...
prayzoñtay voo eemay-dyat-moñ port noomayro...
Go immediately to gate number...

Votre vol a du retard
votr vol a doo ruhtar
Your flight is delayed

*With the single European Market, European Union (EU) citizens are subject only to highly selective spot checks and they can go through the blue customs channel (unless they have goods to declare). There will be no restriction, either by quantity or value, on goods purchased by EU travellers in another EU country provided that they are **for their own personal use**. If you are unsure of certain items, check with the customs officials as to whether duty is required.*

CONTRÔLE DES PASSEPORTS *koñtol day paspor*	**PASSPORT CONTROL**
UE *oo-uh*	**EU**
(Union Européenne)	*(European Union)*
AUTRES PASSEPORTS *ohtr paspor*	**OTHER PASSPORTS**
DOUANE *dwan*	**CUSTOMS**

Do I have to pay duty on this?
Est-ce que je dois payer des droits de douane sur ça?
es kuh zhuh dwa pay-yay day drwa duh dwan soor sa

I bought this as a gift
Je l'ai acheté comme cadeau
zhuh lay ashtay kom kadoh

It is for my own personal use
C'est pour mon usage personnel
say poor moñ oo-zazh pehr-sonel

We are on our way to... *(if in transit through a country)*
Nous allons en...
nooz aloñ oñ...

The children are on this passport
Les enfants sont sur ce passeport
layz oñfoñ soñ soor suh paspor

This is the baby's passport
Voilà le passeport du bébé
vwa-la luh paspor doo bay-bay

25

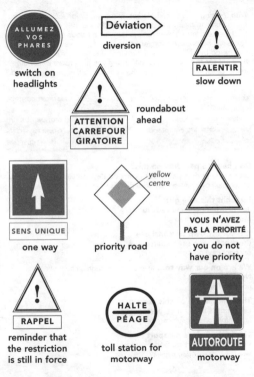

ALLUMEZ VOS PHARES
switch on headlights

Déviation
diversion

RALENTIR
slow down

ATTENTION CARREFOUR GIRATOIRE
roundabout ahead

SENS UNIQUE
one way

yellow centre
priority road

VOUS N'AVEZ PAS LA PRIORITÉ
you do not have priority

RAPPEL
reminder that the restriction is still in force

HALTE PÉAGE
toll station for motorway

AUTOROUTE
motorway

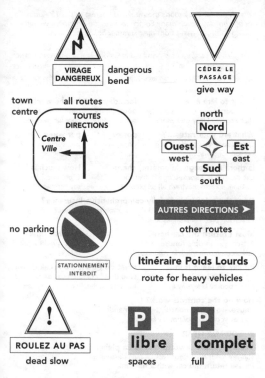

VIRAGE DANGEREUX dangerous bend

CÉDEZ LE PASSAGE give way

town centre — all routes — **TOUTES DIRECTIONS** — *Centre Ville*

north **Nord** — **Ouest** west — **Est** east — **Sud** south

no parking — **STATIONNEMENT INTERDIT**

AUTRES DIRECTIONS ▶ other routes

Itinéraire Poids Lourds route for heavy vehicles

ROULEZ AU PAS dead slow

P libre spaces — **P complet** full

27

CAR HIRE

Watch out for busy roads the weekend nearest to the 15 August, a public holiday, when many French families are on the move, either going to or returning from their summer holidays.

LE PERMIS DE CONDUIRE *luh permee duh kondweer*		**DRIVING LICENCE**
L'ASSURANCE *lasoo-roñs*		**INSURANCE**
LA MARCHE ARRIÈRE *la marsh aree-yehr*		**REVERSE GEAR**

I want to hire a car
Je voudrais louer une voiture
zhuh voodray looay oon vwatoor

for...days
pour...jours
poor...zhoor

for the weekend
pour le week-end
poor luh weekend

What are your rates...?
Quels sont vos tarifs...?
kel soñ voh tareef...

per day
par jour
par zhoor

per week
par semaine
par suhmen

Is there a mileage (kilometre) charge?
Est-ce que le kilométrage est en plus?
es kuh luh keelo-maytrazh eh oñ ploos

How much is it?
C'est combien?
say koñ-byañ

Does the price include fully comprehensive insurance?
Est-ce que le prix comprend l'assurance tous-risques?
es kuh luh pree koñproñ lasoo-roñs too reesk

Must I return the car here?
Est-ce que je dois rendre la voiture ici?
es kuh zhuh dwa roñdr la vwatoor eesee

By what time?
Vers quelle heure?
vehr kel ur

I'd like to leave it in...
Je voudrais la laisser à...
zhuh voodray la lay-say a...

what do I do if we break down?
Que dois-je faire en cas de panne?
kuh dwa-zhuh fehr oñ kah duh pan

How do the controls work?
Pouvez-vous me montrer les commandes?
poovay voo muh moñtray lay komoñd

■ **YOU MAY HEAR**

Veuillez rendre la voiture avec un plein d'essence
vuh-yay roñdr la vwatoor avek uñ plañ dessoñs
Please return the car with a full tank

DRIVING

*The speed limits in France are 50 km/h in built up areas, 90 km/h on ordinary roads, 110 km/h on dual carriageways and 130 km/h on motorways. Don't park in a **zone d'enlèvement** – your car will be towed away! Also watch out when parking in squares. Look out for a sign saying **Interdit de Stationner le samedi Jour de Marché** (No parking on Saturdays, market day). Your car will be towed away. If there are no cars when you park, don't think it's luck, it is probably because the locals know that there is a market on!*

I am looking for a car park
Je cherche un parking
zhuh shehrsh uñ parkeeng

Do I need to pay?
Il faut payer?
eel foh payay

Can I park here?
On peut se garer ici?
oñ puh suh garay eesee

Do I need a parking disk?
Il faut un disque de stationnement?
eel foh uñ deesk duh stasyoñ-moñ

How long can I park for?
Combien de temps peut-on se garer ici?
koñ-byañ duh toñ puht-oñ suh garay eesee?

We're going to....
Nous allons à...
nooz aloñ a...

What's the best route?
Quelle est le meilleur itinéraire?
kel eh luh may-yuhr ee-teenay-rehr

Is the road good?
Est-ce que la route est bonne?
es kuh la root ay bon

Can you show me on the map?
Pouvez-vous me montrer sur la carte?
poovay voo muh moñtray soor la kart

Is the pass open?
Est-ce que le col est ouvert?
es kuh luh kol eh oovehr

How do I get onto the motorway?
Pour rejoindre l'autoroute, s'il vous plaît?
poor ruh-zhwandr lohtohroot seel voo pleh

see also **ROAD SIGNS** ▢ **BREAKDOWN** ▢ **PETROL**   29

SUPER *soopehr*	**4 STAR**
SANS PLOMB *soñ ploñ*	**UNLEADED**
GASOIL *gazwahl*	**DIESEL**

Fill it up, please
Le plein, s'il vous plaît
luh plañ seel voo pleh

Please check the oil / the water
Pouvez-vous vérifier l'huile / l'eau?
poovay voo vayree-fyay lweel / loh

...euros worth of unleaded petrol
...euros d'essence sans plomb
...uhroh daysoñs soñ ploñ

Pump number...
La pompe numéro...
la pomp noo-mayroh...

Where is...?
Où se trouve...?
oo suh troov...

the air line
le compresseur
le koñpreh-sur

the water
l'eau
loh

Can you check the tyre pressure?
Pouvez-vous vérifier la pression des pneus?
poovay voo vay-ree-fyay la preh-syoñ day pnuh

Please fill this can with petrol
Pouvez-vous remplir ce bidon d'essence?
poovay voo roñpleer suh bee-doñ dessoñs

Where do I pay?
Où dois-je payer?
oo dwa-zhuh pay-yay

Do you take credit cards?
Vous acceptez les cartes de crédit?
vooz aksep-tay lay kart duh kraydee

Do you have distilled water?
Avez-vous de l'eau distillée?
avay voo duh loh deestee-lay

I don't want to change the tyres
Je ne veux pas changer les pneus
zhuh nuh vuh pa shoñ-zhay lay pnuh

I checked the tread
J'ai bien vérifié la bande de roulement
zhay byañ vayree-fyay la boñd duh roo-luh-moñ

see also **BREAKDOWN** ☐ **CAR**

ASSISTANCE AUTOMOBILE *aseestoñs ohtohmobeel* **AA** *(French equivalent)*

Can you help me?
Pouvez-vous m'aider?
poovay voo mayday

My car has broken down
Ma voiture est en panne
ma vwatoor eh oñ pan

I can't start the car
Je n'arrive pas à démarrer
zhuh na-reev pa a dayma-ray

The battery is flat
La batterie est à plat
la batree eh ta pla

I've run out of petrol
Je suis en panne d'essence
zhuh swee oñ pan dessoñs

Is there a garage near here?
Il y a un garage près d'ici?
eel ya uñ garazh preh deesee

The engine's overheating
Le moteur chauffe
luh motur shohf

The electrics aren't working
Il y a un faut contact
eel ya uñ foh koñtakt

I need water
Il me faut de l'eau
eel muh foh duh loh

There's a leak
Il y a une fuite
eel ya oon fweet

I've a flat tyre
J'ai un pneu de crevé
zhay uñ pnuh duh kruhvay

I can't get the wheel off
Je n'arrive pas à démonter la roue
zhuh nahreev pa a daymoñtay la roo

Can you tow me to the nearest garage?
Pouvez-vous me remorquer jusqu'au garage le plus proche?
poovay voo muh ruhmor-kay zhooskoh garazh luh ploo prosh

Do you have parts for a (make of car)...?
Avez-vous des pièces de rechange pour une...?
avay voo day pyes duh ruhshoñzh poor oon...

There's something wrong with the... (see CAR PARTS)
J'ai un problème avec le/la/les...
zhay uñ problem avek luh/la/lay...

Can you replace the windscreen?
Pouvez-vous remplacer le pare-brise?
poovay voo roñplasay luh parbreez

see also **CAR PARTS**

The ... doesn't work	**The ... don't work**
Le/La/L' ... ne marche pas	Les ... ne marchent pas
luh/la/l ... nuh marsh pa	*lay ... nuh marsh pa*

accelerator	l'accélérateur *aksay-layra-tur*
battery	la batterie *batree*
bonnet	le capot *kapo*
brakes	les freins *frañ*
choke	le starter *startay*
clutch	l'embrayage *oñbray-yazh*
distributor	le delco *delko*
engine	le moteur *motur*
exhaust pipe	le pot d'échappement *poh dayshap-moñ*
fuse	le fusible *foo-zeebl*
gears	les vitesses *veetess*
handbrake	le frein à main *frañ a mañ*
headlights	les phares *far*
ignition	l'allumage *aloo-mazh*
indicator	le clignotant *klee-nyotoñ*
points	les vis platinées *vees platee-nay*
radiator	le radiateur *radya-tur*
reversing lights	les phares de recul *far duh ruhkool*
seat belt	la ceinture de sécurité *sañtoor duh saykooreetay*
sidelights	les veilleuses *vay-yuhz*
spare wheel	la roue de secours *roo duh suhkoor*
spark plugs	les bougies *boo-zhee*
steering	la direction *deerek-syoñ*
steering wheel	le volant *voloñ*
tyre	le pneu *pnuh*
wheel	la roue *roo*
windscreen	le pare-brise *parbreez*
windscreen washers	le lave-glace *lavglas*
windscreen wiper	l'essuie-glace *eswee-glas*

see also **BREAKDOWN** ☐ **PETROL**

You can book accommodation over the internet using the French Tourist Office website www.franceguide.com.

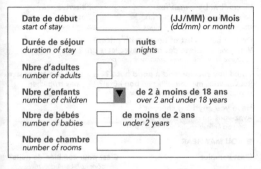

Date de début start of stay	**(JJ/MM) ou Mois** (dd/mm) or month
Durée de séjour duration of stay	**nuits** nights
Nbre d'adultes number of adults	
Nbre d'enfants number of children	**de 2 à moins de 18 ans** over 2 and under 18 years
Nbre de bébés number of babies	**de moins de 2 ans** under 2 years
Nbre de chambre number of rooms	

I'd like (to book) a room...
Je voudrais (réserver) une chambre...
zhuh voodray (rayzehr-vay) oon shoñbr...

double
pour deux personnes
poor duh pehr-son

single
pour une personne
poor oon pehr-son

with bath
avec bain
avek bañ

with shower
avec douche
avek doosh

with double bed
à un lit
a uñ lee

twin-bedded
à deux lits
a duh lee

with an extra bed for a child
avec un autre lit pour un enfant
avek uñ ohtr lee poor uñ oñfoñ

How much is it...?
C'est combien...?
say koñ-byañ...

per night
par nuit
par nwee

per week
par semaine
par suhmen

I'd like to stay ... nights
Je voudrais rester ... nuits
zhuh voodray restay ... nwee

from the 10th to the 15th July
du dix au quinze juillet
doo dees oh kañz zhwee-yeh

cont...

HOTEL (BOOKING)

I'd like two rooms next to each other
Je voudrais deux chambres l'une à côté de l'autre
zhuh voodray duh shoñbr loon a kotay duh lohtr

I'll confirm by e-mail/fax
Je confirmerai par e-mail/fax
zhuh koñfeerm-ray par e-mail/fax

I'll arrive at...
J'arriverai à...
zhahreev-ray a...

Do you have a list of hotels with prices?
Vous avez une liste des hôtels avec leurs prix?
vooz avay oon leest dayz ohtel avek luhr pree

Could you recommend a good hotel?
Pouvez-vous me conseiller un bon hôtel?
poo-vay voo muh koñ-say-yay uñ boñ ohtel

not too expensive
pas trop cher
pa troh shehr

Have you anything cheaper?
Avez-vous quelque chose de moins cher?
avay voo kelkuh shohz duh mwañ shehr

■ **YOU MAY HEAR**

C'est complet
say koñpleh
We're full up

C'est pour combien de nuits?
say poor koñ-byañ duh nwee
For how many nights?

C'est pour combien de personnes?
say poor koñ-byañ duh pehr-son
For how many people?

Votre nom, s'il vous plaît?
votr noñ seel voo pleh
Your name, please?

Veuillez confirmer...
vuh-yay koñfeermay...
Please confirm...

par e-mail
par e-mail
by e-mail

par fax
par fax
by fax

Vous arriverez à quelle heure?
vooz ahreev-ray a kel ur
What time will you arrive?

*You generally have to fill in a registration form (**fiche d'étranger**) and give your passport number.*

Do you have a room for tonight?
Est-ce que vous avez une chambre pour ce soir?
es kuh vooz avay oon shoñbr poor suh swar

I booked a room
J'ai réservé une chambre
zhay rayzehr-vay oon shoñbr

My name is...
Je m'appelle...
zhuh mapel...

Can I see the room?
Pourrais-je voir la chambre?
pooray zhuh vwar la shoñbr

Have you anything else?
Vous avez autre chose?
vooz avay ohtr shoz

Where can I park the car?
Où est-ce que je peux garer la voiture?
oo es kuh zhuh puh garay la vwatoor

What time is...?
À quelle heure est...?
a kel ur eh...

dinner
le dîner
luh deenay

breakfast
le petit-déjeuner
luh puhtee day-zhunay

We'll be back late tonight
Nous rentrerons tard ce soir
noo roñtruh-roñ tar suh swar

Do you lock the door?
Fermez-vous la porte à clé?
fehrmay voo la port a klay

The key, please
La clé, s'il vous plaît
la klay seel voo pleh

Room number...
Chambre numéro...
shoñbr noomayro...

Can you keep this in the safe, please?
Vous pouvez mettre ceci dans le coffre-fort, s'il vous plaît?
voo poovay metr suh-see doñ luh kofruh-for seel voo pleh

Are there any messages for me?
Il y a des messages pour moi?
eel ya day messazh poor mwa

I'm leaving tomorrow
Je pars demain
zhuh par duhmañ

Please prepare the bill
Pouvez-vous préparer la note?
poovay voo praypa-ray la not

see also **PAYING**

ORDURES *ordoor*	**RUBBISH**
EAU POTABLE *oh pohtabl*	**DRINKING WATER**
BLOC SANITAIRE *blok saneetehr*	**WASHING FACILITIES**

Do you have a list of campsites with prices?
Avez-vous un guide des campings avec les prix?
avay voo uñ geed day koñpeeng avek lay pree

Is the campsite sheltered?
Est-ce que le camping est abrité?
es kuh luh koñpeeng eh abreetay

Is the beach far?
C'est loin, la plage?
say lwañ la plazh

Is there a restaurant on the campsite?
Y a-t-il un restaurant dans le camping?
ee a-teel uñ resto-roñ doñ luh koñpeeng

Do you have any vacancies?
Vous avez des emplacements de libre?
vooz avay dayz oñplas-moñ duh leebr

Does the price include...?
Est-ce que le prix comprend...?
es kuh luh pree koñproñ...

hot water
l'eau chaude
loh shohd

electricity
l'électricité
laylek-treeseetay

We'd like to stay for ... nights
Nous voudrions rester ... nuits
noo voodryoñ restay ... nwee

How much is it per night...?
C'est combien la nuit...?
say koñ-byañ la nwee...

for a tent
pour une tente
poor oon toñt

for a caravan
pour une caravane
poor oon karavan

Can I/we camp here overnight?
Peut-on camper ici cette nuit?
puh-toñ koñpay eesee set nwee

see also **SIGHTSEEING & TOURIST OFFICE**

*You can find a variety of places to stay on **www.franceguide.com**, the French Tourist Office website.*

Can we have an extra set of keys?
Pouvons-nous avoir un double des clés?
poo-voñ noo a-vwahr uñ doobl day klay

When does the cleaner come?
Quand est-ce que vient la femme de ménage?
koñ es kuh vyañ la fam duh may-nazh

Who do we contact if there are problems
Qui devons-nous contacter en cas de problème?
kee duhvoñ noo koñtak-tay oñ ka duh problehm

How does the heating work?
Comment marche le chauffage?
komoñ marsh luh shoh-fazh

Is there always hot water?
Est-ce qu'il y a de l'eau chaude en permanence?
es keel ya duh loh shohd oñ pehrmanoñs

Where is the nearest supermarket?
Où est le supermarché le plus proche?
oo ay luh soopehrmarshay luh ploo prosh

Where do we leave the rubbish?
Où est-ce qu'il faut mettre les ordures?
oo es keel foh metr layz ordoor

When is the rubbish collected?
Quand est-ce que le camion-poubelle passe?
koñt es kuh luh kam-yoñ poobel pas

Where is the nearest bottle bank?
Où est-ce qu'on peut recycler le verre?
oo es koñ puh ruhsee-klay luh vehr

What are the neighbours called?
Comment s'appellent les voisins?
komoñ sapel lay vwa-zañ

SHOPPING PHRASES

Opening hours approx. 9 am to 7 pm; some smaller shops close for lunch (between 12 and 2 pm).

Where is...?
Où est...?
oo eh...

Do you have...?
Est-ce que vous avez...?
es kuh vooz avay...

I'm looking for a present for...
Je cherche un cadeau pour...
zhuh shehrsh uñ kadoh poor...

my mother
ma mère
ma mehr

a child
un enfant
uñ oñfoñ

Where can I buy...?
Où est-ce qu'on peut acheter...?
oo es koñ puh ashtay...

toys
des jouets
day zhoo-ay

gifts
des cadeaux
day kadoh

Can you recommend any good shops?
Pouvez-vous me conseiller de bons magasins?
poovay voo muh koñsay-yay duh boñ maga-zañ

Where is the ... department?
Où se trouve le rayon...?
oo suh troov luh rayoñ...

perfume
parfumerie
parfoom-ree

jewellery
bijouterie
beezhoo-tree

I'd like something similar to this
Je voudrais quelque chose dans ce genre-là
zhuh voodray kelkuh shohz doñ suh zhoñr la

It's too expensive for me
C'est trop cher pour moi
say troh shehr poor mwa

Have you anything else?
Vous n'avez rien d'autre?
voo navay ryañ dohtr

Is there a market?
Est-ce qu'il y a un marché?
es keel ya uñ marshay

Which day?
Quel jour?
kel zhoor

■ **YOU MAY HEAR**

Qu'est-ce que vous désirez?
kes kuh voo dayzeeray
What would you like?

see also **SHOPS** ☐ **FOOD** ☐ **CLOTHES** ☐ **POST OFFICE**

SOLDES *sohld*		**SALE**
1 ACHETÉ, 1 GRATUIT *uñ ashtay uñ gratwee*		**BUY ONE GET ONE FREE**
LE RAYON ALIMENTATION *luh rayoñ aleemoñtasyoñ*		**FOOD DEPARTMENT**

baker's	BOULANGERIE	*booloñ-zhuree*
bookshop	LIBRAIRIE	*leebreh-ree*
butcher's	BOUCHERIE	*boosh-ree*
butcher's (pork)	CHARCUTERIE	*sharkoot-ree*
cake shop	PÂTISSERIE	*patees-ree*
cheese shop	FROMAGERIE	*fromazh-ree*
clothes	VÊTEMENTS	*vetmoñ*
DIY	BRICOLAGE	*breeko-lazh*
dry-cleaner's	PRESSING	*presseeng*
electrical goods	APPAREILS ÉLECTRIQUES	*apa-ray-yuh aylek-treek*
fishmonger's	POISSONNERIE	*pwasoñ-ree*
furniture	MEUBLES	*muhbluh*
gifts	CADEAUX	*kadoh*
greengrocer's	FRUITS ET LÉGUMES	*frwee ay laygoom*
grocer's	ÉPICERIE	*aypees-ree*
hairdresser	COIFFEUSE	*kwa-fuz*
health food shop	DIÉTÉTIQUE	*deeyehtehteek*
household articles	ENTRETIEN	*oñtruhtyañ*
hypermarket	HYPERMARCHÉ	*eepehr-marshay*
ironmonger's	QUINCAILLERIE	*kañkye-yuhree*
jeweller's	BIJOUTERIE	*beezhoo-tree*
market	MARCHÉ	*marshay*
perfume shop	PARFUMERIE	*parfoom-ree*
pharmacy	PHARMACIE	*farmasee*
self-service	LIBRE-SERVICE	*leebr-sehrvees*
shoe shop	CHAUSSURES	*shoh-soor*
sports shop	ARTICLES DE SPORT	*arteekl duh spor*
stationer's	PAPETERIE	*papuhtree*
sweet shop	CONFISERIE	*koñfees-ree*
supermarket	SUPERMARCHÉ	*soopehr-marshay*
tobacconist's	TABAC	*taba*
toy shop	JOUETS	*zhoo-ay*

FOOD (GENERAL)

bread	le pain *pañ*
bread stick	la baguette *ba-get*
bread (brown)	le pain complet *pañ koñpleh*
bread roll	le petit pain *puhtee pañ*
butter	le beurre *buhr*
cheese	le fromage *fromazh*
chicken	le poulet *pooleh*
coffee (instant)	le café (instantané) *kafay (añstoñ-ta-nay)*
cream	la crème *krem*
crisps	les chips *sheeps*
eggs	les œufs *uh*
fish	le poisson *pwasoñ*
flour	la farine *fareen*
ham (cooked)	le jambon cuit *zhoñboñ kwee*
ham (cured)	le jambon cru *zhoñboñ kru*
herbal tea	la tisane *tee-zan*
honey	le miel *myel*
jam	la confiture *koñfee-toor*
margarine	la margarine *marga-reen*
marmalade	la confiture d'orange *koñfeetoor do-roñzh*
milk	le lait *leh*
mustard	la moutarde *mootard*
oil	l'huile *weel*
orange juice	le jus d'orange *zhoo do-roñzh*
pasta	les pâtes *pat*
pepper	le poivre *pwavr*
rice	le riz *ree*
salt	le sel *sel*
sugar	le sucre *sookr*
stock cube	le bouillon cube *boo-yoñ koob*
tea	le thé *tay*
tin of tomatoes	la boîte de tomates *bwat duh tomat*
vinegar	le vinaigre *veenaygr*
yoghurt	le yaourt *ya-oort*

see also **MEASUREMENTS & QUANTITIES**

■ FRUIT

apples	les pommes *pom*
apricots	les abricots *abreeko*
bananas	les bananes *banan*
cherries	les cerises *suhreez*
grapefruit	le pamplemousse *poñpluh-moos*
grapes	le raisin *rezañ*
lemon	le citron *seetroñ*
melon	le melon *muhloñ*
nectarines	les nectarines *nektareen*
oranges	les oranges *o-roñzh*
peaches	les pêches *pesh*
pears	les poires *pwahr*
pineapple	l'ananas *ana-nas*
plums	les prunes *proon*
raspberries	les framboises *froñbwaz*
strawberries	les fraises *frez*

■ VEGETABLES

asparagus	les asperges *asperzh*
carrots	les carottes *karot*
cauliflower	le chou-fleur *shoo-flur*
courgettes	les courgettes *koor-zhet*
French beans	les haricots verts *aree-koh vehr*
garlic	l'ail *eye*
leeks	les poireaux *pwa-roh*
lettuce	la laitue *laytoo*
mushrooms	les champignons *shoñpee-nyoñ*
onions	les oignons *o-nyoñ*
peas	les petits pois *puhtee pwa*
peppers	les poivrons *pwa-vroñ*
potatoes	les pommes de terre *pom duh ter*
spinach	les épinards *aypee-nar*
tomatoes	les tomates *tomat*

see also **SHOPPING PHRASES**

CLOTHES

*Size for clothes is **la taille** (tye). For shoes it is **la pointure** (pwañtoor)*

women		men - suits		shoes			
sizes		**sizes**		**sizes**			
UK	EC	UK	EC	UK	EC	UK	EC
10	38	36	46	2	35	7	41
12	40	38	48	3	36	8	42
14	42	40	50	4	37	9	43
16	44	42	52	5	38	10	44
18	46	44	54	6	39	11	45
20	48	46	56				

May I try this on?
Est-ce que je peux l'essayer?
es kuh zhuh puh leh-say-yay

Where are the changing rooms?
Où sont les cabines d'essayage?
oo soñ lay kabeen dessay-yazh

Do you have it...?
L'avez-vous...?
lavay voo...

in a bigger size
en plus grand
oñ ploo groñ

in a smaller size
en plus petit
oñ ploo puhtee

Do you have this in any other colours?
Est-ce que vous l'avez dans d'autres coloris?
es kuh voo lavay doñ dohtr koloree

That's a shame!
C'est dommage!
say domazh

It's...
C'est...
say...

too short
trop court
troh koor

too long
trop long
troh loñ

I'm just looking
Je regarde seulement
zhuh ruhgard suhlmoñ

I'll take it
Je le prends
zhuh luh proñ

■ **YOU MAY HEAR**

Quelle est votre taille?
kel eh votr tye
What size are you?

Quelle pointure faites-vous?
kel pwañtoor feht voo
What shoe size do you take?

see also **NUMBERS**

LE COTON *luh kotoñ*	**COTTON**	**LA SOIE** *la swa*	**SILK**
LA DENTELLE *la doñtel*	**LACE**	**LA LAINE** *la lehn*	**WOOL**

belt	la ceinture *sañtoor*
blouse	le chemisier *shuhmee-zyay*
bra	le soutien-gorge *soo-tyañ gorzh*
coat	le manteau *moñtoh*
dress	la robe *rob*
dressing gown	le peignoir *peh-nywar*
fleece	la laine polaire *lehn pohlehr*
gloves	les gants *goñ*
hat	le chapeau *shapoh*
jacket	la veste *vest*
knickers	le slip *sleep*
nightdress	la chemise de nuit *shuhmeez duh nwee*
pyjamas	le pyjama *pee-zhama*
raincoat	l'imperméable *añ-pehrmay-abl*
sandals	les sandales *soñdal*
scarf (silk)	le foulard *foolar*
scarf (wool)	l'écharpe *aysharp*
shirt	la chemise *shuhmeez*
shoes	les chaussures *shoh-soor*
shorts	le short *short*
skirt	la jupe *zhoop*
slippers	les pantoufles *poñ-toofluh*
socks	les chaussettes *shoh-set*
suit (woman's)	le tailleur *tye-yur*
suit (man's)	le costume *kostoom*
swimsuit	le maillot de bain *mye-yoh duh bañ*
tights	les collants *koloñ*
t-shirt	le t-shirt *tee-shurt*
tracksuit	le survêtement *soorvet-moñ*
trainers	les baskets *bahskeht*
trousers	le pantalon *poñta-loñ*
zip	la fermeture éclair *fehrmeh-toor ayklehr*

see also **SHOPPING** ☐ **SHOPPING PHRASES** ☐ **PAYING**

Have you...?
Avez-vous...?
avay vooz...

a map of the town
un plan de la ville
uñ ploñ duh la veel

a map of the region
une carte de la région
oon kart duh la ray-zhyoñ

Can you show me where ... is on the map?
Pouvez-vous me montrer où est ... sur la carte?
poovay voo muh moñtray oo eh ... soor la kart

Do you have a detailed map of the area?
Vous avez une carte détaillée de la région?
vooz avay oon kart day-ta-yay duh la ray-zhyoñ

Can you draw me a map with directions?
Vous pouvez me dessiner un plan avec les directions?
voo poovay muh deh-seenay uñ ploñ avek lay deerek-syoñ

Do you have a guide book / leaflet in English?
Vous avez un guide / une brochure en anglais?
vooz avay uñ geed / oon bro-shoor oñ oñgleh

I'd like the English language version (of a cassette guide)
Je voudrais la version anglaise (en cassette)
zhuh voodray la vehr-syoñ oñglehz (oñ ka-set)

Where can I/we buy an English newspaper?
Où est-ce qu'on peut acheter des journaux anglais?
oo es koñ puh ashtay day zhoor-noh oñgleh

Do you have any English newspapers / novels?
Vous avez des journaux / des romans anglais?
vooz avay day zhoor-noh / day romoñ oñgleh

When do the English newspapers arrive?
Quand est-ce que vous recevez les journaux anglais?
koñt es kuh voo ruhsuh-vay lay zhoor-noh oñgleh

Please reserve (name newspaper) **for me**
Pouvez-vous me garder un...
poovay voo muh garday uñ...

see also **SIGHTSEEING** □ **TOURIST OFFICE**

Smaller Post Offices are generally shut for lunch (12 to 2 pm).

LA POSTE *la post*	**POST OFFICE**
TIMBRES *tañbr*	**STAMPS**

Is there a post office near here?
Il y a un bureau de poste près d'ici?
eel ya uñ booroh duh post preh deesee

When is it open?
Il ouvre quand?
eel oovruh koñ

Which counter...?
C'est quel guichet...?
say kel gee-shay...

for stamps
pour les timbres
poor lay tañbr

for parcels
pour les colis
poor lay kolee

Three stamps for postcards to Great Britain
Trois timbres pour cartes postales pour la Grande-Bretagne
trwa tañbr poor kart pos-tal poor la groñd bruhta-nyuh

I want to send this letter registered post
Je voudrais envoyer cette lettre en recommandé
zhuh voodray oñvwa-yay set letr oñ ruhkomoñ-day

How much is it to send this parcel?
C'est combien pour envoyer ce colis?
say koñ-byañ poor oñvwa-yay suh kolee

by air
par avion
par a-vyoñ

by surface mail
par voie normale
par vwa normal

It's a gift
C'est un cadeau
say tuñ kadoh

The value of contents is ... euros
La valeur est de... euros
la va-lur eh duh ... uh-roh

■ YOU MAY HEAR

Vous pouvez acheter les timbres au tabac
voo poovay ashtay lay tañbr oh taba
You can buy stamps at the tobacconist's

see also **MONEY** □ **PAYING**

Tapes for video cameras and camcorders can be bought in hi-fi shops – magasin hi-fi

Where can I/we buy video tapes for a camcorder?
Où peut-on acheter des cassettes vidéo pour un caméscope?
oo puh-toñ ashtay day ka-set video poor uñ kamay-skop

A colour film...
Une pellicule couleur...
oon peleekool koo-lur...

with 24 / 36 exposures
de 24 / 36 poses
duh vañt-katr / troñt-sees poz

A video tape for this camcorder
Une cassette vidéo pour ce caméscope, s'il vous plaît
oon ka-set video poor suh kamay-skop seel voo pleh

Have you batteries...?
Avez-vous des piles...?
avay voo day peel...

for this camera / this camcorder
pour cet appareil / ce caméscope
poor set apa-ray-yuh / suh kamay-skop

Can you develop this film?
Pouvez-vous développer cette pellicule?
poovay voo day-vlopay set peleekool

Mat prints, please
En mat, s'il vous plaît
oñ mat seel voo pleh

Glossy prints, please
En brillant, s'il vous plaît
oñ bree-yoñ seel voo pleh

When will the photos be ready?
Quand est-ce que les photos seront prêtes?
koñt es kuh lay foto suh-roñ pret

The film is stuck
La pellicule est coincée
la peleekool eh kwañ-say

Can you take it out for me?
Pouvez-vous me l'enlever?
poovay voo muh loñ-luhvay

Is it OK to take pictures here?
On peut prendre des photos ici?
oñ puh proñdr day foto eesee

Would you take a picture of us, please?
Est-ce que vous pourriez nous prendre en photo, s'il vous plaît?
es kuh voo pooree-ay noo proñdr oñ foto seel voo pleh

see also **SHOPPING**

The tourist office is called le syndicat d'initiative. If you are looking for somewhere to stay they will have details of hotels, campsites, etc. Most museums are closed on Tuesdays.

Where is the tourist office?
Où est le syndicat d'initiative?
oo eh luh saÑdee-ka deenee-sya-teev

What is there to visit in the area?
Qu'est-ce qu'il y a à voir dans la région?
kes keel ya a vwar doÑ la ray-zhyoÑ

in two hours
en deux heures
oÑ duhz ur

Have you any leaflets?
Avez-vous de la documentation?
avay voo duh la dohkoo-moÑta-syoÑ

When can we visit the...?
Quand est-ce qu'on peut visiter le/la...?
koÑt es koÑ puh veezeetay luh/la...

Are there any excursions?
Est-ce qu'il y a des excursions?
es keel ya dayz ekskoor-syoÑ

We'd like to go to...
On voudrait aller à...
oÑ voodray alay a...

When does it leave?
À quelle heure part-il?
a kel ur par teel

Where does it leave from?
Il part d'où?
eel par doo

How much does it cost to get in?
C'est combien l'entrée?
say koÑ-byaÑ loÑtray

Are there any reductions for...?
Est-ce que vous faites des réductions pour...?
es kuh voo feht day raydook-syoÑ poor...

children	students	unemployed	senior citizens
les enfants	les étudiants	les chômeurs	les retraités
layz oÑfoÑ	*layz aytoo-dyoÑ*	*lay shoh-mur*	*lay ruhtrehtay*

see also **MAPS & GUIDES** ☐ **LEISURE/INTERESTS**

Check at the local tourist office for information about local events. You can also find listings on www.franceguide.com.

What is there to do in the evenings?
Qu'est-ce qu'on peut faire le soir?
kes koñ puh fehr luh swar

Do you have a list of events for this month?
Vous avez une liste des festivités pour ce mois-ci?
vooz avay oon leest day festeeveetay poor suh mwa-see

Is there anything for children to do?
Est-ce qu'il y a des choses à faire pour les enfants?
es keel ya day shohz a fehr poor layz oñfoñ

Where is there a play park?
Où est-ce qu'il y a une aire de jeux?
oo es keel ya oon ayr duh zhuh

Where can I/we get tickets...?
Où est-ce qu'on peut acheter des billets...?
oo es koñ puh ashtay day bee-yay...

for tonight
pour ce soir
poor suh swar

for the show
pour le spectacle
poor luh spek-takl

for the football match
pour le match de football
poor luh match duh foot-bal

I'd like ... tickets
Je voudrais ... billets
zhuh voodray ... bee-yay

...adults
...adultes
...adoolt

...children
...enfants
...oñfoñ

Where can I/we go dancing?
Où est-ce qu'on peut aller danser?
oo es koñ puh alay doñsay

How much is it to get in?
Ça coûte combien l'entrée?
sa koot koñ-byañ loñtray

What time does it open?
À quelle heure est-ce que ça ouvre?
a kel ur es kuh sa oovr

What do you do at weekends?
Qu'est-ce que vous faites le week-end?
kes kuh voo feht luh weekend

Where can I/we...? **go fishing** **go riding**
Où est-ce qu'on peut...? pêcher faire du cheval
oo es koñ puh... *pesh-ay* *fehr doo shuhval*

Are there any good ... beaches near here? **sandy**
Est-ce qu'il y a de bonnes plages ... près d'ici? de sable
es keel ya duh boñ plazh ... preh deesee *duh sabluh*

Is there a swimming pool?
Est-ce qu'il y a une piscine?
es keel ya oon peeseen

Where can I/we hire mountain bikes?
Où est-ce qu'on peut louer des VTT?
oo es koñ puh loo-ay day vay-tay-tay

Do you have cycling helmets?
Est-ce que vous avez des casques de cycliste?
es kuh vooz avay day kask day see-kleest

How much is it...? **per hour** **per day**
C'est combien...? de l'heure par jour
say koñ-byañ... *duh lur* *par zhoor*

What do you do in your spare time?
Que faites-vous de votre temps libre?
kuh feht voo duh votr toñ leebr

I like... **to go cycling** **sport** **the theatre**
J'aime... faire du vélo faire du sport le théâtre
zhem... *fehr doo vay-lo* *fehr doo spor* *luh tay-atr*

Are you a member of any clubs?
Vous faites partie d'un club?
voo feht partee duñ club

Do you like playing...? **Do you like...?** *(familiar)*
Vous aimez jouer à/au (etc.)...? Tu aimes...?
voos ehmay zhoo-ay a/oh... *too ehm...*

see also **SPORT** ☐ **SKIING** ☐ **WALKING**

Are there any good concerts on?
Il y a de bons concerts en ce moment?
eel ya duh boñ koñsehr oñ suh momoñ

Where can I get tickets for the concert?
Où est-ce qu'on peut avoir des billets pour le concert?
oo es koñ puh avvar day bee-yay poor luh koñsehr

Where can we hear some classical music / some jazz?
Où est-ce qu'on peut aller écouter de la musique classique / du jazz?
oo es koñ puh alay aykootay duh la moo-zeek klaseek / doo jaz

What sort of music do you like?
Qu'est-ce que vous aimez comme musique?
kes kuh vooz aymay kom moo-zeek

I like...
J'aime...
zhem...

Which is your favourite group / singer?
Quel est votre groupe / chanteur préféré?
kel eh votr groop / shoñtur prayfay-ray

Can you play any musical instrument?
Vous savez jouer d'un instrument de musique?
voo savay zhoo-ay duñ añstroomoñ duh moo-zeek

I play...	**the guitar**	**piano**	**clarinet**
Je joue...	de la guitare	du piano	de la clarinette
zhuh zhoo...	*duh la gee-tar*	*doo pyano*	*duh la klaree-net*

Have you been to any good concerts?
Vous êtes allés à de bons concerts?
vooz eht za-lay a duh boñ koñsehr

Do you like opera?
Vous aimez l'opéra?
vooz aymay lopayra

Do you like reggae?
Tu aimes le reggae? *(familiar)*
t-aym luh reggae

SOUS-TITRÉ *soo-teetray*	SUBTITLED
LA SÉANCE *la sayoñs*	PERFORMANCE
VO *(version originale) versyoñ oreezheenal*	IN THE ORIGINAL LANGUAGE

What's on at the cinema?
Qu'est-ce qu'il passe au cinéma?
kes keel pass oh seenay-ma

When does the film start / finish?
Le film commence / finit à quelle heure?
luh feelm komoñs / feenee a kel ur

Is it dubbed or subtitled?
C'est doublé ou sous-titré?
say dooblay oo soo-teetray

How much are the tickets?
C'est combien les billets?
say koñ-byañ lay bee-yay

I'd like two seats at ... euros
Je voudrais deux places à ... euros
zhuh voodray duh plas a ... uh-roh

What films have you seen recently?
Quels films avez-vous vus récemment?
kel feelm avay voo voo ray-sahmoñ

What is (English name of film) **called in French?**
Comment est-ce que ... s'appelle en français?
komoñ es kuh ... sapel oñ froñseh

Who is your favourite actor?
Quel est votre acteur préféré?
kel eh votr aktur prayfay-ray

Who is your favourite actress?
Quelle est votre actrice préférée?
kel eh votr aktrees prayfay-ray

see also **ENTERTAINMENT** □ **LEISURE/INTERESTS**

LA PIÈCE *la pyes*	**PLAY**
LA REPRÉSENTATION *la ruhpray-zoñta-syoñ*	**PERFORMANCE**
À L'ORCHESTRE *a lorkestr*	**IN THE STALLS**
AU BALCON *oh balkoñ*	**IN THE CIRCLE**
LE FAUTEUIL *luh fohtuh-yuh*	**SEAT**
LE VESTIAIRE *luh ves-tyehr*	**CLOAKROOM**

What is on at the theatre?
Qu'est-ce qu'on joue au théâtre?
kes koñ zhoo oh tay-atr

How do we get there?
Pour y aller?
poor ee alay

What is on at the opera?
Qu'est-ce qu'on joue à l'opéra?
kes koñ zhoo a lopayra

What prices are the tickets?
Les billets sont à combien?
lay bee-yay soñ ta koñ-byañ

I'd like two tickets...
Je voudrais deux billets...
zhuh voodray duh bee-yay...

for tonight
pour ce soir
poor suh swar

for tomorrow night
pour demain soir
poor duhmañ swar

for 5th August
pour le cinq août
poor luh sañk oo

in the stalls
à l'orchestre
a lorkestr

in the circle
au balcon
oh balkoñ

How long is the interval?
L'entracte dure combien de temps?
loñtract door koñ-byañ duh toñ

Is there a bar?
Il y a un bar?
eel ya uñ bar

When does the performance begin / end?
Quand est-ce que la représentation commence / finit?
koñt es kuh la ruhpray-zoñta-syoñ komoñs / feenee

I enjoyed the play
J'ai bien aimé la pièce
zhay byañ ehmay la pyes

It was very good
C'était une très bonne pièce
saytay oon treh boñ pyes

see also **ENTERTAINMENT** ☐ **LEISURE/INTERESTS**

LA TÉLÉCOMMANDE *taylaykomoñd*	REMOTE CONTROL
LE FEUILLETON *luh fuh-yuh-toñ*	SOAP
LE MAGNÉTOSCOPE *luh ma-nyaytoskop*	VIDEO RECORDER
LES INFORMATIONS *layz añforma-syoñ*	NEWS
METTRE EN MARCHE *metruh oñ marsh*	TO SWITCH ON
ÉTEINDRE *ay-tañdr*	TO SWITCH OFF
UNE ÉMISSION *oon aymee-syoñ*	PROGRAMME
LES DESSINS ANIMÉS *lay dehsañ a-neemay*	CARTOONS

Where is the television?
Où est la télévision?
oo eh la taylay-veezyoñ

Can we watch television?
On peut regarder la télévision?
oñ puh ruhgarday la taylay-veezyoñ

What is on television?
Qu'est-ce qu'il y a à la télé?
kes keel ya a la taylay

When is the news?
Les informations sont à quelle heure?
layz añforma-syoñ soñ ta kel uhr

Do you have any English-speaking channels?
Est-ce qu'il y a des chaînes en anglais?
es keel ya day shen oñ oñglay

When are the children's programmes?
À quelle heure sont les émissions pour les enfants?
a kel ur soñ layz aymee-syoñ poor layz oñfoñ

Do you have any English videos?
Avez-vous des vidéos en anglais?
avay voo day video oñ oñglay

Could you video this programme?
Pourriez-vous enregistrer cette émission?
pooree-ay vooz oñruhzhee-stray set aymee-syoñ

Is there a television?
Il y a une télévision?
eel ya oon taylay-veezyoñ

LE MATCH/LE JEU *luh match/luh zhuh*	**MATCH/GAME**
LE TERRAIN/LE COURT *luh teh-rañ/luh koor*	**PITCH/COURT**

Where can I/we...?
Où est-ce qu'on peut...?
oo es koñ puh...

play tennis
jouer au tennis
zhoo-ay oh tenees

play golf
jouer au golf
zhoo-ay oh golf

go swimming
faire de la natation
fehr duh la nata-syoñ

go jogging
faire du jogging
fehr doo jogging

How much is it per hour?
C'est combien l'heure?
say koñ-byañ lur

Do you have to be a member?
Est-ce qu'il faut être membre?
es kel foh etr moñbr

Can we hire...?
Est-ce qu'on peut louer...?
es koñ puh loo-ay...

rackets
des raquettes
day ra-ket

golf clubs
des clubs de golf
day club duh golf

We'd like to go to see (name team) **play**
Nous voudrions aller voir jouer l'équipe de...
noo voo-dryoñ alay vwar zhoo-ay lay-keep duh...

Where can I/we get tickets?
Où est-ce qu'on peut avoir des billets?
oo es koñ puh avwar day bee-yay

Which is your favourite football team?
Quelle est votre équipe de football préférée?
kel eh votr ay-keep duh footbal prayfay-ray

What sports do you play?
Qu'est-ce que vous faites comme sports?
kes kuh voo feht kom spor

■ YOU MAY HEAR

Le match vous est transmis en direct depuis...
luh match vooz eh troñsmee oñ deerekt duhpwee...
The match is brought live to you from...

LE FORFAIT *luh forfeh*	SKI PASS
DÉBUTANT *daybootañ*	BEGINNER
INTERMÉDIAIRE *añtehrmaydyehr*	INTERMEDIATE
AVANCÉ *avoñsay*	ADVANCED
LE SKI DE FOND *luh skee duh foñ*	CROSS-COUNTRY SKIING
LE SKI DE PISTE *luh skee duh peest*	DOWNHILL SKIING

I want to hire skis
Je voudrais louer des skis
zhuh voodray loo-ay day skee

Are poles included in the price?
Est-ce que les bâtons sont compris dans le prix?
es kuh lay batoñ soñ koñpree doñ luh pree

Can you adjust my bindings, please?
Pourriez-vous régler mes fixations, s'il vous plaît?
pooree-ay voo rayglay may feeksa-syoñ seel voo pleh

How much is a pass for...?   **a day**   **a week**
C'est combien le forfait pour...?   une journée   une semaine
say koñ-byañ luh forfay poor...   *oon zhoor-nay*   *oon suhmen*

Do you have a map of the pistes?
Avez-vous une carte des pistes?
avay voo oon kart day peest

When does the last chair-lift go up?
À quelle heure part la dernière benne?
a kel ur par la dehr-nyehr ben

■ **YOU MAY HEAR**

Vous avez déjà fait du ski?   Quelle pointure faites-vous?
vooz avay day-zha feh doo skee   *kel pwañ-toor feht voo*
Have you ever skied before?   What is your shoe size?

Quelle longueur de skis voulez-vous?
kel loñg-ur duh skee voolay voo
What length skis do you want?

see also **LEISURE/INTERESTS** ☐ **SPORT** ☐ **WALKING**   55

Are there any guided walks?
Y a-t-il des promenades guidées?
ee a-teel day promnad geeday

Do you have a guide to local walks?
Avez-vous un guide des promenades dans la région?
avay vooz uñ geed day promnad doñ la ray-zhyoñ

Do you know any good walks?
Vous connaissez de bonnes promenades?
voo koneh-say duh bon promnad

How many kilometres is the walk?
La promenade fait combien de kilomètres?
la promnad feh koñ-byañ duh keelo-metr

How long will it take?
Ça prendra combien de temps?
sa proñ-dra koñ-byañ duh toñ

Is it very steep?
Est-ce que ça monte dur?
es kuh sa moñt door

We'd like to go climbing
Nous aimerions faire de l'escalade
nooz ehmuh-ryoñ fehr duh leska-lad

Do I/we need walking boots?
Est-ce qu'il faut des chaussures de marche?
es keel foh day shoh-soor duh marsh

Should we take...?
Est-ce qu'il faut emporter...?
es keel foh oñportay...

waterproofs
un imperméable
uñ añ-pehrmay-abl

water	food	a compass
de l'eau	quelque chose à manger	une boussole
duh loh	*kelkuh zhohz a moñ-zhay*	*oon boosol*

What time does it get dark?
À quelle heure est-ce qu'il commence à faire nuit?
a kel ur es keel komoñs a fehr nwee

see also **MAPS & GUIDES**

*The international code for France is **00 33** plus the French number
you require less the first **0**. Other codes are: Belgium – **00 32**,
Luxembourg – **00 352**, Switzerland – **00 41**. To phone the UK from
abroad, dial **00 44** plus the UK area code less the first **0**. You
always dial the area code and number in France. Even for local
calls. (Paris **01**, NW France **02**, NE **03**, SE & Corsica **04**, SW **05**.)*

French phone numbers are given in 2 digits				
01	**44**	**79**	**04**	**57**
zéro un	quarante-quatre	soixante-dix-neuf	zéro quatre	cinquante-sept

I'd like to make a phone call
Je voudrais téléphoner
zhuh voodray taylay-fonay

A phonecard, please
Une télécarte, s'il vous plaît
oon taylay-kart seel voo pleh

Do you have a mobile?
Vous avez un portable?
vooz avay uñ por-tabl

Can I use your mobile?
Je peux emprunter votre portable?
zhuh puh oñprañtay vohtr por-tabl

My mobile number is...
Le numéro de mon portable est...
lun noo-mayro duh moñ por-tabl eh...

Monsieur Brun, please
Monsieur Brun, s'il vous plaît
muhsyuh bruñ seel voo pleh

Is there a pay phone?
Il y a un téléphone public?
eel ya uñ taylay-fon poobleek

for ... euros
de ... euros
duh ... uh-roh

What's your mobile number?
Quel est le numéro de votre portable?
kel eh luh noo-mayro duh votr por-tabl

Extension...
le poste...
luh post...

I'd like to speak to...
Je voudrais parler à...
zhuh voodray parlay a...

This is Jim Brown
C'est de la part de Jim Brown
say duh la par duh jim brown

It's Mr Brooke
Monsieur Brooke à l'appareil
muhsyuh brooke a lapa-ray-yuh

How do I get an outside line?
Comment on fait pour avoir une ligne extérieure?
komoñ oñ feh poor avvar oon leen-yuh ekstay-ree-uhr

I'll call back...
Je vous rappellerai...
zhuh voo ra-pehlray...

later
plus tard
ploo tar

tomorrow
demain
duhmañ

■ YOU MAY HEAR

Âllo
alo
Hello

C'est de la part de qui?
say duh la par duh kee
Who's calling?

Un instant, s'il vous plaît...
uñ añstoñ seel voo pleh...
Just a moment...

Je vous le/la passe
zhuh voo luh/la pass
I'm putting you through

C'est occupé
sayt okoopay
It's engaged

Pouvez-vous rappeler plus tard?
poovay voo ra-play ploo tar
Please try later

Voulez-vous laisser un message?
voolay voo lay-say uñ messazh
Do you want to leave a message?

Veuillez laisser votre message après le bip sonore
vuh-yay lay-say votr messazh apreh luh beep soñor
Please leave a message after the tone

S'il vous plaît, éteignez votre portable
seel voo pleh ayten-yay votr por-tabl
Please turn your mobile off

I will text you
Je t'enverrai un message
zhuh toñvuh-ray uñ messazh

Can you text me?
Tu peux m'envoyer un message?
too puh moñ-voyay uñ messazh

see you tomorrow
@ 2m1 (à demain)

see you later
@+ (à plus tard)

hello
bjr (bonjour) or slt (salut)

thank you
mr6 (merci)

please
svp (s'il vous plaît)

who
ki (qui)

what
k or koa (quoi)

someone
qqn (quelqu'un)

something
qqch (quelque chose)

Are you busy?
toqp (t'es occupé?)

Are you OK?
tok (t'es OK?)

weekend
we (week-end)

What's up/new?
k29 or koa29 (quoi de neuf)

now
NOW (maintenant)

soon
BI1TO (bientôt)

don't mention it
p2k (pas de quoi)

it doesn't matter
cpg (c'est pas grave)

in any case
entouk (en tout cas)

why
pk or pkoa (pourquoi)

when
qd or kan (quand)

because
parske (parce que)

there is/are
ya (il y a)

when you like
qtv (quand tu veux)

I'm sorry
dsl (desolé)

I love you
je t'm (je t'aime)

I'm going (there)
jv (j'y vais)

see also **E-MAIL**

An informal way of addressing an e-mail is Salut... and ending it with à bientôt (speak to you soon). For more formal e-mails, begin either Cher... (for a man) and Chère... (for a woman) and end with amicalement.

tél: .... (phone)	on forms mél is used for
mél: .... (e-mail)	e-mail address

Do you have an e-mail?
Vous avez une adresse e-mail?
vooz avay oon ad-ress ee-mehl

What is your e-mail address?
Quelle est votre adresse e-mail?
kel ay votr ad-ress ee-mehl

How do you spell it?
Comment ça s'écrit?
komoñ sa saykree

All one word
En un seul mot
oñ uñ suhl moh

All lower case
Tout en minuscules
too oñ mee-nooskool

My e-mail address is...
Mon adresse e-mail est...
moñ ad-ress ee-mehl eh...

caroline.smith@anycompany.co.uk
caroline point smith arrobase anycompany point co point uk
caroline pwañ smith a-ro-baz anycompany pwañ say oh pwañ oo ka

Can I send an e-mail?
Je peux envoyer un e-mail?
zhuh puh oñ-vwa-yay uñ ee-mehl

Did you get my e-mail?
Est-ce que vous avez reçu mon e-mail?
ess-kuh vooz av-ay ruh-soo moñ ee-mehl

see also **TEXT** ☐ **INTERNET** ☐ **FAX** ☐ **BUSINESS**

ACCUEIL *akuh-yuh*	HOME
NOM D'UTILISATEUR *noñ dooteelee-zah-tuhr*	USERNAME
NAVIGUER SUR INTERNET *naveegay soor añterneh*	TO BROWSE
FOIRE AUX QUESTIONS *fwar oh kestyoñ*	FAQ (FREQUENTLY ASKED QUESTIONS)
MOTEUR DE RECHERCHE *moh-tuhr duh ruhshehrsh*	SEARCH ENGINE
MOT DE PASSE *moh duh pas*	PASSWORD
CONTACTEZ-NOUS *kontaktay-noo*	CONTACT US
RETOUR VERS LE SOMMAIRE *ruhtoor vehr luh som-mehr*	BACK TO MENU
PLAN DU SITE *ploñ doo seet*	SITEMAP

Are there any internet cafés here?
Est-ce qu'il y a des cyber-cafés par ici?
es keel ya day cyber-kafay par eesee

How much is it to log on for an hour?
Combien coûte une heure de connection?
koñbyañ koot oon uhr duh koneksyoñ

Do you have a website?
Avez-vous un site web?
avay voo uñ seet web

The website address is www.collins.co.uk
L'adresse web est www.collins.co.uk
ladres web eh doo-bluh-vay doo-bluh-vay doo-bluh-vay pwañ collins pwañ say oh pwañ oo ka

Do you know any good sites for...?
Connaissez-vous de bons sites pour...?
konehsay-voo duh boñ seet poor...

Which is the best search engine to use?
Quel est le meilleur moteur de recherche?
kel eh luh may-yuh motuhr duh ruhshehrsh

I can't log on
Je n'arrive pas à me connecter
zhuh nareev pa a muh konektay

see also TEXT ☐ E-MAIL ☐ FAX ☐ BUSINESS   61

International codes: France **00 33** *(1-Paris), Belgium* **00 32**, *Luxembourg* **00 352**, *Switzerland* **00 41**. *The code from abroad for the UK is* **00 44**.

ADDRESSING A FAX	
À/DE	TO/FROM
OBJET :	RE:
NOMBRE DE PAGES	NUMBER OF PAGES
VEUILLEZ TROUVER CI-JOINT...	PLEASE FIND ATTACHED...

Can I send a fax from here?
Est-ce que je peux envoyer un fax d'ici?
es kuh zhuh puh oñvwa-yay uñ fax deesee

Do you have a fax?
Avez-vous un fax?
avay voo uñ fax

I want to send a fax
Je voudrais envoyer un fax
zhuh voodray oñvwa-yay uñ fax

What is your fax number?
Quel est votre numéro de fax?
kel eh votr noomayro duh fax

My fax number is...
Mon numéro de fax est...
moñ noomayro duh fax eh...

Did you get my fax?
Vous avez bien reçu mon fax?
vooz avay byan ruh-soo moñ fax

Please resend your fax
Veuillez nous renvoyer votre fax
vuh-yay noo roñvwa-yay votr fax

I can't read it
Je n'arrive pas à le lire
zhuh nahreev pa a luh leer

The fax is constantly engaged
Le fax est constamment occupé
luh fax eh koñstamoñ okoopay

see also **INTERNET** ☐ **E-MAIL** ☐ **BUSINESS**

Tuesday 17 May 2004	mardi 17 mai 2004
Dear Sirs	Messieurs *(commercial letter)*
Dear Sir/Madam	Monsieur/Madame
Yours faithfully	Je vous prie d'agréer, Monsieur/Madame, l'expression de mes salutations distinguées
Dear Mr.../Mrs...	Cher Monsieur.../Chère Madame...
Yours sincerely	Je vous prie d'agréer, M..../Mme..., l'expression de mes sentiments les plus dévoués
Dear Aude	Chère Aude
Best regards	Salutations *or* Cordialement
Dear Pierre	Cher Pierre
Love	Je t'embrasse *or* Grosses bises

What is your address?
Quelle est votre adresse?
kel eh votr a-dres

What is your postcode (zip)?
Quel est votre code postal?
kel eh votr kod postal

Addressing an envelope

M. et Mme Bertillon
16, rue des Poissons
14290 Orbec
France

number of house and road
postcode and town
country

see also **INTERNET** ☐ **E-MAIL** ☐ **FAX** ☐ **BUSINESS**

MONEY

Banks are generally open 9 am to 4.30 pm Monday to Friday, but as this varies you are best advised to go in the morning.

DISTRIBUTEUR *dees-tree-bootuhr*	**CASH DISPENSER**
INSÉREZ VOTRE CARTE *añsayray votr kart*	**INSERT YOUR CARD**
ATTENDEZ S.V.P. *at-toñday svp*	**PLEASE WAIT**
COMPOSEZ VOTRE CODE SECRET *koñpozay votr kod suhkret*	**ENTER YR PIN NUMBER**
PUIS VALIDEZ *pwee valeeday*	**AND PRESS ENTER**
RETRAIT ESPÈCES *ruhtreh espes*	**CASH WITHDRAWAL**
TAPEZ LE MONTANT *tapay luh moñtoñ*	**PRESS AMOUNT REQUIRED**
PRENEZ VOS BILLETS *pruhnay voh beeyay*	**TAKE YOUR CASH**

Where can I change some money?
Où est-ce que je peux changer de l'argent?
oo es kuh zhuh puh shoñ-zhay duh lar-zhoñ

I want to change these traveller's cheques
Je voudrais changer ces travellers
zhuh voodray shoñ-zhay say travellers

When does the bank open?
La banque ouvre quand?
la boñk oovr koñ

When does the bank close?
La banque ferme quand?
la boñk fehrm koñ

Can I pay with pounds / euros?
Je peux payer en livres sterling / euros?
zhuh puh pay-yay oñ leevr sterling / uh-roh

Can I use my credit card to get euros?
Je peux avoir des euros avec ma carte de crédit?
zhuh puh avwar day zuh-roh avek ma kart duh kraydee

Can I use my card with this cash dispenser?
Je peux utiliser ma carte dans ce distributeur?
zhuh puh ooteelee-zay ma kart doñ suh deestreeboo-tur

Do you have any loose change?
Vous avez de la monnaie?
vooz avay duh la monay

64   *see also* **PAYING**

L'ADDITION *ladeesyoñ*	BILL *(restaurant)*
LA NOTE *la not*	BILL *(hotel)*
LA FACTURE *la faktoor*	INVOICE
LA CAISSE *la kehs*	CASH DESK

How much is it?
C'est combien? / Ça fait combien?
say koñ-byañ / sa feh koñ-byañ

How much will it be?
Ça fera combien?
sa fuh-ra koñ-byañ

Can I pay...?
Je peux payer...?
zhuh puh pay-yay...

by credit card
par carte de crédit
par carte duh kraydee

by cheque
par chèque
par shek

Put it on my bill *(hotel)*
Mettez-le sur ma note
metay luh soor ma not

The bill, please
L'addition, s'il vous plaît
ladeesyoñ seel voo pleh

Do you take credit cards?
Vous acceptez les cartes de crédit?
vooz aksep-tay lay kart duh kraydee

My credit card number is...
Mon numéro de carte de crédit, c'est le...
moñ noo-mayroh duh kart duh kraydee say luh...

Expiry date...
Date d'expiration...
dat dekspeera-syoñ...

Valid until...
Valide jusqu'à...
valeed zhoos-ka...

Could you give me a receipt, please?
Pourriez-vous me donner un reçu, s'il vous plaît?
pooree-ay voo muh donay uñ ruhsoo seel voo pleh

Do I pay in advance?
Est-ce qu'il faut payer à l'avance?
es keel foh pay-yay ala-voñs

I'm sorry
Je suis désolé(e)
zhuh swee dayzo-lay

I've nothing smaller *(no change)*
Je n'ai pas de monnaie
zhuh nay pa duh monay

see also **SHOPPING** ☐ **MONEY**

LE RETRAIT DE BAGAGES *luh ruhtreh duh bagazh*	**BAGGAGE RECLAIM**
LA CONSIGNE *la koñsee-nyuh*	**LEFT LUGGAGE**
LE CHARIOT À BAGAGES *luh sharyoh a bagazh*	**LUGGAGE TROLLEY**

My luggage hasn't arrived yet
Mes bagages ne sont pas encore arrivés
may bagazh nuh soñ pa oñkor aree-vay

My suitcase has been damaged on the flight
Ma valise a été abîmée pendant le vol
ma valeez a aytay abee-may poñdoñ luh vol

What has happened to the luggage on the flight from...?
Où sont passés les bagages du vol en provenance de...?
oo soñ pas-ay lay bagazh doo vol oñ prohvuh-noñs duh...

Can you help me with my luggage, please?
S'il vous plaît, pouvez-vous m'aider à porter mes bagages?
seel voo pleh poovay voo mayday a portay may bagazh

When does the left luggage office open / close?
Quand est-ce que la consigne ouvre / ferme?
koñt es kuh la koñsee-nyuh oovr / fehrm

I'd like to leave this suitcase...
Je voudrais consigner cette valise...
zhuh voodray koñseen-yay set valeez...

until 4 o'clock
jusqu'à seize heures
zhoo-ska sehz ur

overnight
pour la nuit
poor la nwee

till Saturday
jusqu'à samedi
zhoo-ska samdee

Can I leave my luggage here?
Je peux laisser mes bagages ici?
zhuh puh lay-say may bagazh eesee

I'll collect it at...
Je viendrai les chercher à...
zhuh vyañdray lay shehrshay a...

■ YOU MAY HEAR

Vous pouvez les laisser ici jusqu'à dix-huit heures
voo poovay lay lay-say eesee zhoo-ska deez-weet ur
You can leave your luggage here until 6 o'clock

see also **TRAIN** □ **AIR TRAVEL**

LE CORDONNIER *luh kordon-yay*   **SHOE REPAIR SHOP**
RÉPARATIONS MINUTE *raypa-ra-syoñ meenoot*   **REPAIRS WHILE YOU WAIT**

This is broken
C'est cassé
say kassay

Where can I get this repaired?
Où est-ce que je peux le faire réparer?
oo es kuh zhuh puh luh fehr raypa-ray

My ... is broken
Mon/Ma ... est cassé(e)
moñ/ma ... eh kassay

My ... are broken
Mes ... sont cassé(e)s
may ... soñ kassay

Is it worth repairing?
Ça vaut la peine de le faire réparer?
sa voh la pehn duh luh fehr raypa-ray

Can you repair...?
Pouvez-vous réparer...?
poovay voo raypa-ray...

these shoes
ces chaussures
say shoh-soor

my watch
ma montre
ma moñtr

How much will it be?
Ça reviendra à combien?
sa ruhvyañ-dra a koñ-byañ

Can you do it straight away?
Vous pouvez le faire tout de suite?
voo poovay luh fehr too d-sweet

How long will it take?
Ça prendra combien de temps?
sa proñd-ra koñ-byañ duh toñ

When will it be ready?
Ça sera prêt quand?
sa suh-ra preh koñ

Where can I have my shoes reheeled?
Où est-ce que je peux faire mettre de nouveaux talons à mes chaussures? *oo es kuh zhuh puh fehr metr duh noovoh taloñ a may shoh-soor*

I need...
Il me faut...
eel muh foh...

some glue
de la colle
duh la kol

some Sellotape®
du scotch®
doo scotch

some buttons
des boutons
day bootoñ

Do you have a needle and thread?
Vous avez du fil et une aiguille?
vooz avay doo feel ay oon aygwee-yuh

The lights have fused
Les plombs ont sauté
lay ploñ oñ soh-tay

see also **BREAKDOWN**

LAUNDRY

LE PRESSING *luh preh-seeng*	**DRY-CLEANER'S**
LA LAVERIE AUTOMATIQUE *la lav-ree ohto-ma-teek*	**LAUNDERETTE**
LA LESSIVE EN POUDRE *la luhseev oñ poodr*	**WASHING POWDER**

Where can I do some washing?
Où est-ce que je peux faire un peu de lessive?
oo es kuh zhuh puh fehr uñ puh duh leseev

Do you have a laundry service?
Vous avez un service de blanchisserie?
vooz avay uñ sehrvees duh bloñshees-ree

When will my things be ready?
Quand est-ce que mes affaires seront prêtes?
koñt es kuh mayz afehr suh-roñ pret

Is there … near here?	**a launderette**	**a dry-cleaner's**
Il y a … près d'ici?	une laverie automatique	un pressing
eel ya … pray deesee	*oon lav-ree ohto-ma-teek*	*uñ pressing*

When does it open?	**When does it close?**
Ça ouvre à quelle heure?	Ça ferme à quelle heure?
sa oovr a kel ur	*sa fehrm a kel ur*

What coins do I need?
Qu'est-ce qu'il me faut comme pièces de monnaie?
kes keel muh foh kom pyes duh monay

Where can I dry my clothes?
Où est-ce que je peux faire sécher le linge?
oo es kuh zhuh puh fehr sayshay luh lañzh

Can you iron these clothes?
Pouvez-vous repasser ce linge?
poovay voo ruhpa-say suh lañzh

Can I borrow an iron?
Je peux vous emprunter un fer à repasser?
zhuh puh vooz oñprañ-tay uñ fehr a ruhpa-say

   see also **HOTEL (RECEPTION)**

This doesn't work
Ça ne marche pas
sa nuh marsh pa

The ... doesn't work
Le/La ... ne marche pas
luh/la ... nuh marsh pa

The ... don't work
Les ... ne marchent pas
lay ... nuh marsh pa

light	**lock**	**heating**	**air conditioning**
la lumière	la serrure	le chauffage	la climatisation
la loo-myehr	*la sehroor*	*luh shoffazh*	*la kleema-teeza-syoñ*

There's a problem with my room
Ma chambre ne va pas
ma shoñbr nuh va pa

It's noisy
Il y a beaucoup de bruit
eel ya bohkoo duh brwee

It's too hot...
Il fait trop chaud...
eel feh troh shoh...

It's too cold...
Il fait trop froid...
eel feh troh frwa...

in my room
dans ma chambre
doñ ma shoñbr

It's too hot / too cold (food)
C'est trop chaud / trop froid
say troh shoh / troh frwa

The meat is cold
La viande est froide
la vyoñd eh frwad

This isn't what I ordered
Ce n'est pas ce que j'ai commandé
suh neh pa suh kuh zhay komoñday

It's dirty
C'est sale
say sal

To whom should I complain?
À qui dois-je m'adresser pour faire une réclamation?
a kee dwa-zh madressay poor fehr oon rayklama-syoñ

It's faulty
Il y a un défaut
eel ya uñ dayfoh

I want a refund
Je veux être remboursé(e)
zhuh vuh etr roñboor-say

see also **HOTEL (RECEPTION)** ▢ **REPAIRS** ▢ **PROBLEMS** 69

Can you help me?
Pouvez-vous m'aider?
poovay voo mayday

I speak very little French
Je parle très peu le français
zhuh parl treh puh luh froñseh

Does anyone here speak English?
Est-ce qu'il y a quelqu'un qui parle anglais ici?
es keel ya kelkuñ kee parl oñgleh eesee

I've lost my key
J'ai perdu ma clé
zhay pehrdoo ma klay

I've locked myself out
Je me suis enfermé(e) dehors
zhuh muh swee oñfehr-may duh-ohr

I would like to speak to whoever is in charge
Je voudrais parler au responsable
zhuh voodray parlay oh ruhspoñ-sabl

I'm lost
Je me suis perdu(e)
zhuh muh swee pehrdoo

How do I get to...?
pour aller à/au (etc.)...?
poor alay a/oh...

I missed...	**my train**	**my plane**	**my connection**
J'ai raté...	mon train	mon avion	ma correspondance
zhay ratay...	*moñ trañ*	*moñ a-vyoñ*	*ma kores-poñ-doñs*

I've missed my flight because there was a strike
J'ai raté mon avion à cause d'une grève
zhay ratay moñ a-vyoñ a kohz doon grehv

The coach has left without me
Le car est parti sans moi
luh kar eh partee soñ mwa

Can you show me how this works?
Pouvez-vous me montrer comment ça marche?
poovay voo muh moñtray komoñ sa marsh

I have lost my purse
J'ai perdu mon porte-monnaie
zhay pehrdoo moñ port-monay

I need to get to...
Je dois aller à/au (etc.)...
zhuh dwa alay a/oh...

Leave me alone!
Laissez-moi tranquille!
laysay mwa troñkeel

Go away!
Allez-vous en!
alay vooz oñ

EMERGENCIES

POLICE *polees*	**POLICE**
AMBULANCE *oñboo-loñs*	**AMBULANCE**
POMPIERS *poñpyay*	**FIRE BRIGADE**
COMMISSARIAT *komee-sar-ya*	**POLICE STATION**
GENDARMERIE *zhoñdarm-ree*	**POLICE STATION** (in villages)
URGENCES *oorzhoñs*	**A&E**

Help!
Au secours!
oh skoor

Fire!
Au feu!
oh fuh

Can you help me?
Pouvez-vous m'aider?
poovay voo mayday

There's been an accident!
Il y a eu un accident!
eel ya oo uñ aksee-doñ

Someone has been injured
Il y a un blessé
eel ya uñ blessay

He's been knocked down by a car
Il a été renversé par une voiture
eel a aytay roñvehrsay par oon vwatoor

Please call...
S'il vous plaît, appelez...
seel voo pleh apuhlay...

the police
la police
la polees

an ambulance
une ambulance
oon oñboo-loñs

Where is the police station?
Où est le commissariat?
oo eh luh komee-sar-ya

I want to report a theft
je veux signaler un vol
zhuh vuh seen-yalay uñ vol

I've been robbed / attacked
On m'a volé / attaqué
oñ ma volay / ata-kay

I've been raped
On m'a violée
oñ ma vee-o-lay

Someone's stolen...
On m'a volé...
oñ ma volay...

my handbag
mon sac à main
moñ sak a mañ

my money
mon argent
moñ arzhoñ

My car has been broken into
On a forcé ma voiture
oñ a forsay ma vwatoor

cont...

71

My car has been stolen
On m'a volé ma voiture
oñ ma volay ma vwatoor

I want to speak to a policewoman
Je veux parler à une femme agent de police
zhuh vuh parlay a oon fam azhoñ duh polees

I need to make a telephone call
Il faut que je passe un coup de téléphone
eel foh kuh zhuh pas uñ koo duh taylay-fon

I need a report for my insurance
Il me faut un constat pour mon assurance
eel muh foh uñ konsta poor moñ asoo-roñs

I didn't know the speed limit
Je ne savais pas quelle était la limite de vitesse
zhuh nuh sah-vay pa kel aytay la leemeet duh vee-tes

How much is the fine?
C'est une amende de combien?
say toon amoñd duh koñ-byañ

Where do I pay it?
Où dois-je la payer?
oo dwa-zhuh la pay-yay

Do I have to pay it straight away?
Est-ce qu'il faut la payer immédiatement?
es keel foh la pay-yay eemay-dyat-moñ

I'm very sorry, officer
Je suis vraiment désolé(e), monsieur l'agent
zhuh swee vraymoñ dayzo-lay muhsyuh la-zhoñ

■ **YOU MAY HEAR**

Vous avez brûlé un feu rouge
vooz avay broolay uñ fuh roozh
You went through a red light

Vous n'avez pas cédé la priorité à droite
vooz navay pa sayday la pree-oh-reetay a drwat
You didn't give way to traffic coming from the right

see also **BODY** ☐ **DOCTOR**

LA PHARMACIE *la farmasee*	**PHARMACY/CHEMIST**
LA PHARMACIE DE GARDE *la farmasee duh gard*	**DUTY CHEMIST**

I'm ill
Je suis malade
zhuh swee malad

Can you give me something for...?
Avez-vous quelque chose pour le/la *(etc.)*...?
avay voo kelk shoz poor luh/la...

a headache	**car sickness**	**flu**	**diarrhoea**
le mal de tête	le mal des transports	la grippe	la diarrhée
luh mal duh tet	*luh mal day troñspor*	*la greep*	*la dya-ray*

sunburn
les coups de soleil
lay koo duh sohlay-yuh

Is it safe for children?
C'est sans danger pour les enfants?
say soñ doñzhay poor layz oñfoñ

How much should I give them?
Combien je dois leur en donner?
koñ-byañ zhuh dwa lur oñ donay

■ **YOU MAY HEAR**

Prenez-en trois fois par jour avant / pendant / après le repas
pruhnayzoñ trwa fwa par zhoor avoñ / poñdoñ / apray luh ruhpa
Take it three times a day before / with / after meals

■ **WORDS YOU MAY NEED**

antiseptic	un antiseptique	*oñtee-septeek*
aspirin	de l'aspirine	*aspee-reen*
condoms	les préservatifs	*praysehrva-teef*
cotton wool	le coton hydrophile	*kotoñ eedro-feel*
dental floss	du fil dentaire	*feel doñtehr*
insect repellent	la crème anti-insecte	*krem oñtee-añsekt*
lip salve	le baume pour les lèvres	*bohm poor lay lehvr*
period pains	les règles douloureuses	*reh-gluh dooloo-ruhz*
plasters	le sparadrap	*spara-dra*
sore throat	le mal de gorge	*mal duh gorzh*
tampons	les tampons	*toñpoñ*
toothpaste	le dentifrice	*doñtee-frees*

see also **BODY** □ **DOCTOR**   73

In French the possessive (my, his, her, etc.) is generally not used with parts of the body, e.g.

I've broken my **leg**   Je me suis cassé **la** jambe
He's hurt his **ankle**   Il s'est fait mal **à la** cheville

ankle	la cheville	*shuhveey*
arm	le bras	*bra*
back	le dos	*doh*
bone	l'os	*os*
ear	l'oreille	*o-ray-yuh*
eye, eyes	l'œil, les yeux	*uhy, yuh*
finger	le doigt	*dwa*
foot	le pied	*pyay*
hair	les cheveux	*shuhvuh*
hand	la main	*mañ*
head	la tête	*tet*
heart	le cœur	*kur*
hip	la hanche	*oñsh*
joint	l'articulation	*artee-koola-syoñ*
kidney	le rein	*rañ*
knee	le genou	*zhuhnoo*
leg	la jambe	*zhoñb*
liver	le foie	*fwa*
mouth	la bouche	*boosh*
muscle	le muscle	*mooskl*
nail	l'ongle	*oñgl*
nose	le nez	*nay*
penis	le pénis	*paynees*
stomach	l'estomac	*esto-ma*
throat	la gorge	*gorzh*
thumb	le pouce	*poos*
toe	l'orteil	*ortay-yuh*
vagina	le vagin	*vahzhuñ*
wrist	le poignet	*pwa-nyay*

   see also **DOCTOR** □ **PHARMACY**

HÔPITAL *opeetal*	**HOSPITAL**
URGENCES *oorzhoñs*	**A & E**
CONSULTATIONS *koñsooltasyoñ*	**SURGERY HOURS**

I need a doctor
J'ai besoin d'un médecin
zhay buh-zwañ duñ maydsañ

I have a pain here (point)
J'ai mal ici
zhay mal eesee

My son / My daughter is ill
Mon fils / Ma fille est malade
moñ fees / ma feey eh malad

He / She has a temperature
Il / Elle a de la fièvre
eel / el a duh la fyeh-vr

I'm diabetic
Je suis diabétique
zhuh swee dya-bay-teek

I'm pregnant
Je suis enceinte
zhuh swee oñsañt

I'm on the pill
Je prends la pilule
zhuh proñ la peelool

I'm allergic to penicillin
Je suis allergique à la pénicilline
zhuh swee alehr-zheek a la paynee-seeleen

My blood group is...
Mon groupe sanguin est...
moñ groop soñgañ eh...

Will he have to go to hospital?
Faut-il le transporter à l'hôpital?
foh-teel luh troñsportay a lopee-tal

Will I have to pay?
Est-ce que je dois payer?
es kuh zhuh dwa pay-yay

How much will it cost?
Combien ça va coûter?
koñ-byañ sa va kootay

I need a receipt for the insurance
Il me faut un reçu pour l'assurance
eel muh foh uñ ruhsoo poor lasoo-roñs

■ YOU MAY HEAR

Il faut que vous alliez à l'hôpital
eel foh kuh voo zal-yay a lopee-tal
You will have to go to hospital

Ce n'est pas très grave
suh neh pa treh grav
It's not serious

see also **EMERGENCIES** □ **PHARMACY** □ **BODY**

UN PLOMBAGE *uñ ploñbazh*	**A FILLING**
UNE COURONNE *oon kooron*	**A CROWN**
LE DENTIER *luh doñtay*	**DENTURES**

I need to see a dentist
J'ai besoin de voir un dentiste
zhay buhzwañ duh vwar uñ doñteest

He / She has toothache
Il / Elle a mal aux dents
eel / el a mal oh doñ

Can you do a temporary filling?
Pouvez-vous me faire un plombage momentané?
poovay voo muh fehr uñ ploñbazh momoñtanay

Can you give me something for the pain?
Pouvez-vous me donner quelque chose contre la douleur?
poovay voo muh donay kelkuh shohz koñtr la doo-lur

I think I have an abscess
Je crois que j'ai un abcès
zhuh crwa kuh zhay uñ abseh

It hurts
Ça me fait mal
sa muh feh mal

Can you repair my dentures?
Pouvez-vous me réparer mon dentier?
poovay voo muh raypa-ray moñ doñtyay

Do I have to pay?
Je dois payer?
zhuh dwa payay

How much will it be?
Combien ça va coûter?
koñ-byañ sa va kootay

I need a receipt for my insurance
Il me faut un reçu pour mon assurance
eel muh foh uñ ruhsoo poor moñ asoo-roñs

■ YOU MAY HEAR

Il faut l'arracher
eel foh larashay
It has to come out

Je vais vous faire une piqûre
zhuh vay voo fehr oon peekoor
I'm going to give you an injection

 see also **PHARMACY**

What facilities do you have for disabled people?
Qu'est-ce que vous avez comme aménagements pour les handicapés?
kes kuh vooz avay kom amay-nazh-moñ poor layz oñdeekapay

Are there any toilets for the disabled?
Est-ce qu'il y a des toilettes pour handicapés?
es keel ya day twalet poor oñdeekapay

Do you have any bedrooms on the ground floor?
Avez-vous des chambres au rez-de-chaussée?
avay voo day shoñbr oh ray duh shohsay

Is there a lift?
Est-ce qu'il y a un ascenseur?
es keel ya uñ asoñ-sur

Where is the lift?
Où est l'ascenseur?
oo eh lasoñ-sur

Are there any ramps?
Est-ce qu'il y a des rampes?
es keel ya day roñp

How many steps are there?
Il y a combien de marches?
eel ya koñ-byañ duh marsh

Do you have wheelchairs?
Est-ce qu'il y a des fauteuils roulants?
es keel ya day foht-uhy rooloñ

Can you visit ... in a wheelchair?
On peut visiter ... en fauteuil roulant?
oñ puh veezeetay ... oñ foht-uhy rooloñ

Is there a reduction for disabled people?
Est-ce qu'il y a une réduction pour les handicapés?
es keel ya oon raydook-syoñ poor layz oñdeekapay

Is there somewhere I can sit down?
Est-ce qu'il y a un endroit où on peut s'asseoir?
es keel ya uñ oñ-drwa oo oñ puh saswar

see also **HOTEL**

*We have used the familiar **tu** form for these phrases.*

What would you like for breakfast?
Qu'est-ce que tu veux manger pour le petit-déjeuner?
kes kuh too vuh moñzhay poor luh puh-tee dayzhuhnay

What would you like to eat?
Qu'est-ce que tu veux manger?
kes kuh too vuh moñ-zhay

What would you like to drink?
Qu'est-ce que tu veux boire?
kes kuh too vuh bwar

Did you sleep well?
Tu as bien dormi?
too a byañ dor-mee

What would you like to do today?
Qu'est-ce que tu veux faire aujourd'hui?
kes kuh too vuh fehr oh-zhoor-dwee

I will pick you up at...
Je passerai te prendre à...
zhuh pass-ray tuh proñdr a...

May I phone home?
Est-ce que je peux téléphoner chez moi?
ess kuh zhuh puh te-le-fohnay shay mwa

I like...
J'aime bien...
zhem byañ...

I don't like...
Je n'aime pas...
zhuh nem pa...

Take care
Prends soin de toi
proñ swañ duh twa

Thanks for everything
Merci pour tout
mehr-see poor too

Thank you very much
Merci beaucoup
mehr-see boh-koo

I've had a great time
J'ai passé des moments formidables
zhay pass-ay day momoñ formeedabl

see also **POLITE EXPRESSIONS**

Public transport is free for children under 4. Children between 4 and 12 pay half price.

A child's ticket
Un billet tarif enfant
un beeyay tareef oñfoñ

He/She is ... years old
Il/Elle a ... ans
eel/el a ... oñ

Is there a reduction for children?
Est-ce qu'il y a une reduction pour les enfants?
es keel ee a oon raydook-syoñ poor layz oñfoñ

Do you have a children's menu?
Est-ce que vous avez un menu enfant?
es kuh vooz avay uñ muhnoo poor oñfoñ

Is it OK to take children?
On peut y aller avec des enfants?
on puh ee alay avek dayz oñfoñ

What is there for children to do?
Quelles sont les activités prévues pour les enfants?
kel son layz akteevee-tay pray-voo poor layz oñfoñ

Is there a play park near here?
Est-ce qu'il y a une aire de jeux près d'ici?
es keel ya oon ehr duh zhuh preh deesee

Is it safe for children?
C'est sans danger pour les enfants?
say son donzhay poor layz oñfoñ

Do you have...?
Avez-vous...?
avay voo...

a high chair
une chaise de bébé
oon shehz duh baybay

a cot
un lit d'enfant
uñ lee doñfoñ

I have two children
J'ai deux enfants
zhay duhz oñfoñ

He/She is 10 years old
Il/Elle a dix ans
eel/el a deez oñ

Do you have any children?
Est-ce que vous avez des enfants?
es kuh vooz avay dayz oñfoñ

LA RÉUNION DU CONSEIL *la rayoonyoñ doo koñsay-yuh*	**BOARD MEETING**
LA SALLE DE RÉUNION *la sal duh rayoonyoñ*	**CONFERENCE ROOM**
LE DIRECTEUR GÉNÉRAL *luh deerektuhr zhaynayral*	**MANAGING DIRECTOR**
LA RÉUNION *la rayoonyoñ*	**MEETING**
LE COMPTE RENDU *luh koñt roñdoo*	**MINUTES**
UN ÉCHANTILLON *uñ ayshoñteeyoñ*	**A SAMPLE**
PRÉSIDER LA RÉUNION *prayseeday la rayoonyoñ*	**TO CHAIR A MEETING**
DRESSER UN CONTRAT *dresay uñ koñtra*	**TO DRAW UP A CONTRACT**
LA FOIRE COMMERCIALE *la fwar komersyal*	**TRADE FAIR**
LE CHIFFRE D'AFFAIRES *luh shifr dafehr*	**TURNOVER**

I'd like to arrange a meeting with...
J'aimerais fixer une réunion avec...
zhem-ray feeksay oon ray-oon-yoñ avek...

Are you free to meet...?
Êtes-vous libre pour qu'on se rencontre...?
eht voo leebr poor koñ suh roñkoñtr...

on the 4th May
le 4 mai
luh katr may

for breakfast
pour le petit-déjeuner
poor luh puhtee dayzhuh-nay

for lunch
pour le déjeuner
poor luh dayzhuh-nay

for dinner
pour le dîner
poor luh deenay

I will confirm...
Je confirmerai...
zhuh koñfeerm-ray...

by e-mail
par e-mail
par ee-mail

by fax
par fax
par fax

I'm staying at Hotel...
Je suis à l'Hôtel...
zhuh swee a lohtel...

How do I get to your office?
Pour aller à votre bureau?
poor alay a votr boo-roh

Please let ... know that I will be ... minutes late
Veuillez faire savoir à ... que je serai en retard de ... minutes
vuh-yay fehr savwar a ... ke zhuh suh-ray oñ ruhtar duh ... meenoot

I have an appointment with...
J'ai rendez-vous avec...
zhay roñday-voo avek...

at ... o'clock
à ... heures
a ... ur

Here is my card
Voici ma carte de visite
vwasee ma kart duh veezeet

I'm delighted to meet you at last!
Je suis enchanté(e) de faire enfin votre connaissance!
zhuh swee oñshoñtay duh fehr oñfañ votr koneh-soñs

My French isn't very good
Mon français n'est pas très bon
moñ froñseh nay pa treh boñ

Please speak slowly
S'il vous plaît, parlez lentement
seel voo pleh parlay loñt-moñ

I'm sorry I'm late
Je suis désolé(e), je suis en retard
zhuh swee dayzo-lay zhuh swee oñ ruhtar

My flight was delayed
Mon vol avait du retard
moñ vol aveh doo ruhtar

May I introduce you to...
Je voudrais vous présenter à...
zhuh voodray voo prayzoñtay a...

Can I offer you dinner?
Est-ce que je peux vous inviter à dîner?
es kuh zhuh puh vooz añveetay a deenay

at my hotel?
à mon hôtel?
a moñ ohtel

■ **YOU MAY HEAR**

Est-ce que vous avez rendez-vous?
es kuh vooz avay roñday-voo
Do you have an appointment?

...n'est pas au bureau
...neh paz oh booroh
...isn't in the office

Il / Elle sera de retour dans cinq minutes
eel / el suh-ra duh ruhtoor doñ sañk meenoot
He / She will be back in five minutes

see also **TELEPHONE** ❑ **E-MAIL** ❑ **INTERNET** ❑ **FAX**

ALPHABET

The French alphabet is the same as the English. Below are the words used for clarification when spelling something out.

How do you spell it?
Comment ça s'écrit?
komoñ sa say-kree

A as in Anatole, b as in Berthe
A comme Anatole, b comme Berthe
a kom ana-tol bay kom behrt

A	a	**Anatole**	ana-tol	
B	bay	**Berthe**	behrt	
C	say	**Célestin**	sayles-tañ	
D	day	**Désiré**	dayzee-ray	
E	uh	**Eugène**	uh-zhen	
F	ef	**François**	froñswah	
G	zhay	**Gaston**	gastoñ	
H	ash	**Henri**	oñree	
I	ee	**Irma**	eerma	
J	zhee	**Joseph**	zhohzef	
K	ka	**Kléber**	klaybehr	
L	el	**Louis**	lw-ee	
M	em	**Marcel**	marsel	
N	en	**Nicolas**	neekoh-la	
O	oh	**Oscar**	oskar	
P	pay	**Pierre**	pyehr	
Q	koo	**Quintal**	kañtal	
R	ehr	**Raoul**	ra-ool	
S	es	**Suzanne**	soozan	
T	tay	**Thérèse**	tayrez	
U	oo	**Ursule**	oorsool	
V	vay	**Victor**	veektor	
W	doo-bluh-vay	**William**	weel-yam	
X	eex	**Xavier**	kza-vyay	
Y	ee grek	**Yvonne**	eevon	
Z	zed	**Zoé**	zoh-ay	

◼ LIQUIDS

1/2 litre...	un demi-litre de...	uñ duhmee leetr duh...
a litre of...	un litre de...	uñ leetr duh...
1/2 bottle of...	une demi-bouteille de...	oon duhmee-bootay-yuh duh...
a bottle of...	une bouteille de...	oon bootay-yuh duh...
a glass of...	un verre de...	uñ vehr duh...

◼ WEIGHTS

100 grams of...	cent grammes de...	soñ gram duh...
1/2 kilo of...	un demi-kilo de...	uñ duhmee keelo duh...
a kilo of...	un kilo de...	uñ keelo duh...

◼ FOOD

a slice of...	une tranche de...	oon troñsh duh...
a portion of...	une portion de...	oon por-syoñ de...
a dozen...	une douzaine de...	oon doozen duh...
a box of...	une boîte de...	oon bwat duh...
a packet of...	un paquet de...	uñ pakay duh...
a tin of...	une boîte de...	oon bwat duh...
a carton of...	une brique de...	oon breek duh...
a jar of...	un pot de...	uñ poh duh...

◼ MISCELLANEOUS

500 euros of...	500 euros de...	sañk uh-roh duh...
a third	un tiers	uñ tyehr
a quarter	un quart	uñ kar
ten per cent	dix pour cent	dee poor soñ
more...	plus de...	ploo duh...
less...	moins de...	mwañ duh...
enough of...	assez de...	assay duh...
double	le double	luh doobl
twice	deux fois	duh fwa

NUMBERS

0	**zéro** *zayro*	**1st**	**premier(ière)** 1er/ère
1	**un** *uñ*		*pruh-myay (yehr)*
2	**deux** *duh*	**2nd**	**deuxième** 2e
3	**trois** *trwa*		*duh-zyem*
4	**quatre** *katr*	**3rd**	**troisième** 3e
5	**cinq** *sañk*		*trwa-zyem*
6	**six** *sees*	**4th**	**quatrième** 4e
7	**sept** *set*		*katree-yem*
8	**huit** *weet*	**5th**	**cinquième** 5e
9	**neuf** *nuhf*		*sañ-kyem*
10	**dix** *dees*	**6th**	**sixième** 6e
11	**onze** *oñz*		*see-zyem*
12	**douze** *dooz*	**7th**	**septième** 7e
13	**treize** *trez*		*seh-tyem*
14	**quatorze** *katorz*	**8th**	**huitième** 8e
15	**quinze** *kañz*		*wee-tyem*
16	**seize** *sez*	**9th**	**neuvième** 9e
17	**dix-sept** *dees-set*		*nuh-vyem*
18	**dix-huit** *deez-weet*	**10th**	**dixième** 10e
19	**dix-neuf** *deez-nuhf*		*dee-zyem*
20	**vingt** *vañ*		
21	**vingt et un** *vañt ay uñ*		
22	**vingt-deux** *vañt-duh*		
23	**vingt-trois** *vañt-trwa*		
30	**trente** *troñt*		
40	**quarante** *karoñt*		
50	**cinquante** *sañkoñt*		
60	**soixante** *swasoñt*		
70	**soixante-dix** *swasoñt dees*		
71	**soixante et onze** *swasoñ tay-oñz*		
72	**soixante-douze** *swasoñt dooz*		
80	**quatre-vingts** *katr-vañ*		
81	**quatre-vingt-un** *katr-vañ un*		
82	**quatre-vingt-deux** *katr-vañ duh*		
90	**quatre-vingt-dix** *katr-vañ-dees*		
91	**quatre-vingt-onze** *katr-vañ-oñz*		
100	**cent** *soñ*		
110	**cent dix** *soñ dees*		
200	**deux cents** *duh soñ*		
250	**deux cent cinquante** *duh soñ sañkoñt*		
1,000	**mille** *meel*		
1 million	**un million** *uñ mee-lyoñ*		

days

LUNDI *lañdee*		**MONDAY**
MARDI *mardee*		**TUESDAY**
MERCREDI *merkruhdee*		**WEDNESDAY**
JEUDI *zhuhdee*		**THURSDAY**
VENDREDI *voñdruhdee*		**FRIDAY**
SAMEDI *samdee*		**SATURDAY**
DIMANCHE *deemoñsh*		**SUNDAY**

seasons

PRINTEMPS *prañtoñ*	**SPRING**
ÉTÉ *aytay*	**SUMMER**
AUTOMNE *ohtoñ*	**AUTUMN**
HIVER *eevehr*	**WINTER**

months

JANVIER *zhoñvyay*	**JANUARY**
FÉVRIER *fevree-yay*	**FEBRUARY**
MARS *mars*	**MARCH**
AVRIL *avreel*	**APRIL**
MAI *may*	**MAY**
JUIN *zhwañ*	**JUNE**
JUILLET *zhwee-yeh*	**JULY**
AOÛT *oot*	**AUGUST**
SEPTEMBRE *septoñbr*	**SEPTEMBER**
OCTOBRE *oktobr*	**OCTOBER**
NOVEMBRE *novoñbr*	**NOVEMBER**
DÉCEMBRE *daysoñbr*	**DECEMBER**

What is today's date?
Quelle est la date aujourd'hui?
kel eh la dat oh-zhoor-dwee

It's 8 May 2004
C'est le huit mai deux mille quatre
say luh wee may duh meel katr

It's the 5th of March
Nous sommes le 5 mars
noo som luh sañk mars

1st January
Le premier janvier
luh pruhm-yay zhoñvee-ay

on Saturday	**on Saturdays**	**every Saturday**
samedi	le samedi	tous les samedis
samdee	*luh samdee*	*too lay samdee*

this Saturday	**next Saturday**	**last Saturday**
samedi qui vient	samedi prochain	samedi dernier
samdee kee vyañ	*samdee proshañ*	*samdee dehr-nyay*

in June	**at the beginning of June**	**at the end of June**
en juin	début juin	fin juin
oñ zhwañ	*dayboo zhwañ*	*fañ zhwañ*

before summer	**during the summer**	**after summer**
avant l'été	pendant l'été	après l'été
avoñ laytay	*poñdoñ laytay*	*apreh laytay*

see also **NUMBERS**

The 24-hour clock is used a lot more in Europe than in Britain. After 1200 midday, it continues: **1300**–treize heures, **1400**–quatorze heures, **1500**–quinze heures, etc. until **2400**–vingt-quatre heures. With the 24-hour clock, the words **quart** (quarter) and **demie** (half) aren't used:

13.15 (1.15 pm)	*treize heures quinze*
19.30 (7.30 pm)	*dix-neuf heures trente*
22.45 (10.45 pm)	*vingt-deux heures quarante-cinq*

What time is it?
Il est quelle heure? / Quelle heure est-il?
eel eh kel ur / kel ur eht-eel

It's ... Il est... *eel eh...*	2 o'clock deux heures *duhz ur*	3 o'clock trois heures *trwaz ur*	6 o'clock *(etc.)* six heures *seez ur*

It's 1 o'clock Il est une heure *eel eh oon ur*	It's midday Il est midi *eel eh meedee*	It's midnight Il est minuit *eel eh meenwee*

9	**neuf heures** *nuhf ur*
9.10	**neuf heures dix** *nuhf ur dees*
quarter past 9	**neuf heures et quart** *nuhf ur ay kar*
9.20	**neuf heures vingt** *nuhf ur vañ*
9.30	**neuf heures et demie / neuf heures trente** *nuhf ur ay duhmee / nuhf ur troñt*
9.35	**dix heures moins vingt-cinq** *deez ur mwañ vañt sañk*
quarter to 10	**dix heures moins le quart** *deez ur mwañ luh kar*
10 to 10	**dix heures moins dix** *deez ur mwañ dees*

When does it... ?
Il ... à quelle heure?
eel ... a kel ur

open / close / begin / finish
ouvre / ferme / commence / finit
oovr / fehrm / komoñs / feenee

at 3 o'clock	**before 3 o'clock**	**after 3 o'clock**
à trois heures	avant trois heures	après trois heures
a trwaz ur	*avoñ trwaz ur*	*apray trwaz ur*

today	**tonight**	**tomorrow**	**yesterday**
aujourd'hui	ce soir	demain	hier
oh-zhoor-dwee	*suh swar*	*duhmañ*	*eeyehr*

the day before yesterday
avant-hier
avoñt yehr

the day after tomorrow
après-demain
apray duhmañ

in the morning	**in the afternoon**	**in the evening**
le matin	l'après-midi	le soir
luh matañ	*lapray meedee*	*luh swar*

this morning	**this afternoon**	**this evening/tonight**
ce matin	cet après-midi	ce soir
suh matañ	*set apray meedee*	*suh swar*

It's nearly 6 o'clock
Il est presque six heures
eel eh preskuh seez ur

at half past 7	**at about 10 o'clock**
à sept heures et demie	vers dix heures
a set ur ay duhmee	*vehr deez ur*

in an hour's time	**in half an hour**	**two hours ago**
dans une heure	dans une demi-heure	il y a deux heures
doñs oon ur	*doñs oon duhmee ur*	*eel ya duhz ur*

soon	**early**	**late**
bientôt	de bonne heure	tard
byañtoh	*duh bon ur*	*tar*

later
plus tard
ploo tar

I'll do it...	**as soon as possible**	**...at the latest**
Je le ferai...	aussitôt que possible	...au plus tard
zhuh luh fuh-ray...	*ohsee-toh kuh po-seebl*	*...oh ploo tar*

see also **NUMBERS**

salon de thé

Generally attached to a cake shop, pâtisserie, where you can sit down and sample some of the cakes. Can be quite expensive.

Crêperie

Specialising in sweet and savoury pancakes (galettes). Good for light inexpensive meals.

Libre-service

Self-service

BISTRO

Usually cheaper and smaller than Brasserie

glacier

Ice-cream parlour

gaufres

waffles

Restaurant

Generally open 11.30 am to 2.30 pm and 7.30 to 10.30 pm. The menu is posted outside.

table d'hôte

Home cooking using local produce.

BRASSERIE

All-day food place often attached to a bar-café

Frites 500m

Signals a road-side café 500 metres away. Mediocre food (mostly chips).

*If you just ask for **un café** you will be served a small strong black coffee. You should specify the type of coffee you want:*

un café crème	*uñ kafay krem*	**white coffee**
un grand crème	*uñ groñ krem*	**large white coffee**
un café au lait	*uñ kafay oh leh*	**coffee with hot milk**

a coffee	**a sweet cider**	**an orangeade**	**...please**
un café	un cidre doux	une orangeade	...s'il vous plaît
uñ kafay	*uñ seedr doo*	*oon oroñzhad*	*...seel voo pleh*

a tea...	**with milk**	**with lemon**	**no sugar**
un thé...	au lait	au citron	sans sucre
uñ tay...	*oh leh*	*oh seetroñ*	*soñ sookr*

for two	**for me**	**for him / her**	**for us**
pour deux personnes	pour moi	pour lui / elle	pour nous
poor duh pehr-son	*poor mwa*	*poor lwee / el*	*poor noo*

with ice, please
avec des glaçons, s'il vous plaît
avek day glasoñ seel voo pleh

Some mineral water	**sparkling / still**
De l'eau minérale	gazeuse / plate
duh loh meenay-ral	*gazuhz / plat*

Would you like to have a drink?	**What will you have?**
Vous voulez prendre quelque chose?	Qu'est-ce que vous prenez?
voo voolay proñdr kelkuh shohz	*kes kuh voo pruhnay*

I'm very thirsty!	**It's my round!**	**I'm paying!**
J'ai très soif	C'est ma tournée!	C'est moi qui paie!
zhay treh swaf	*say ma toornay*	*say mwa kee pay*

■ OTHER DRINKS TO TRY

un chocolat *rich-tasting hot chocolate*
un citron pressé *freshly-squeezed lemon: add water and sugar*
un diabolo *lemonade and cordial:* **menthe** *mint,* **fraise** *strawberry*
une tisane *herb tea:* **verveine** *verbena,* **tilleul** *lime*

see also **IN A RESTAURANT**

READING THE MENU

Restaurants exhibit their menus outside. Often there is a choice of two or three menus at different prices as well as à la carte dishes. French families often go to a restaurant for Sunday lunch, so it is advisable to book in advance.

| Boisson non comprise | drink not included |

Plat du jour à 7 € 50	dish of the day 7 € 50
poisson	fish
ou viande *garnis*	or meat with veg and French fries
ou volaille	or poultry

menu du midi	lunchtime menu
entrée + plat + café	starter + main course + coffee

Carte	*Menu*
Entrées	**Starters**
potages	soups
assiette de charcuterie	assorted pâté & salami
assiette de crudités	assorted raw veg & dip
Viandes	**Meat**
Gibier et Volaille	**Game & Poultry**
Poissons	**Fish**
fruits de mer	seafood
Légumes	**Vegetables**
Fromages	**Cheese**
Desserts	**Dessert**
Boissons	**Drinks**

For those who are vegetarian, or who prefer vegetarian dishes, turn to the VEGETARIAN topic on page 92 for further phrases.

Hello, we'd like to eat
Bonjour, nous voudrions manger
boñzhoor noo voodree-yoñ moñzhay

A table for two?
Une table pour deux?
oon tabl poor duh

Can you recommend a good restaurant?
Pouvez-vous nous recommander un bon restaurant?
poovay voo noo ruhko-moñday uñ boñ resto-roñ

I'd like to book a table for ... people
Je voudrais réserver une table pour ... personnes
zhuh voodray rayzehr-vay oon tabl poor ... pehr-son

for tonight	**for tomorrow night**	**at 7.30**
pour ce soir	pour demain soir	à dix-neuf heures trente
poor suh swar	*poor duhmañ swar*	*a deez-nuhf ur troñt*

The menu, please
Le menu, s'il vous plaît
luh muhnoo seel voo pleh

What is the dish of the day?
Quel est le plat du jour?
kel eh luh pla doo zhoor

I'll have the menu at ... euros, please
Je prends le menu à ... euros, s'il vous plaît
zhuh proñ luh muhnoo a ... uh-roh seel voo pleh

Can you recommend a local dish?
Pouvez-vous nous recommander un plat régional?
poovay voo noo ruhko-moñday uñ pla rayzho-nal

What is in this?
Qu'est-ce qu'il y a dedans?
kes keel ya duh doñ

I'll have this
Je prends ça
zhuh proñ sa

More bread...	**More water...**	**please**
Encore du pain...	Encore de l'eau...	s'il vous plaît
oñkor doo pañ...	*oñkor duh loh...*	*seel voo pleh*

The bill, please
L'addition, s'il vous plaît
ladee-syoñ seel voo pleh

Is service included?
Est-ce que le service est compris?
es kuh luh sehrvees eh koñpree

see also **EATING PLACES** ▯ **WINES & SPIRITS**

Don't expect great things – the French love good meat!

Are there any vegetarian restaurants here?
Est-ce qu'il y a des restaurants végétariens ici?
es keel ya day resto-roñ vay-zhayta-ryañ eesee

I am vegetarian
Je suis végétarien(ne)
zhuh swee vay-zhayta-ryañ(-ryen)

Do you have any vegetarian dishes?
Vous avez des plats végétariens?
vooz avay day pla vay-zhayta-ryañ

What fish dishes do you have?
Qu'est-ce que vous avez comme poisson?
kes kuh vooz avay kom pwasoñ

I'd like pasta as a main course
Je voudrais des pâtes comme plat principal
zhuh voodray day pat kom pla pruñseepal

I don't like meat
Je n'aime pas la viande
zhuh nehm pa la vyoñd

What do you recommend?
Qu'est-ce que vous me conseillez?
kes kuh voo muh koñsay-yay

Is it made with vegetable stock?
Est-ce que c'est fait avec du bouillon de légumes?
es kuh say feh avek doo boo-yoñ duh laygoom

■ POSSIBLE DISHES

tagliatelles *pasta*
salade verte *green salad:* niçoise *tomatoes, olives, tuna, eggs*
artichauts à la sauce fromage *artichokes in cheese sauce*
soupe à l'oignon *French onion soup*
tarte à l'oignon *onion tart*
ratatouille *courgettes, tomatoes, peppers, onions, aubergines*
pizzas *various pizzas*
crêpes *sweet and savoury pancakes with various filling*

The wine list, please
La carte des vins, s'il vous plaît
la kart day vañ seel voo pleh

white wine / red wine
du vin blanc / du vin rouge
doo vañ bloñ / doo vañ roozh

Can you recommend a good wine?
Pouvez-vous nous recommander un bon vin?
poovay voo noo ruhko-moñday uñ boñ vañ

A bottle...
Une bouteille...
oon bootay-yuh...

A carafe...
Un pichet...
uñ pee-shay...

of the house wine
de la cuvée du patron
duh la koovay doo patroñ

Barsac *sweet white wine*
Beaujolais *light fruity wines to be drunk young (Burgundy)*
Bergerac *red and white wines (Dordogne)*
Blanc de blancs *any white wine made from white grapes only*
Blanquette de Limoux *dry sparkling white wine (southwest)*
Bordeaux *region producing red (claret), dry and sweet wines*
Bourgueuil *light, fruity red wine to be drunk very young (Loire)*
Brouilly *among the finest Beaujolais: fruity, supple, full of flavour*
Cabernet Sauvignon *red wine with a slight blackcurrant aroma*
Cahors *dark, long-lived, powerful red wine from the south west*
Chablis *very dry, full-bodied white wine (Burgundy)*
Chambertin *one of the finest red Burgundies (Burgundy)*
Champagne *sparkling white/rosé (Champagne)*
Chardonnay *a white grape variety widely used in sparkling wines*
Châteauneuf-du-Pape *good,full-bodied red wine (Rhône)*
Côtes de Beaune *full-bodied red (Burgundy)*
Côtes du Rhône *full-bodied red (Rhône)*
Côtes du Roussillon *good ordinary red (Languedoc-Roussillon)*
Entre-deux-mers *medium-dry white wine from Bordeaux*
Fitou *dark red, sturdy wine (Languedoc-Roussillon)*
Gewürztraminer *fruity, spicy white wine (Alsace)*
Mâcon *good ordinary red and white wines (Burgundy)*
Médoc *principal wine-producing area of Bordeaux*

cont...

Mersault *dry white wine (Burgundy)*
Monbazillac *sweet white wine (Dordogne)*
Muscadet *very dry white wine (Loire)*
Pouilly-Fuissé *light dry white wine (Burgundy)*
Pouilly-Fumé *spicy, dry white wine (Loire)*
Rosé d'Anjou *light, fruity rosé (Loire)*
Saint-Emilion *good full-bodied red wine (Bordeaux)*
Sancerre *dry white wine (Loire)*
Sauternes *sweet white wine (Bordeaux)*
Sylvaner *dry white wine (Alsace)*
Vouvray *dry, sweet and sparkling white wines (Loire)*

■ SPIRITS & LIQUEURS

What liqueurs do you have?
Qu'est-ce que vous avez comme digestifs?
kes kuh vooz avay kom deezheh-steef

Armagnac *fine grape brandy from southwest France*
Calvados *apple brandy made from cider (Normandy)*
Cassis *blackcurrant liqueur:* **kir** *white wine and cassis apéritif*
Chartreuse *aromatic herb liqueur made by Carthusian monks*
Cognac *high quality white grape brandy*
Cointreau *orange-flavoured liqueur*
Crème de menthe *peppermint-flavoured liqueur*
Eau de vie *very strong brandy (often made from plum, pear, etc.)*
Grand Marnier *tawny-coloured, orange-flavoured liqueur*
Izarra vert *green-coloured herb liqueur:* **jaune** *sweeter*
Kirsch *cherry-flavoured spirit from Alsace*
Mirabelle *plum spirit from Alsace*
Pastis *aniseed-based apéritif (like Pernod) to which water is added*

A

...à la/à l'/au/aux... 'in the style of...', or 'with...'
  au feu de bois cooked over a wood fire
  au four baked
  au porto in port
abats offal, giblets
abricot apricot
Abricotine liqueur brandy with apricot flavouring
agneau lamb
agrumes citrus fruit
aïado roast shoulder of lamb stuffed with garlic and other ingredients
aiglefin haddock
aïgo bouïdo garlic soup
ail garlic
aile wing
aïoli rich garlic mayonnaise originated in the south and gives its name to the dish it is served with: cold steamed fish and vegetables. The mayonnaise is served on the side
airelles bilberries, cranberries
alicot puréed potato with cheese
allumettes very thin chips

amande almond
amuse-bouche nibbles

arlésienne, à l' with tomatoes, onions, aubergines, potatoes and rice
armagnac fine grape brandy from the Landes area
armoricaine, ...à l' cooked with brandy, wine, tomatoes and onions
ananas pineapple
anchoïade anchovy paste usually served on grilled French bread
anchois anchovies
andouille, andouillette spicy tripe sausage
anglaise, ...à l' poached or boiled
anguille eel
anis aniseed
arachide peanut (uncooked)
araignée de mer spider crab
artichaut artichoke
  artichauts à la barigoule artichokes in wine, with carrots, garlic, onions
  artichauts châtelaine artichokes stuffed with mushrooms

asperge asparagus
aspic de vollaille chicken in aspic
assiette dish, platter
assiette anglaise plate of assorted cold meats
assiette de charcuterie plate of assorted pâtés and salami
assiette de crudités selection of raw vegetables served with dip
assiette de pêcheur assorted fish
aubergine aubergine
aubergines farcies stuffed aubergines
aurin grey mullet
auvergnat, ...à l' with cabbage, sausage and bacon
avocat avocado

B

babas au rhum rum baba
baccala frittu dried salt cod fried Corsica style
Badoit mineral water, very slightly sparkling
baeckoffe hotpot of pork, mutton and beef baked with potato layers from Alsace
baguette stick of French bread

banane banana
bananes flambées bananas flambéed in brandy
bar sea-bass
barbue brill
bardatte cabbage stuffed with rabbit or hare
barquette small boat-shaped flan
basilic basil
baudroie fish soup with vegetables, garlic and herbs, monkfish
bavarois moulded cream and custard pudding, usually served with fruit
Béarnaise, à la sauce similar to mayonnaise but flavoured with tarragon. Traditionally served with steak
bécasse woodcock
béchamel classic white sauce made with milk, butter and flour
beignets fritters, doughnuts
Bénédictine herb liqueur on a brandy base
betterave beetroot
beurre butter
beurre blanc, ...à la sauce of white wine and shallots with butter

bien cuit well done

bière beer
  bière pression draught beer
  bière blonde lager
  bière brune bitter

bifteck steak

bigorneau periwinkle

biologique organic

bis wholemeal (of bread or flour)

biscuit de Savoie sponge cake

bisque smooth rich seafood soup
  bisque de homard lobster soup

blanquette white meat stew served with a creamy white sauce
  blanquette de veau veal stew in white sauce
  blanquette de volaille chicken stew in white sauce

blé wheat

blette Swiss chard

bleu very rare

bœuf beef
  bœuf bourguignon beef in burgundy, onions and mushrooms
  bœuf en daube rich beef stew with wine, vegetables and herbs

bombe moulded ice cream dessert

bonite bonito, small tuna fish

bonne femme,
  ...à la cooked in white wine with mushrooms

bordelaise, ...à la cooked in a sauce of red wine, shallots and herbs

bouchée vol-au-vent
  bouchée à la reine vol-au-vent filled with chicken or veal in a white sauce

boudin pudding
  boudin blanc white pudding
  boudin noir black pudding

bouillabaisse rich seafood soup flavoured with saffron originally from Marseilles

bouilleture d'anguilles eels cooked with prunes and red wine

bouilli boiled

bouillon stock
  bouillon de légumes vegetable stock
  bouillon de poule chicken stock

boulangère, ...à la baked with potatoes and onions

97

boulettes meatballs
bourgeoise, ...à la with carrots, onions, bacon, celery and braised lettuce
bourguignonne, ...à la cooked in red wine, with onions, bacon and mushrooms
bourride fish stew traditionally served with garlic mayonnaise (aïoli)
brandade de morue dried salt cod puréed with cream and olive oil
brème bream
brioche sweet bun
brioche aux fruits sweet bun with glacé fruit
brochet pike
brochette kebab
brocoli broccoli
brugnon nectarine
bulot whelk

C

cabillaud fresh cod
cacahuète peanut
café coffee
café au lait coffee with hot milk
café crème white coffee
café décaféiné decaffeinated coffee
café expresso espresso coffee
café glacé iced coffee
café irlandais Irish coffee
café noir black coffee
caille quail
caille sur canapé quail served on toast
caillettes rolled liver stuffed with spinach
cajou, noix de cashew nut
calisson almond sweet
calmar (or **calamar**) squid
calvados apple brandy made from cider (Normandy)
canard duck
canard à l'orange roast duck with orange sauce
canard périgourdin roast duck with prunes, *pâté de foie gras* and truffles
canard Rouennais stuffed roast duck covered in red wine sauce
caneton duckling
cannelle cinnamon
câpres capers
carbonnade de bœuf braised beef
cardon cardoon
cari curry
carotte carrot
carottes Vichy carrots cooked in butter and sugar

carpe carp
  carpe farcie carp stuffed with mushrooms or *foie gras*
carré persillé roast lamb Normandy style (with parsley)
carrelet plaice
carte des vins wine list
cassis blackcurrant, blackcurrant liqueur
cassoulet bean stew with pork or mutton and sausages. There are many regional variations
caviar caviar
  caviar blanc mullet roe
  caviar niçois a paste made with anchovies and olive oil
cédrat large citrus fruit, similar to a lemon
céleri celery; celeriac
  céleri rémoulade celeriac in a mustard and herb dressing
céleri-rave celeriac
cèpes boletus mushrooms, wild mushrooms
  cèpes marinés wild mushrooms marinated in oil, garlic and herbs
cerfeuil chervil
cerise cherry

cervelas smoked pork sausages, saveloy
cervelle brains (usually lamb or calf)

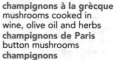

champignon mushroom
  champignons à la grècque mushrooms cooked in wine, olive oil and herbs
  champignons de Paris button mushrooms
  champignons périgourdine mushrooms with truffles and *foie gras*
chanterelle chanterelle (wild golden-coloured mushroom)
chantilly whipped cream
charlotte custard and fruit in lining of almond fingers
Chartreuse aromatic herb liqueur made by Carthusian monks
chasseur literally hunter-style, cooked with white wine, shallots, mushrooms and herbs
châtaigne chestnut
châteaubriand thick fillet steak
châtelaine, ...à la with artichoke hearts and chestnut purée
chaud(e) hot

chaudrée rochelaise a selection of fish stewed in red wine

chauffé heated

chausson a pasty filled with meat or seafood

chausson aux pommes apple turnover

cheval, à topped with a fried egg

chèvre goat

chevreuil venison

chichi doughnut shaped in a stick

chicorée chicory, endive

chocolat chocolate

chocolat chaud hot chocolate

chou cabbage

choucroute sauerkraut

choucroute garnie sauerkraut with various types of sausages

chou-fleur cauliflower

choux brocolis broccoli

choux de Bruxelles Brussels sprouts

ciboule (or **cive**) spring onion

ciboulette chives

cidre cider, sparkling (bouché) or still, quite strong

cidre brut dry cider

cidre doux sweet cider

citron lemon

citron pressé freshly squeezed lemon juice with water and sugar

citron vert lime

citrouille pumpkin

civet thick stew

civet de langouste crayfish in wine sauce

civet de lièvre hare stewed in wine, onions and mushrooms

clafoutis cherry pudding

claire type of oyster

clou de girofle clove

cochon pig

coco coconut

cocotte, en cooked in a small earthenware casserole

cœur heart

cœurs d'artichauts artichoke hearts

cœurs de palmier palm hearts

cognac high quality white grape brandy

coing quince

Cointreau orange-flavoured liqueur

colbert,...à la fried, with a coating of egg and breadcrumbs colin hake

compote de fruits mixed stewed fruit

concombre cucumber

condé rich rice pudding with fruits

confit pieces of meat preserved in fat
  confit d'oie goose meat preserved in its own fat
  confit de canard duck meat preserved in its own fat

confiture jam
  confiture d'oranges marmalade

congre conger eel

consommé clear soup, generally made from meat or fish stock

contre-filet sirloin fillet (beef)

coq au vin chicken cooked in red wine

coquelet cockerel

coques cockles

coquillages shellfish

coquilles Saint-Jacques scallops
  coquilles Saint-Jacques à la provençale scallops with garlic sauce
  coquilles Saint-Jacques scallops cooked in shell with a breadcrumb and white sauce topping

coquillettes pasta shells

cornichon gherkin

côtelette cutlet
  côtelettès de veau veal cutlets

côte rib, chop
  côtes de porc pork chops

cotriade fish stew (Brittany)

cou neck

coulibiac salmon cooked in puff pastry

coulis puréed fruit sauce

coupe goblet with ice cream

courge marrow

cousinat chestnut and cream soup

crabe crab

craquelots smoked herring

crème cream
  crème anglaise fresh custard
  crème au beurre butter cream with egg yolks and sugar
  crème brûlée rich custard with caramelised sugar on top
  crème caramel baked custard with caramelised sugar sauce
  crème chantilly slightly sweetened whipped cream

crème fraîche sour cream

crème pâtissière thick fresh custard used in tarts and desserts

crème renversée (or **crème caramel**) custard with a caramelised top

crème de cream of... (soup)

crème d'Argenteuil white asparagus soup

crème de cresson watercress soup

crème de marrons chestnut purée

crème de menthe peppermint-flavoured liqueur

crêpes sweet and savoury pancakes

crêpes fourrées filled pancakes

crêpes Suzette pancakes with a Cointreau or Grand Marnier sauce usually flambéed

crépinette type of sausage

crevette prawn

crevette grise shrimp

crevette rose large prawn

crevettes en terrine potted prawns

croûte, en in pastry

croûtes, croûtons, ...aux served with cubes of toasted or fried bread

cru raw

crudités assortment of raw vegetables (grated carrots, sliced tomatoes, etc) served as a starter

crustacés shellfish

cuisses de grenouille frogs' legs

cuit cooked

culotte rump steak

Curaçao orange-flavoured liqueur

D

darne fillet or steak

datte date

daube casserole with wine, herbs and garlic

dauphinoise, ...à la cooked in milk

daurade sea bream

diable, ...à la strong mustard seasoning

diabolo menthe mint cordial and lemonade

dinde turkey

diots au vin blanc pork sausages in white wine

duxelles fried mushrooms and shallots with cream

E

eau water
  eau de Seltz soda water
  eau-de-vie brandy (often
    made from plum, pear, etc)
  eau minérale mineral water
  eau minérale gazeuse
    sparkling mineral water
  eau du robinet tap water
échalote shallot
échine loin of pork
écrevisse freshwater crayfish
églefin haddock
emballé wrapped
en brochette cooked like a
  kebab (on a skewer)
encornet squid
endive chicory
entrecôte rib steak
entrées starters
entremets sweets (desserts)
épaule shoulder
éperlan whitebait
épice spice
épinards spinach
escalope escalope
escargots snails (generally
  cooked with strong
  seasonings)
  escargots à la
    bourguignonne snails with
    garlic butter

espadon sword-
fish
estouffade de
  boeuf beef
  stew cooked in
  red wine, herbs,
  onions, mushrooms
  and diced bacon
estragon tarragon
esturgeon sturgeon

F

faisan pheasant
farci(e) stuffed
faux-filet sirloin
faverolles haricot beans
favou(ille) tiny crab
fenouil fennel
férigoule thyme (in
  provençal dialect)
feuille leaf
feuilleté in puff pastry
fèves broad beans
figue fig
filet fillet steak
  filet de bœuf en croûte
    steak in pastry
  filet de bœuf tenderloin
  filet mignon small fillet
    steak
financière, ...à la rich sauce
  made with Madeira wine
  and truffles

fine de claire type of oyster

fines herbes mixed, chopped herbs

flageolet type of small green haricot bean

flamande, ...à la served with potatoes, cabbage, carrots and pork

flambé(e) doused with brandy or another spirit and set alight, usually cooked at your table

flétan halibut

flocons d'avoine oat flakes

florentine with spinach, usually served with mornay sauce

foie liver (usually calf's)
foie de volailles chicken livers
foie gras goose liver pâté

fond d'artichaut artichoke heart

fondue a shared dish which is served in the middle of the table. Each person uses a long fork to dip their bread or meat into the pot
fondue (au fromage) melted cheeses into which chunks of bread are dipped

fondue bourguignonne small chunks of meat dipped into boiling oil and eaten with different sauces. The meat equivalent to cheese fondue

forestière, ...à la with bacon and mushroom

fougasse type of bread with various fillings

fourré(e) stuffed

frais (fraîche) fresh

fraise strawberry
fraises des bois wild strawberries

framboise raspberry

frappé iced

fricassée a stew, usually chicken or veal, and vegetables

frisée curly endive

frit(e) fried

friture fried food, usually small fish

froid(e) cold

fromage cheese
fromage blanc soft white cheese
fromage frais creamy fresh cheese

froment wheat

fruit fruit
fruit de la passion passion fruit

fruits de mer shellfish, seafood
fumé(e) smoked
fumet fish stock

G

galantine meat in aspic
galette savoury buckwheat pancake
gambas large prawns
garbure thick vegetable and meat soup
gargouillau pear tart
garni(e) garnished i.e. served with something
garnitures side dishes
gâteau cake, gateau
  gâteau Saint-Honoré choux pastry cake filled with custard
gaufres waffles (often cream-filled)
gazeuse sparkling
gelée jelly, aspic
genièvre juniper berry
génoise sponge cake
germes de soja bean sprouts
gésier gizzard
gibier game
gigot d'agneau leg of lamb

gigot de mer large fish baked whole
gingembre ginger
glace ice cream
goyave guava
Grand Marnier tawny-coloured, orange-flavoured liqueur
gratin, au topped with cheese and breadcrumb and grilled
gratin dauphinois potatoes cooked in cream, garlic and Swiss cheese
gratinée Lyonnaise clear soup with eggs flavoured with Port wine and served with toasted french bread and grated cheese
grenade pomegranate
greque, ...à la cooked in olive oil, garlic and herbs, can be served hot or cold
grenouilles frogs' legs
  grenouilles meunière frogs' legs cooked in butter
grillade grilled meat
grillé(e) grilled
gros mollet lump fish
groseille redcurrant
groseille à maquereau gooseberry

H

hachis mince
hareng herring
haricots beans
haricots beurre butter beans
haricots blancs haricot beans
haricots rouges red kidney beans
haricots verts green beans, French beans

herbes (fines herbes) herbs

hollandaise, sauce sauce made of butter, egg yolks and lemon juice, served warm

homard lobster
homard à l'armoricaine lobster cooked with onions, tomatoes and wine
homard thermidor lobster served in cream sauce, topped with parmesan

hors d'œuvre variés selection of appetizers

huile oil
huile d'arachide groundnut oil
huile de tournesol sunflower oil

huître oyster

I

îles flottantes soft meringues floating on fresh custard

Izarra vert green-coloured herb liqueur

J

jambon ham
jambon de Bayonne cured raw ham from the Basque country
jambon de Paris boiled ham

jardinière, ...à la with peas and carrots, or other fresh vegetables

julienne vegetables cut into fine strips

jus juice, meat-based glaze or sauce
jus de pomme apple juice
jus d'orange orange juice

K

kir white wine and **cassis** aperitif

kirsch a kind of **eau-de-vie** made from cherries (Alsace)

kugelhopf hat-shaped sugar-covered cake from Alsace

L

lait milk
  lait demi-écrémé semi-skimmed milk
  lait écrémé skimmed milk
  lait entier full-cream milk

laitue lettuce

lamproie à la bordelaise lamprey in red wine

langouste crayfish (saltwater)
  langouste froide crayfish served cold with mayonnaise and salad

langoustines large scampi

langue tongue

lapin rabbit

lard fat, streaky bacon
  lard fumé smoked bacon

lardon strip of fat, diced bacon

laurier bayleaf

légumes vegetables

lentilles lentils

levure yeast

lièvre hare

limande lemon sole

limousine, ...à la cooked with chestnuts and red cabbage

lotte de mer monkfish

loup de mer sea-bass

Lyonnaise, ...à la with onions

M

macaron macaroon

macédoine (de fruits) fresh fruit salad

macédoine de légumes mixed cooked vegetables

madeleine small sponge cake

magret de canard duck breast

maïs, maïs doux maize, sweetcorn

mange-tout sugar peas

mangue mango

maquereau mackerel

marcassin young wild boar

marinière, ...à la a sauce of white wine, onions and herbs (mussels or clams)

marmite casserole

marjolaine marjoram

marron chestnut
  marrons glacés candied chestnuts
  marrons Mont Blanc chestnut purée and cream on a rum-soaked sponge cake

matelote fresh-fish stew
  matelote à la normande sea-fish stew with cider, calvados and cream

médaillon thick, medal-sized slices of meat

melon melon

menthe mint, mint tea

merguez spicy, red sausage

meringues à la chantilly meringues filled with whipped cream

merlan whiting

merluche hake

mérou grouper

merveilles fritters flavoured with brandy

mignonnette small fillet of lamb

mijoté stewed

mille-feuille thin layers of pastry filled with cream

mirabelle small yellow plum, plum brandy from Alsace

mont-blanc pudding made with chestnuts and cream

Mornay, sauce cream and cheese sauce

morue dried salt cod

moules mussels

moules marinière mussels cooked in white wine

moules poulette mussels in wine, cream and mushroom sauce

mourtairol beef, chicken, ham and vegetable soup

mousse au chocolat chocolate mousse

mousseline mashed potatoes with cream and eggs

moutarde mustard

mouton mutton, sheep or lamb

mûre blackberry

muscade nutmeg

myrtille bilberry

N

navet turnip

nectarine nectarine

niçoise, ...à la with garlic and tomatoes

noisette hazelnut

noisettes d'agneau small round pieces of lamb

noix walnut, general term for a nut

nouilles noodles

O

œuf egg

œufs à la causalade fried eggs with bacon

œufs à la coque soft-boiled eggs

œufs au plat fried eggs

œufs à la tourangelle eggs served with red wine sauce

œufs Bénédicte poached eggs on toast, with ham and hollandaise sauce

œufs brouillés scrambled eggs

œufs durs hard-boiled eggs

œufs en cocotte eggs baked in individual containers

œufs frits fried eggs

oie goose

oie farcie aux pruneaux goose stuffed with prunes

oignon onion

olive olive

omelette omelette

omelette brayaude cheese and potato omelette

omelette nature plain omelette

omelette norvégienne baked Alaska

onglet cut of beef

orange orange

orangeade orangeade

orge barley

os bone

oseille sorrel

oursin sea urchin

P

pain bread, loaf of bread

pain au choco-lat croissant with chocolate filling

pain bagnat bread roll with egg, olives, salad, tuna, anchovies and olive oil

pain bis brown bread

pain complet wholemeal bread

pain d'épice ginger cake

pain de mie white sliced loaf

pain de seigle rye bread

pain grillé toast

palmier caramelized puff pastry

palombe wood pigeon

palourde clam

pamplemousse grapefruit

panais parsnip

pané(e) with breadcrumbs

panini toasted Italian sandwich

panisse thick chickpea flour pancake

papillote, en in filo pastry

parfait rich home-made ice cream

Paris Brest ring-shaped cake filled with praline-flavoured cream

parisienne, ...à la sautéed in butter with white wine, sauce and shallots

parmentier with potatoes

pastèque watermelon

pastis aniseed-based aperitif

patate douce sweet potato

pâté pâté
  pâté de foie de volailles chicken liver pâté
  pâté en croûte pâté encased in pastry

pâtes pasta
  pâtes fraîches fresh pasta

paupiettes meat slices stuffed and rolled

pavé thick slice

pays d'auge, ...à la cream and cider

paysanne, ...à la cooked with diced bacon and vegetables

pêche peach
  pêches melba poached peaches served with a raspberry sauce and vanilla ice cream or whipped cream

pélandron type of string bean

perche perch (fish)
  perche du Menon perch cooked in champagne

perdreau (perdrix) partridge

Périgueux, sauce with truffles

Pernod aperitif with aniseed flavour (**pastis**)

persil parsley

persillé(e) with parsley

petit-beurre butter biscuit

petit farcis stuffed tomatoes, aubergines, courgettes and peppers

petit pain roll

petits fours bite-sized cakes and pastries

petits pois small peas

petit-suisse a smooth mixture of cream and curds

pieds et paquets mutton or pork tripe and trotters

pigeon pigeon

pignons pine nuts

pilon drumstick (chicken)

piment chilli
  piment doux sweet pepper
  piment fort chilli

pimenté peppery hot

pintade/pintadeau guinea fowl

pipérade tomato, pepper and onion omelette

piquant spicy

piquante, ...à la gherkins, vinegar and shallots

pissaladière a kind of pizza made mainly in the Nice region, filled with onions, anchovies and black olives

pistache pistachio

pistou garlic, basil and olive oil sauce – similar to **pesto**

plat dish
  plat principal main course

plate still

plie plaice

poché(e) poached

poêlé pan-fried

pimenté peppery hot

point, ...à medium rare

poire pear
  poires belle Hélène poached pears with vanilla ice cream and chocolate sauce

poireau leek

pois peas

pois cassés split peas

pois-chiches chickpeas

poisson fish

poitevin pork-stuffed cabbage

poitrine breast

poivre pepper

poivron sweet pepper
  poivron rouge red pepper
  poivron vert green pepper

pomme apple

pomme (de terre) potato
  pommes à l'anglaise boiled potatoes
  pommes à la vapeur steamed potatoes
  pommes allumettes match-stick chips
  pommes dauphine potato croquettes
  pommes duchesse potato mashed then baked in the oven
  pommes frites fried potatoes
  pommes Lyonnaise potatoes fried with onions
  pommes mousseline potatoes mashed with cream
  pommes rissolées small potatoes deep-fried

pompe aux grattons pork flan

porc pork

pot au feu beef and vegetable stew

potage soup, generally creamed or thickened

potée auvergnate cabbage and meat soup

potiron type of pumpkin

poulet chicken

poulet basquaise chicken stew with wine, tomatoes, mushrooms and peppers

poulet célestine chicken cooked in white wine with mushrooms and onion

poulet demi-deuil chicken breasts in a wine sauce

poulet Vallée d'Auge chicken cooked with cider, calvados, apples and cream

poulpe à la niçoise octopus in tomato sauce

pousses de soja bean sprouts

poussin baby chicken

poutargue mullet roe paste

praire clam

praliné hazelnut flavoured

primeurs spring vegetables

provençale, ...à la cooked with tomatoes, peppers, garlic and white wine

prune plum, plum brandy

purée mashed potatoes

Q

quatre-quarts cake made with equal parts of butter, flour, sugar, eggs

quenelles poached fish or meat mousse balls served in a sauce

quenelles de brochet pike mousse in cream sauce

quetsch type of plum

queue de bœuf oxtail

quiche Lorraine flan with egg, fresh cream and diced back bacon

R

râble saddle

radis radishes

ragoût stew, casserole

raie skate

raifort horseradish

raisin grape

raisin sec sultana, raisin

raïto red wine, olive, caper, garlic and shallot sauce

ramier wood pigeon

râpé(e) grated

rascasse scorpion fish

ratatouille tomatoes, aubergines, courgettes and garlic cooked in olive oil

rave turnip

raviolis pasta parcels of meat (in provençal dialect)
reine-claude greengage
rillettes coarse pork pâté
  rillettes de canard coarse duck pâté
ris de veau calf sweetbread
riz rice
rognon kidney
  rognons blancs testicles
  rognons sautés sauce madère sautéed kidneys served in Madeira sauce
romaine cos lettuce
romarin rosemary
romsteak rump steak
rond de gigot large slice of leg of lamb
rosbif roast beef
rôti roast
rouget red mullet
rouille spicy version of garlic mayonnaise (*aïoli*) served with fish stew or soup
roulade meat or fish, stuffed and rolled
roulé sweet or savoury roll
rutabaga swede

S

sabayon dessert made with egg yolks, sugar and Marsala wine

sablé shortbread
safran saffron
saignant rare

Saint-Hubert game consommé flavoured with wine
salade lettuce, salad
  salade aveyronnaise cheese salad (made with Roquefort)
  salade de fruits fruit salad
  salade de saison mixed salad and/or greens in season
  salade lyonnaise salad dressed with croutons and bacon
  salade niçoise many variations on a famous theme: the basic ingredients are green beans, anchovies, black olives, green peppers
  salade russe mixed cooked vegetables in mayonnaise
  salade verte green salad
salé salted/spicy
salsifis salsify
sandwich sandwich
  sandwich croque-monsieur grilled gruyère cheese and ham sandwich

sandwich croque-madame grilled cheese and bacon, sausage, chicken or egg sandwich

sanglier wild boar

sarrasin buckwheat

sarriette savoury (herb)

sauce sauce

saucisse/saucisson sausage

saumon salmon
  saumon fumé smoked salmon
  saumon poché poached salmon

sauté(e) sautéed

sauté d'agneau lamb stew

savarin a filled ring-shaped cake

savoyarde, ...à la with gruyère cheese

scarole endive, escarole

sec dry or dried

seiche cuttlefish

sel salt

selle d'agneau saddle of lamb

semoule semolina

socca thin chickpea flour pancake

sole sole
  sole Albert sole in cream sauce with mustard

sole cardinal sole cooked in wine, served with lobster sauce

sole Normande sole cooked in a cream, cider and shrimp sauce

sole Saint Germain grilled sole with butter and tarragon sauce

sole-limande lemon sole

soufflé light fluffy dish made with egg yolks and stiffly beaten egg whites combined with cheese, ham, fish, etc

soupe hearty thick soup
  soupe à l'oignon onion soup usually served with a crisp chunk of French bread in the dish with grated cheese on top
  soupe à la bière beer soup
  soupe au pistou vegetable soup with garlic and basil
  soupe aux choux cabbage soup with pork
  soupe de poisson fish soup

soupe anglaise trifle

steak steak
  steak au poivre steak with peppercorns
  steak tartare minced raw steak mixed with raw egg, chopped onion, tartare or worcester sauce, parsley and capers

St Raphael aperitif (with quinine)

sucre sugar

sucré sweet

suprême de volaille breast of chicken in cream sauce

T

tagine North African casserole

tapendade olive paste

tarte open tart, generally sweet
  tarte aux fraises strawberry tart
  tarte aux pommes apple tart
  tarte flambée thin pizza-like pastry topped with onion, cream and bacon
  tarte Normande apple tart
  tarte tatin upside down tart with caramelized apples or pears
  tarte tropézienne sponge cake filled with custard cream topped with nuts

tartine open sandwich

terrine terrine, pâté
  terrine de campagne pork and liver terrine
  terrine de porc et gibier pork and game terrine

tête de veau calf's head

tétras grouse

thé tea
  thé au citron tea with lemon
  thé au lait tea with milk
  thé sans sucre tea without sugar

thermidor lobster grilled in its shell with cream sauce

thon tuna fish

tilleul lime tea

timbale round dish in which a mixture of usually meat or fish is cooked. Often lined with pastry and served with a rich sauce
  timbale d'écrevisses crayfish in a cream, wine and brandy sauce
  timbale de fruits pastry base covered with fruits

tisane herbal tea

tomate tomato
  tomates à la provençale grilled tomatoes steeped in garlic
  tomates farcies stuffed tomatoes

tomme type of cheese

tournedos thick fillet steak
  tournedos Rossini thick fillet steak on fried bread with goose liver and truffles on top

tourte à la viande meat pie usually made with veal and pork

tripe tripe

tripes à la mode de Caen tripe cooked with vegetables, herbs, cider and calvados

truffade potato pie with garlic and cheese originating in Auvergne

truffe truffle

truffiat potato cake

truite trout

truite aux amandes trout covered with almonds

turbot turbot

V

vacherin large meringue filled with cream, ice cream and fruit

vapeur, ...à la steamed

veau calf, veal

veau sauté Marengo veal cooked in a casserole with white wine and garlic

velouté thick creamy white sauce made with fish, veal or chicken stock. Also used in soups

venaison venison

verdure, en garnished with green vegetables

verjus juice of unripe grapes

vermicelle vermicelli

véronique, ...à la grapes, wine and cheese

verveine herbal tea made with verbena

viande meat

viande séchée thin slices of cured beef

vichyssoise leek and potato soup, served cold

viennoise fried in egg and breadcrumbs

vin wine

vin blanc white wine

vin de pays local wine

vin de table table wine

vin rosé rosé wine

vin rouge red wine

vinaigrette dressing of oil and vinegar

vinaigre vinegar

violet sea squirt

volaille poultry

Y

yaourt yoghurt

Z

zewelwai onion flan

a(n) un (m)/une (f)

abbey l'abbaye (f)

able: to be able to pouvoir

abortion l'avortement (m)

about (approximately) vers ;
environ
(concerning) au sujet de
about 100 euros environ
cent euros
about 10 o'clock vers dix
heures

above au-dessus (de)
above the bed au-dessus
du lit
above the farm au-dessus
de la ferme

abroad à l'étranger

abscess l'abcès (m)

accelerator l'accélérateur (m)

accent l'accent (m)

to accept accepter
do you accept this card?
vous acceptez cette carte?

access l'access (m)

accident l'accident (m)

**accident & emergency
department** les urgences

accommodation le logement

to accompany accompagner

account le compte

account number le numéro
de compte

to ache faire mal
it aches ça fait mal

acid l'acide (m)

actor l'acteur (m),/l'actrice (f)

adaptor (electrical)
l'adaptateur (m)

address l'adresse (f)
here's my address voici
mon adresse
what is the address?
quelle est l'adresse?

address book le carnet
d'adresse

admission charge l'entrée (f)

to admit (to hospital)
hospitaliser

adult m/f l'adulte (f)
for adults pour adultes

advance: in advance
à l'avance

advertisement (in paper)
l'annonce (f)
(on TV) la publicité

to advise conseiller

A&E les urgences

aeroplane l'avion (m)

aerosol l'aérosol (m)

afraid: to be afraid of avoir
peur de

after après

afternoon l'après-midi (m)
in the afternoon l'après-
midi
this afternoon cet après-
midi
tomorrow afternoon
demain après-midi

aftershave l'après-rasage (m)

again encore

against contre

A

age l'âge (m)

agency l'agence (f)

ago: *a week ago* il y a une semaine

to agree être d'accord

agreement l'accord (m)

AIDS le SIDA

airbag (in car) l'airbag (m)

airbed le matelas pneumatique

air-conditioning la climatisation

air freshener le désodorisant

airline la ligne aérienne

air mail: *by airmail* par avion

airplane l'avion (m)

airport l'aéroport (m)

airport bus la navette pour l'aéroport

air ticket le billet d'avion

aisle le couloir

alarm l'alarme (f)

alarm clock le réveil

alcohol l'alcool (m)

alcohol-free sans alcool

alcoholic drink la boisson alcoolisée

all tout(e)/tous/toutes

allergic allergique
I'm allergic to... je suis allergique à...

allergy l'allergie (f)

to allow permettre
it's not allowed c'est interdit

all right (agreed) d'accord
are you all right? ça va?

almost presque

alone tout(e) seul(e)

Alps les Alpes

already déjà

also aussi

altar l'autel (m)

always toujours

a.m. du matin

am: *I am* je suis

amber (traffic light) orange

ambulance l'ambulance (f)

America l'Amérique (f)

American américain(e)

amount (total) le montant

anaesthetic l'anesthésique (m)
a local anaesthetic une anesthésie locale
a general anaesthetic une anesthésie générale

anchor l'ancre (f)

and et

angina l'angine de poitrine (f)

angry fâché(e)

animal l'animal (m)

aniseed l'anis (m)

ankle la cheville

anniversary l'anniversaire (m)

to announce annoncer

announcement l'annonce (f)

annual annuel(-elle)

another un(e) autre
another beer une autre bière

answer la réponse
to answer répondre à
answerphone le répondeur
antacid le comprimé contre
les brûlures d'estomac
antibiotic l'antibiotique (m)
antifreeze l'antigel (m)
antihistamine
l'antihistaminique (m)
antiques les antiquités
antique shop le magasin
d'antiquités
antiseptic l'antiseptique (m)
any de (du/de la/des)
have you any apples?
vous avez des pommes?
anyone quelqu'un/personne
anything quelque chose/rien
anywhere quelque part
apartment l'appartement (m)
appendicitis l'appendicite (f)
apple la pomme
application form
le formulaire
appointment le rendez-vous
I have an appointment
j'ai rendez-vous
approximately environ
April avril
architect m/f l'architecte
architecture l'architecture (f)
are: you are vous êtes
we are nous sommes
they are ils/elles sont
arm le bras

armbands *(for swimming)*
les bracelets gonflables
armchair le fauteuil
to arrange arranger
to arrest arrêter
arrival l'arrivée (f)
to arrive arriver
art l'art (m)
art gallery le musée
arthritis l'arthrite (f)
artificial artificiel
artist l'artiste (m/f)
ashtray le cendrier
to ask demander
to ask a question poser
une question
aspirin l'aspirine (f)
asthma l'asthme (m)
I have asthma je suis
asthmatique
at à
at my/your home chez
moi/vous
at 8 o'clock à huit heures
at once tout de suite
at night la nuit
Atlantic Ocean l'Océan
atlantique (m)
attack *(mugging)*
l'agression (f)
(medical) la crise
to attack agresser
attic le grenier
attractive séduisant(e)
auction la vente aux enchères

A

audience le public
August août
aunt la tante
au pair la jeune fille au pair
Australia l'Australie *(f)*
Australian australien(ne)
author l'écrivain ; l'auteur *(m)*
automatic automatique
automatic car la voiture à boîte automatique
auto-teller le distributeur automatique (de billets)
autumn l'automne *(m)*
available disponible
avalanche l'avalanche *(f)*
avenue l'avenue *(f)*
average moyen(ne)
to avoid éviter
awake: *I was awake all night* je n'ai pas dormi de toute la nuit
awful affreux(-euse)
axle *(car)* l'essieu *(m)*

B

baby le bébé
baby food les petits pots
baby milk *(formula)* le lait maternisé
baby's bottle le biberon
baby seat *(car)* le siège pour bébés
babysitter le/la babysitter
baby wipes les lingettes

back *(of body)* le dos
backpack le sac à dos
bacon le bacon ; le lard
bad *(food, weather)* mauvais(e)
badminton le badminton
bag le sac
 (suitcase) la valise
baggage les bagages
baggage allowance le poids (de bagages) autorisé
baggage reclaim la livraison des bagages
bait *(for fishing)* l'appât *(m)*
baked au four
baker's la boulangerie
balcony le balcon
bald *(person)* chauve
 (tyre) lisse
ball *(large: football, etc)* le ballon
 (small: golf, tennis, etc) la balle
ballet le ballet
balloon le ballon
banana la banane
band *(music)* le groupe
bandage le pansement
bank *(money)* la banque
 (river) la rive ; le bord
bank account le compte en banque
banknote le billet de banque
bar le bar
bar of chocolate la tablette de chocolat

barbecue le barbecue
  to have a barbecue faire
  un barbecue
barber's le coiffeur
to bark aboyer
barn la grange
barrel *(wine, beer)* le tonneau
basement le sous-sol
basil le basilic
basket le panier
basketball le basket-ball
bat *(baseball, cricket)* la batte
  (animal) la chauve-souris
bath le bain
  to have a bath prendre
  un bain
bathing cap le bonnet de
  bain
bathroom la salle de bains
  with bathroom avec salle
  de bains
battery *(for car)* la batterie
  (for radio, camera) la pile
bay *(along coast)* la baie
B&B la chambre d'hôte
to be être
beach la plage
  private beach la plage
  privée
  sandy beach la plage de
  sable
  nudist beach la plage de
  nudistes
beach hut la cabine
bean le haricot
beard la barbe
beautiful beau (belle)

because parce que
to become devenir
bed le lit
  double bed le grand lit ;
  le lit de deux personnes
  single bed le lit d'une
  personne
  sofa bed le canapé-lit
  twin beds les lits jumeaux
bed clothes les draps et
  couvertures
bedroom la chambre à
  coucher
bee l'abeille *(f)*
beef le bœuf
beer la bière
before avant
to begin commencer
behind derrière
beige beige
Belgian belge
Belgium la Belgique
to believe croire
bell *(church, school)* la cloche
  (doorbell) la sonnette
to belong to appartenir à
below sous
belt la ceinture
bend *(in road)* le virage
berth *(train, ship, etc)* la
  couchette
beside *(next to)* à côté de
  beside the bank à côté
  de la banque
best le/la meilleur(e)
bet le pari

B

to bet on faire un pari sur
better meilleur(e)
  better than meilleur que
between entre
bib *(baby's)* le bavoir
bicycle la bicyclette ; le vélo
bicycle repair kit la trousse
  de réparation (pour vélo)
bidet le bidet
big grand(e), gros(se)
bike *(pushbike)* le vélo
  (motorbike) la moto
bike lock l'antivol *(m)*
bikini le bikini
bill *(restaurant)* l'addition *(f)*
  (hotel) la note
  (for work done) la facture
bin *(dustbin)* la poubelle
bin liner le sac poubelle
binoculars les jumelles
bird l'oiseau *(m)*
biro le stylo
birth la naissance
birth certificate l'acte de
  naissance *(m)*
birthday l'anniversaire *(m)*
  happy birthday! bon
  anniversaire!
  my birthday is on... mon
  anniversaire c'est le...
birthday card la carte
  d'anniversaire
birthday present le cadeau
  d'anniversaire
biscuits les biscuits
bit: *a bit (of)* un peu (de)

bite *(animal)* la morsure
  (insect) la piqûre
to bite *(animal)* mordre
  (insect) piquer
bitten *(by animal)* mordu(e)
  (by insect) piqué(e)
bitter amer(-ère)
black noir(e)
black ice le verglas
blanket la couverture
bleach l'eau de Javel *(f)*
to bleed saigner
blender *(for food)* le mixeur
blind *(person)* aveugle
blind *(for window)* le store
blister l'ampoule *(f)*
block of flats l'immeuble *(m)*
blocked bouché(e)
  the sink is blocked l'évier
  est bouché
blond *(person)* blond(e)
blood le sang
blood group le groupe
  sanguin
blood pressure la tension
  (artérielle)
blood test l'analyse de
  sang *(f)*
blouse le chemisier
blow-dry le brushing
blue bleu(e)
  dark blue bleu foncé
  light blue bleu clair
boar *(wild)* le sanglier
to board embarquer

122

boarding card la carte d'embarquement

boarding house la pension (de famille)

boat le bateau
(rowing) la barque

boat trip l'excursion en bateau (f)

body le corps

to boil faire bouillir

boiled bouilli(e)

boiler la chaudière

bomb la bombe

bone l'os (m)
(fish) l'arête (f)

bonfire le feu

book le livre

to book (reserve) réserver

booking la réservation

booking office le bureau de location

bookshop la librairie

boots les bottes
(short) les bottillons

border (of country) la frontière

boring ennuyeux(-euse)

born: to be born naître

to borrow emprunter

boss le chef

both les deux

bottle la bouteille
    a bottle of wine une bouteille de vin
    a bottle of water une bouteille d'eau

a half-bottle une demi-bouteille

bottle opener l'ouvre-bouteilles (m)

bottom (of pool, etc) le fond

bowl (for soup, etc) le bol

bow tie le nœud papillon

box la boîte

box office le bureau de location

boxer shorts le caleçon

boy le garçon

boyfriend le copain

bra le soutien-gorge

bracelet le bracelet

brain le cerveau

brake(s) le(s) frein(s)

to brake freiner

brake fluid le liquide de freins

brake lights les feux de stop

brake pads les plaquettes de frein

branch (of tree) la branche
(of company, etc) la succursale

brand (make) la marque

brass le cuivre

brave courageux(-euse)

bread le pain
(French stick) la baguette
(thin French stick) la ficelle
sliced bread le pain de mie en tranches

bread roll le petit pain

to break casser

B

breakable fragile
breakdown (car) la panne
  (nervous) la dépression
breakdown van la
  dépanneuse
breakfast le petit déjeuner
breast le sein
to breast-feed allaiter
to breathe respirer
brick la brique
bride la mariée
bridegroom le marié
bridge le pont
briefcase la serviette
Brillo® pad le tampon Jex®
to bring apporter
Britain la Grande-Bretagne
British britannique
brochure la brochure ;
  le dépliant
broken cassé(e)
  my leg is broken je me
  suis cassé la jambe
broken down en panne
bronchitis la bronchite
bronze le bronze
brooch la broche
broom (brush) le balai
brother le frère
brother-in-law le beau-frère
brown marron
bruise le bleu
brush la brosse
bubble bath le bain moussant
bucket le seau

buffet car (train) la voiture-
  buffet
to build construire
building l'immeuble (m)
bulb (light) l'ampoule (f)
bumbag la banane
bumper (on car) le pare-chocs
bunch (of flowers) le bouquet
  (of grapes) la grappe
bungee jumping le saut à
  l'élastique
bureau de change le bureau
  de change
burger le hamburger
burglar le/la
  cambrioleur(-euse)
burglar alarm le système
  d'alarme
to burn brûler
bus le bus
  (coach) le car
bus pass la carte de bus
bus station la gare routière
bus stop l'arrêt de bus (m)
bus ticket le ticket de bus
business les affaires
  on business pour affaires
business card la carte de
  visite
business class la classe
  affaires
businessman/woman
  l'homme/la femme d'affaires
business trip le voyage
  d'affaires
busy occupé(e)

but mais

butcher's la boucherie

butter le beurre

button le bouton

to buy acheter

by (via) par
  (beside) à côté de
  by bus en bus
  by car en voiture
  by ship en bateau
  by train en train

bypass (road) la rocade

C

cab (taxi) le taxi

cabaret le cabaret

cabin (on boat) la cabine

cabin crew l'équipage (m)

cablecar le téléphérique ;
  la benne

café le café
  internet café le cybercafé

cafetière la cafetière

cake (large) le gâteau
  (small) la pâtisserie ; le petit
  gâteau

cake shop la pâtisserie

calculator la calculatrice

calendar le calendrier

call (telephone) l'appel (m)

to call (speak, phone) appeler

calm calme

camcorder le caméscope

camera l'appareil photo (m)

camera case l'étui (m)

camera shop le magasin
  de photo

to camp camper

camping gas le butane

camping stove le camping-
  gaz®

campsite le camping

can (to be able to) pouvoir
  (to know how to) savoir
  I can je peux/sais
  we can nous
  pouvons/savons

can la boîte

can opener l'ouvre-boîtes (m)

Canada le Canada

Canadian canadien(ne)

canal le canal

to cancel annuler

cancellation l'annulation (f)

cancer le cancer

candle la bougie

canoe le kayak

canoeing: to go canoeing
  faire du canoë-kayak

cap (hat) la casquette
  (contraceptive) le
  diaphragme

capital (city) la capitale

car la voiture

car alarm l'alarme de
  voiture (f)

car ferry le ferry

car hire la location de
  voitures

car insurance l'assurance
  automobile (f)

car keys les clés de voiture
car phone le téléphone de voiture
car park le parking
car parts les pièces pour voiture
car radio l'autoradio (m)
car seat (for child) le siège pour enfant
carwash le lavage automatique
carafe le pichet
caravan la caravane
carburettor le carburateur
card la carte
  birthday card la carte d'anniversaire
  business card la carte de visite
  playing cards les cartes à jouer
cardboard le carton
cardigan le gilet
careful: to be careful faire attention
  careful! attention!
carpet (rug) le tapis
  (fitted) la moquette
carriage (railway) la voiture
carrot la carotte
to carry porter
carton (cigarettes) la cartouche
  (milk, juice) le brick
case (suitcase) la valise
cash l'argent liquide (m)
to cash (cheque) encaisser

cash desk la caisse
cash dispenser (ATM) le distributeur automatique (de billets)
cashier le/la caissier(-ière)
cashpoint le distributeur automatique (de billets)
casino le casino
casserole dish la cocotte
cassette la cassette
cassette player le magnéto-phone
castle le château
casualty dept les urgences
cat le chat
cat food la nourriture pour chats
catalogue le catalogue
catch (bus, train) prendre
cathedral la cathédrale
Catholic catholique
cave la grotte
cavity (in tooth) la carie
CD le CD
CD player le lecteur de CD
ceiling le plafond
cellar la cave
cellphone le téléphone cellulaire
cemetery le cimetière
centimetre le centimètre
central central(e)
central heating le chauffage central
central locking le verrouillage central

centre le centre
century le siècle
ceramic la céramique
cereal la céréale
certain *(sure)* certain(e)
certificate le certificat
chain la chaîne
chair la chaise
chairlift le télésiège
chalet le chalet
chambermaid la femme de chambre
champagne le champagne
change *(scoins)* la monnaie
to change changer
  to change money changer de l'argent
  to change clothes se changer
  to change bus changer d'autobus
  to change train changer de train
changing room la cabine d'essayage
Channel *(English)* la Manche
chapel la chapelle
charcoal le charbon de bois
charge *(fee)* le prix
to charge prendre
charger *(battery)* le chargeur
charter flight le vol charter
cheap bon marché
cheaper moins cher
cheap rate le tarif réduit
to check vérifier

to check in enregistrer
check-in (desk)
  l'enregistrement des bagages *(m)*
  (at hotel) la réception
cheek la joue
cheers! santé!
cheese le fromage
chef le chef de cuisine
chemist's la pharmacie
cheque le chèque
cheque book le carnet de chèques
cheque card la carte d'identité bancaire
chest *(body)* la poitrine
chewing gum le chewing-gum
chicken le poulet
chickenpox la varicelle
child l'enfant *(m)*
child safety seat *(car)* le siège pour enfant
children les enfants
  for children pour enfants
chimney la cheminée
chin le menton
china la porcelaine
chips les frites
chocolate le chocolat
  drinking-chocolate le chocolat en poudre
  hot chocolate le chocolat chaud
chocolates les chocolats
choir la chorale

to choose choisir

chop (meat) la côtelette

chopping board la planche à découper

christening le baptême

Christian name le prénom

Christmas Noël (m)
merry Christmas! joyeux Noël!

Christmas card la carte de Noël

Christmas Eve la veille de Noël

church l'église (f)

cigar le cigare

cigarette la cigarette

cigarette lighter le briquet

cigarette paper le papier à cigarette

cinema le cinéma

circle (theatre) le balcon

circuit breaker le disjoncteur

circus le cirque

cistern (toilet) le réservoir de chasse d'eau

city la ville

city centre le centre-ville

class la classe
first-class de première classe
second-class de seconde classe

clean propre

to clean nettoyer

cleaner la femme de ménage

cleanser (for face) le démaquillant

clear clair(e)

client le client/la cliente

cliff (along coast) la falaise
(in mountains) l'escarpement (m)

to climb (mountain) faire de la montagne

climbing boots les chaussures de montagne

Clingfilm® le Scellofrais®

clinic la clinique

cloakroom le vestiaire

clock l'horloge (f)

close by proche

to close fermer

closed (shop, etc) fermé(e)

cloth (rag) le chiffon
(fabric) le tissu

clothes les vêtements

clothes line la corde à linge

clothes pegs les pinces à linge

clothes shop le magasin de vêtements

cloudy nuageux(-euse)

club le club

clutch (in car) l'embrayage (m)

coach (bus) le car ; l'autocar (m)

coach station la gare routière

coach trip l'excursion en car

coal le charbon

coast la côte

coastguard le garde-côte

coat le manteau
coat hanger le cintre
cockroach le cafard
cocktail le cocktail
cocoa le cacao
code le code
coffee le café
  white coffee le café au lait
  black coffee le café noir
  cappuccino le cappuccino
  decaffeinated coffee le café décaféiné
coil *(IUD)* le stérilet
coin la pièce de monnaie
Coke® le Coca®
colander la passoire
cold froid
  I'm cold j'ai froid
  it's cold il fait froid
cold water l'eau froide *(f)*
cold *(illness)* le rhume
  I have a cold j'ai un rhume
cold sore le bouton de fièvre
collar le col
collar bone la clavicule
colleague le/la collègue
to collect *(someone)* aller chercher
collection la collection
colour la couleur
colour-blind daltonien(ne)
colour film *(for camera)* la pellicule couleur
comb le peigne
to come venir
  (to arrive) arriver

to come back revenir
to come in entrer
  come in! entrez!
comedy la comédie
comfortable confortable
company *(firm)* la compagnie ; la société
compartment le compartiment
compass la boussole
to complain faire une réclamation
complaint la plainte
to complete remplir
compulsory obligatoire
computer l'ordinateur *(m)*
computer disk *(floppy)* la disquette
computer game le jeu électronique
computer program le programme informatique
concert le concert
concert hall la salle de concert
concession la réduction
concussion la commotion (cérébrale)
conditioner l'après-shampooing *(m)*
condom le préservatif
conductor *(in orchestra)* le chef d'orchestre
conference la conférence
to confirm confirmer
confirmation la confirmation

C

confused: *I am confused*
je m'y perds

congratulations!
félicitations!

connection *(train, bus, etc)*
la correspondance

constipated constipé(e)

consulate le consulat

to consult consulter

to contact contacter

contact lenses les verres
de contact

contact lens cleaner le
produit pour nettoyer les
verres de contact

to continue continuer

contraceptive le contraceptif

contract le contrat

convenient: *it's not
convenient* ça ne
m'arrange pas

convulsions les convulsions

to cook *(be cooking)* cuisiner
to cook a meal préparer
un repas

cooked cuisiné

cooker la cuisinière

cool frais (fraîche)

cool-bag *(for picnic)* le sac
isotherme

cool-box *(for picnic)* la
glacière

copper le cuivre

copy *(duplicate)* la copie

to copy copier

cork le bouchon

corkscrew le tire-bouchon

corner le coin

cornflakes les corn-flakes

corridor le couloir

cortisone la cortisone

cosmetics les produits de
beauté

cost le coût

to cost coûter
how much does it cost?
ça coûte combien?

costume *(swimming)* le maillot
(de bain)

cot le lit d'enfant

cottage la maison de
campagne

cotton le coton

cotton bud le coton-tige®

cotton wool le coton
hydrophile

couchette la couchette

cough la toux

to cough tousser

cough mixture le sirop pour
la toux

cough sweets les pastilles
pour la gorge

counter *(shop, bar, etc)*
le comptoir

country *(not town)*
la campagne
(nation) le pays

countryside le paysage

couple *(two people)* le couple
a couple of... deux ...

courgette la courgette

courier service le service de messageries

course *(syllabus)* le cours *(of meal)* le plat

cousin le/la cousin(e)

cover charge *(restaurant)* le couvert

cow la vache

crafts les objets artisanaux

craftsperson l'artisan(e)

cramps *(period pain)* les règles douloureuses

crash *(car)* l'accident *(m)* ; la collision

crash helmet le casque

cream *(food, lotion)* la crème
  soured cream la crème fermentée
  whipped cream la crème fouettée

credit card la carte de crédit

crime le crime

crisps les chips

croissant le croissant

cross la croix

to cross *(road, etc)* traverser

cross-country skiing le ski de fond

cross-channel ferry le ferry qui traverse la Manche

crossing *(by sea)* la traversée

crossroads le carrefour ; le croisement

crossword puzzle les mots croisés

crowd la foule

crowded bondé(e)

crown la couronne

cruise la croisière

crutches les béquilles

to cry *(weep)* pleurer

crystal le cristal

cucumber le concombre

cufflinks les boutons de manchette

cul-de-sac le cul-de-sac

cup la tasse

cupboard le placard

currant le raisin sec

currency la devise ; la monnaie

current *(air, water)* le courant

curtain le rideau

cushion le coussin

custom *(tradition)* la tradition

customer le/la client(e)

customs la douane *(duty)* les droits de douane

customs declaration la déclaration de douane

to cut couper

cut la coupure

cutlery les couverts

to cycle faire du vélo

cycle track la piste cyclable

cycling le cyclisme

cyst le kyste

cystitis la cystite

daily (each day) tous les jours

dairy produce les produits laitiers

dam le barrage

damage les dégâts

damp humide

dance le bal

to dance danser

danger le danger

dangerous dangereux(-euse)

dark l'obscurité (f)
after dark la nuit tombée

date la date

date of birth la date de naissance

daughter la fille

daughter-in-law la belle-fille ; la bru

dawn l'aube (f)

day le jour
per day par jour
every day tous les jours

dead mort(e)

deaf sourd(e)

dear (expensive, in letter) cher (chère) (m(f))

debts les créances

decaffeinated décaféiné(e)
decaffeinated coffee le café décaféiné

December décembre

deckchair la chaise longue

to declare déclarer
nothing to declare rien à déclarer

deep profond(e)

deep freeze le congélateur

deer le cerf

to defrost décongeler

to de-ice (windscreen) dégivrer

delay le retard
how long is the delay? il y a combien de retard?

delayed retardé(e)

delicatessen l'épicerie fine (f)

delicious délicieux(-euse)

demonstration la manifestation

dental floss le fil dentaire

dentist le/la dentiste

dentures le dentier

deodorant le déodorant

to depart partir

department le rayon

department store le grand magasin

departure le départ

departure lounge la salle d'embarquement

deposit les arrhes

to describe décrire

description la description

desk (furniture) le bureau (information) l'accueil (m)

dessert le dessert

details les détails

detergent le détergent

detour la déviation

to develop (photos) faire développer

diabetes le diabète
diabetic diabétique
  I'm diabetic je suis diabétique
to dial *(a number)* composer
dialling code l'indicatif *(m)*
dialling tone la tonalité
diamond le diamant
diapers les couches (pour bébé)
diaphragm le diaphragme
diarrhoea la diarrhée
diary l'agenda *(m)*
dice le dé
dictionary le dictionnaire
to die mourir
diesel le gas-oil
diet le régime
  I'm on a diet je suis au régime
  special diet le régime spécial
different différent(e)
difficult difficile
to dilute diluer ; ajouter de l'eau à
dinghy le canot
dining room la salle à manger
dinner *(evening meal)* le dîner
  to have dinner dîner
diplomat le diplomate
direct *(train, etc)* direct(e)
directions les indications
  to ask for directions demander le chemin
directory *(telephone)* l'annuaire *(m)*

directory enquiries (le service des) renseignements
dirty sale
disability: *to have a disability* être handicapé(e)
disabled *(person)* handicapé(e)
to disagree ne pas être d'accord
to disappear disparaître
disaster la catastrophe
disco la discothèque
discount le rabais
to discover découvrir
disease la maladie
dish le plat
dishtowel le torchon à vaisselle
dishwasher le lave-vaisselle
disinfectant le désinfectant
disk *(floppy)* la disquette
to dislocate *(joint)* disloquer
disposable jetable
distant lointain(e)
distilled water l'eau distillée *(f)*
district *(of town)* le quartier
to disturb déranger
diversion la déviation
divorced divorcé(e)
DIY shop le magasin de bricolage
dizzy pris(e) de vertige
to do faire
doctor le médecin
documents les papiers

D

dog le chien
dog food la nourriture pour chiens
dog lead la laisse
doll la poupée
dollar le dollar
domestic flight le vol intérieur
donor card la carte de donneur d'organes
door la porte
doorbell la sonnette
double double
double bed le grand lit
double room la chambre pour deux personnes
doughnut le beignet
down: to go down descendre
downstairs en bas
drain *(house)* le tuyau d'écoulement
draught le courant d'air
there's a draught il y a un courant d'air
draught lager la bière pression
drawer le tiroir
drawing le dessin
dress la robe
to dress s'habiller
dressing *(for food)* la vinaigrette
(for wound) le pansement
dressing gown le peignoir
drill *(tool)* la perceuse électrique

drink la boisson
to drink boire
drinking water l'eau potable *(f)*
to drive conduire
driver *(of car)* le conducteur/ la conductrice
driving licence le permis de conduire
drought la sécheresse
to drown se noyer
drug *(medicine)* le médicament
(narcotics) la drogue
drunk ivre ; soûl(e)
dry sec (sèche)
to dry sécher
dry-cleaner's le pressing
dummy *(for baby)* la tétine
during pendant
dust la poussière
duster le chiffon
dustpan and brush la pelle et la balayette
duty-free hors taxe
duvet la couette
duvet cover la housse de couette
dye la teinture
dynamo la dynamo

E

each chacun/chacune
ear l'oreille *(f)*
earlier plus tôt

early tôt

to earn gagner

earphones le casque

earplugs les boules Quiès®

earrings les boucles d'oreille

earth la terre

earthquake le tremblement de terre

east l'est (m)

Easter Pâques
happy Easter! joyeuses Pâques!

easy facile

to eat manger

economy (class) économique

egg l'œuf (m)
fried eggs les œufs sur le plat
hard-boiled egg l'œuf dur
scrambled eggs les œufs brouillés
soft-boiled egg l'œuf à la coque

either ... or soit ... soit

elastic band l'élastique (m)

elastoplast® le sparadrap

elbow le coude

electric électrique

electric blanket la couverture chauffante

electric razor le rasoir électrique

electrician l'électricien (m)

electricity l'électricité (f)

electricity meter le compteur électrique

elevator l'ascenseur (m)

e-mail le e-mail
to e-mail sb envoyer un e-mail à qn

e-mail address l'adresse électronique
(on forms) le mél

embassy l'ambassade (f)

emergency l'urgence (f)

emergency exit la sortie de secours

empty vide

end la fin

engaged (to marry) fiancé(e)
(phone, toilet, etc) occupé(e)

engine le moteur

England l'Angleterre (f)

English anglais(e)
(language) l'anglais (m)

Englishman/-woman l'Anglais(e) (m/f)

to enjoy aimer
I enjoy swimming j'aime nager
I enjoy dancing j'aime danser
enjoy your meal! bon appétit!

enough assez
that's enough ça suffit

enquiry desk les renseignements

to enter entrer

entertainment les divertissements

entrance l'entrée (f)

entrance fee le prix d'entrée

E

envelope l'enveloppe (f)
epileptic épileptique
epileptic fit la crise d'épilepsie
equipment l'équipement (m)
equal égal
eraser la gomme
error l'erreur (f)
escalator l'escalator (m)
to escape s'échapper
essential indispensable
estate agency l'agence immobilière (f)
euro l'euro (m)
eurocheque l'eurochèque (m)
Europe l'Europe (f)
European européen(ne)
European Union l'Union européenne (f)
evening le soir
this evening ce soir
tomorrow evening demain soir
in the evening le soir
7 o'clock in the evening sept heures du soir
evening dress *(man)* la tenue de soirée
(woman) la robe du soir
evening meal le dîner
every chaque
everyone tout le monde
everything tout
everywhere partout
examination l'examen (m)
example: *for example* par exemple

excellent excellent(e)
except sauf
excess baggage l'excédent de bagages (m)
exchange l'échange (m)
to exchange échanger
exchange rate le taux de change
exciting passionnant(e)
excursion l'excursion (f)
excuse: *excuse me!* excusez-moi!
(to get by) pardon!
exercise l'exercice (m)
exhaust pipe le pot d'échappement
exhibition l'exposition (f)
exit la sortie
expenses les frais
expensive cher (chère)
expert m/f l'expert(e)
to expire *(ticket, etc)* expirer
to explain expliquer
explosion l'explosion (f)
to export exporter
express *(train)* le rapide
express *(parcel, etc)* en exprès
extension *(electrical)* la rallonge
extra *(additional)* supplémentaire
(more) de plus
eye l'œil (m)
eyes les yeux
eyebrows les sourcils

eye drops les gouttes pour les yeux

eyelashes les cils

eyeliner l'eye-liner (m)

eye shadow le fard à paupières

F

fabric le tissu

face le visage

face cloth/glove le gant de toilette

facial les soins du visage

facilities les installations

factory l'usine (f)

to faint s'évanouir

fainted évanoui(e)

fair (hair) blond(e)
(just) juste

fair (funfair) la fête foraine

fake faux (fausse)

fall (autumn) l'automne (m)

to fall tomber
he has fallen il est tombé

false teeth le dentier

family la famille

famous célèbre

fan (handheld) l'éventail (m)
(electric) le ventilateur
(sports) le supporter

fan belt la courroie de ventilateur

fancy dress le déguisement

far loin
is it far? c'est loin?

fare (bus, metro, etc) le prix du billet

farm la ferme

farmer le fermier

farmhouse la ferme

fashionable à la mode

fast rapide
too fast trop vite

to fasten (seatbelt) attacher

fat gros (grosse)
(noun) la graisse

father le père

father-in-law le beau-père

fault (defect) un défaut
it's not my fault ce n'est pas de ma faute

favour le service

favourite préféré(e)

fax le fax
by fax par fax

fax number le numéro de fax

to fax (document) faxer
(person) envoyer un fax à

February février

to feed nourrir

to feel sentir
I feel sick j'ai la nausée
I don't feel well je ne me sens pas bien

feet les pieds

felt-tip pen le feutre

female (animal) la femelle

ferry le ferry

festival le festival

to fetch aller chercher

fever la fièvre

few peu
  a few quelques-un(e)s
fiancé(e) le fiancé/la fiancée
field le champ
to fight se battre
file *(computer)* le fichier
  (for papers) le dossier
to fill remplir
to fill in *(form)* remplir
to fill up *(with petrol)* faire
  le plein
  fill it up! *(car)* le plein!
fillet le filet
filling *(in tooth)* le plombage
film le film
  (for camera) la pellicule
filter *(on cigarette)* le filtre
to find trouver
fine *(penalty)* la contravention
finger le doigt
to finish finir
finished fini(e)
fire le feu ; l'incendie *(m)*
fire alarm l'alarme
  d'incendie *(f)*
fire brigade les pompiers
fire engine la voiture de
  pompiers
fire escape *(staircase)*
  l'échelle de secours *(f)*
fire exit la sortie de secours
fire extinguisher
  l'extincteur *(m)*
fireplace la cheminée
fireworks les feux d'artifice
firm la compagnie

first premier(-ière)
first aid les premiers
  secours
first aid kit la trousse de
  secours
first-class de première
  classe
first name le prénom
fish le poisson
to fish pêcher
fisherman le pêcheur
fishing la pêche
  to go fishing aller à la pêche
fishing permit le permis de
  pêche
fishing rod la canne à pêche
fishmonger's le/la
  marchand(e) de poisson
fit *(medical)* l'attaque *(f)*
to fit: *it doesn't fit me* ça
  ne me va pas
to fix *(repair)* réparer
  can you fix it? vous
  pouvez le réparer?
fizzy gazeux(-euse)
flag le drapeau
flames les flammes
flash *(for camera)* le flash
flashlight la lampe de poche
flask le Thermos®
flat l'appartement *(m)*
flat *(level)* plat
  (beer) éventé
flat tyre le pneu dégonflé
flavour le goût
  (of ice cream) le parfum

F

flaw le défaut

fleas les puces

flesh la chair

flex *(electrical)* le fil

flight le vol

flip flops les tongs

flippers les palmes

flood l'inondation *(f)*
flash flood la crue subite

floor *(of room)* le sol
(storey) l'étage
(on the) ground floor (au) rez-de-chaussée
(on the) first floor (au) premier étage
(on the) second floor (au) deuxième étage
which floor? quel étage?

floorcloth la serpillère

florist's shop le magasin de fleurs

flour la farine

flower la fleur

flu la grippe

fly la mouche

to fly *(person)* aller en avion
(bird) voler

fly sheet le double toit

fog le brouillard

foggy: it was foggy il y avait du brouillard

foil le papier alu(minium)

to fold plier

to follow suivre

food la nourriture

food poisoning l'intoxication alimentaire *(f)*

foot le pied
to go on foot aller à pied

football le football

football match le match de football

football pitch le terrain de football

football player le/la joueur(-euse) de football

footpath le sentier

for pour
for me/you/us pour moi/vous/nous
for him/her pour lui/elle

forbidden interdit(e)

forehead le front

foreign étranger(-ère)

foreign currency les devises étrangères

foreigner l'étranger(ère) *(m(f))*

forest la forêt

forever toujours

to forget oublier

fork *(for eating)* la fourchette
(in road) l'embranchement *(m)*

form *(document)* le formulaire
(shape, style) la forme

fortnight la quinzaine

forward en avant

foul *(football)* la faute

fountain la fontaine

four-wheel drive vehicle le quatre-quatre ; le 4 x 4

ENGLISH–FRENCH

F

fox le renard
fracture la fracture
fragile fragile
fragrance le parfum
frame *(picture)* le cadre
France la France
  in/to France en France
free *(not occupied)* libre
  (costing nothing) gratuit(e)
freezer le congélateur
French français(e)
  (language) le français
French fries les frites
French people les Français
frequent fréquent(e)
fresh frais (fraîche)
fresh water l'eau douce *(f)*
Friday vendredi
fridge le frigo
fried frit(e)
friend *m/f* l'ami(e)
frog la grenouille
frogs' legs les cuisses
  de grenouille
from de
  I'm from England je suis
  anglais(e)
  I'm from Scotland je suis
  écossais(e)
front le devant
  in front of... devant...
front door la porte d'entrée
frost le gel
frozen gelé(e)
  (food) surgelé(e)
fruit le fruit

dried fruit les fruits secs
fruit juice le jus de fruit
fruit salad la salade de fruits
to fry frire
frying-pan la poêle
fuel le combustible
fuel gauge l'indicateur de
  niveau d'essence
fuel pump la pompe
  d'alimentation
fuel tank le réservoir
  d'essence
full plein(e)
  (occupied) complet(ète)
full board la pension complète
fumes *(exhaust)* les gaz
  d'échappement
fun: *to have fun* s'amuser
funeral les obsèques
funfair la fête foraine
funny *(amusing)* amusant(e)
fur la fourrure
furnished meublé(e)
furniture les meubles
fuse le fusible
fuse box la boîte à fusibles
future l'avenir *(m)*

G

gallery la galerie
game le jeu
  (meat) le gibier
garage *(for petrol)* la station-
  service
  (for parking, repair) le garage

garden le jardin

garlic l'ail (m)

gas le gaz

gas cooker la gazinière

gas cylinder la bouteille de gaz

gastritis la gastrite

gate la porte

gay (person) homo

gear la vitesse
in first gear en première
in second gear en seconde

gearbox la boîte de vitesses

generous généreux(-euse)

gents (toilet) les toilettes pour hommes

genuine authentique

German allemand(e)
(language) l'allemand (m)

German measles la rubéole

Germany l'Allemagne (f)

to get (obtain) obtenir
(to fetch) aller chercher

to get in (vehicle) monter

to get off (bus, etc)
descendre

gift le cadeau

gift shop la boutique de souvenirs

girl la fille

girlfriend la copine

to give donner

to give back rendre

glacier le glacier

glass le verre
a glass of water un verre d'eau

glasses les lunettes

glasses case l'étui à lunettes

gloves les gants

glue la colle

to go aller
I'm going to... je vais ...
we're going to hire a car nous allons louer une voiture

to go back retourner

to go in entrer

to go out (leave) sortir

goat la chèvre

God Dieu (m)

goggles (for swimming)
les lunettes de natation

gold l'or
is it gold? c'est en or?

golf le golf

golf ball la balle de golf

golf clubs les clubs de golf

golf course le terrain de golf

good bon (bonne)
(that's) good! (c'est) bien!

good afternoon bonjour

goodbye au revoir

good day bonjour

good evening bonsoir

good morning bonjour

good night bonne nuit

goose l'oie (f)

gram le gramme

grandchildren les petits-enfants

G

granddaughter la petite-fille
grandfather le grand-père
grandmother la grand-mère
grandparents les grands-parents
grandson le petit-fils
grapes le raisin
grass l'herbe (f)
grated (cheese) râpé(e)
grater la râpe
greasy gras (grasse)
great (big) grand(e)
   (wonderful) formidable
Great Britain la Grande-Bretagne
green vert(e)
green card (insurance) la carte verte
greengrocer's le magasin de fruits et légumes
greetings card la carte de vœux
grey gris(e)
grill (part of cooker) le gril
grilled grillé(e)
grocer's l'épicerie (f)
ground la terre ; le sol
ground floor le rez-de-chaussée
   on the ground floor au rez-de-chaussée
groundsheet le tapis de sol
group le groupe
guarantee la garantie
guard (on train) le chef de train

guest (house guest) l'invité(e)
   (in hotel) le/la client(e)
guesthouse la pension
guide (tourist guide) le/la guide
guidebook le guide
guided tour la visite guidée
guitar la guitare
gun (rifle) le fusil
   (pistol) le pistolet
gym (gymnasium) le gymnase
gym shoes les chaussures de sport

H

haemorrhoids les hémorroïdes
hail la grêle
hair les cheveux
hairbrush la brosse à cheveux
haircut la coupe (de cheveux)
hairdresser le/la coiffeur(-euse)
hairdryer le sèche-cheveux
hair dye la teinture pour les cheveux
hair gel le gel pour cheveux
hairgrip la pince à cheveux
hair mousse la mousse coiffante
hair spray la laque
half la moitié
   half an hour une demi-heure
half board la demi-pension

half fare le demi-tarif

half-price à moitié prix

ham *(cooked)* le jambon *(cured)* le jambon cru

hamburger le hamburger

hammer le marteau

hand la main

handbag le sac à main

hand luggage les bagages à main

hand-made fait main

handicapped handicapé(e)

handkerchief le mouchoir

handle la poignée

handlebars le guidon

handsome beau (belle)

hanger *(coathanger)* le cintre

hangover la gueule de bois

to hang up *(telephone)* raccrocher

hang-gliding le deltaplane *to go hang-gliding* faire du deltaplane

to happen arriver ; se passer *what happened?* qu'est-ce qui s'est passé?

happy heureux(-euse) *happy birthday!* bon anniversaire!

harbour le port

hard *(not soft)* dur(e) *(not easy)* difficile

hard disk le disque dur

hardware shop la quincaillerie

to harm someone faire du mal à quelqu'un

harvest *(grape)* les vendanges

hat le chapeau

to have avoir

to have to devoir

hay fever le rhume des foins

he il

head la tête

headache le mal de tête *I have a headache* j'ai mal à la tête

headlights les phares

headphones les écouteurs

head waiter le maître d'hôtel

health la santé

health food shop la boutique de produits diététiques

healthy sain(e)

to hear entendre

hearing aid la prothèse auditive

heart le cœur

heart attack la crise cardiaque

heartburn les brûlures d'estomac

heater l'appareil de chauffage *(m)*

heating le chauffage

to heat up faire chauffer

heavy lourd(e)

heel le talon

H

heel bar le talon-minute

height la hauteur

helicopter l'hélicoptère *(m)*

hello bonjour!
(on telephone) allô?

helmet le casque

help! au secours!

to help aider
can you help me? vous
pouvez m'aider?

hem l'ourlet *(m)*

hepatitis l'hépatite *(f)*

her son/sa/ses
her passport son
passeport
her room sa chambre
her suitcases ses valises

herb l'herbe *(f)*

herbal tea la tisane

here ici
here is... voici...

hernia la hernie

hi! salut!

to hide *(something)* cacher
(oneself) se cacher

high haut(e)

high blood pressure la
tension

high chair la chaise de bébé

high tide la marée haute

hill la colline

hill-walking la randonnée
(de basse montagne)

him il ; lui

hip la hanche

hip replacement la pose
d'une
prothèse de la hanche

hire la location
car hire la location
de voitures
bike hire la location
de bicyclettes
boat hire la location
de bateaux
ski hire la location de skis

to hire louer

hired car la voiture de
location

his son/sa/ses
his passport son
passeport
his room sa chambre
his suitcases ses valises

historic historique

history l'histoire *(f)*

to hit frapper

to hitchhike faire du stop

HIV le VIH

hobby le passe-temps

to hold
(contain) contenir

hold-up *(in traffic)*
l'embouteillage *(m)*

hole le trou

holiday les vacances
on holiday en vacances

home la maison
at my/your/our home chez
moi/vous/nous

homesick: *to be homesick* avoir le mal du pays
 I'm homesick j'ai le mal du pays

homosexual homosexuel(le)

honest honnête

honey le miel

honeymoon la lune de miel

hood (of car) le capot

hook (fishing) l'hameçon (m)

to hope espérer
 I hope so/not j'espère que oui/non

horn (of car) le klaxon

hors d'œuvre le hors-d'œuvre

horse le cheval

horse racing les courses de chevaux

horse-riding: *to go horse-riding* faire du cheval

hosepipe le tuyau d'arrosage

hospital l'hôpital (m)

hostel (youth hostel) l'auberge de jeunesse (f)

hot chaud(e)
 I'm hot j'ai chaud
 it's hot (weather) il fait chaud

hot-water bottle la bouillotte

hotel l'hôtel (m)

hour l'heure (f)
 half an hour une demi-heure
 1 hour une heure
 2 hours deux heures

house la maison

househusband l'homme au foyer

housewife la femme au foyer

house wine le vin en pichet

housework: *to do the housework* faire le ménage

hovercraft l'aéroglisseur (m)

how? (in what way) comment?
 how much/many? combien?
 how are you? comment allez-vous?

hungry: *to be hungry* avoir faim
 I'm hungry j'ai faim

to hunt chasser

hunting permit le permis de chasse

hurry: *I'm in a hurry* je suis pressé

to hurt: *to hurt somebody* faire du mal à quelqu'un
 that hurts ça fait mal

husband le mari

hut (bathing/beach) la cabine (mountain) le refuge

hydrofoil l'hydrofoil (m)

hypodermic needle l'aiguille hypodermique (f)

I

I je

ice la glace
 (cube) le glaçon
 with/without ice avec/sans glaçons

I

ice cream la glace
ice lolly l'esquimau *(m)*
ice rink la patinoire
to ice skate faire du patin
  (à glace)
ice skates les patins (à glace)
idea l'idée *(f)*
identity card la carte
  d'identité
if si
ignition l'allumage *(m)*
ignition key la clé de
  contact
ill malade
illness la maladie
immediately
  immédiatement
immersion heater le
  chauffe-eau électrique
immigration l'immigration *(f)*
immunisation l'immunisation
to import importer
important important(e)
impossible impossible
to improve améliorer
in dans
  in 2 hours' time dans deux
    heures
  in France en France
  in Canada au Canada
  in London à Londres
in front of devant
included compris(e)
inconvenient gênant
to increase augmenter
indicator *(car)* le clignotant

indigestion l'indigestion *(f)*
indigestion tablets les
  comprimés pour les
  troubles digestifs
indoors à l'intérieur
infection l'infection *(f)*
infectious infectieux(-euse)
information les
  renseignements
information desk les
  renseignements
information office le bureau
  de renseignements
ingredients les ingrédients
inhaler l'inhalateur *(m)*
injection la piqûre
to injure blesser
injured blessé(e)
injury la blessure
inn l'auberge *(f)*
inner tube la chambre à air
inquiries les renseignements
inquiry desk le bureau de
  renseignements
insect l'insecte *(m)*
insect bite la piqûre
  (d'insecte)
insect repellent le produit
  antimoustiques
inside à l'intérieur
instant coffee le café
  instantané
instead of au lieu de
instructor le moniteur/la
  monitrice

insulin l'insuline (f)
insurance l'assurance (f)
insurance certificate
  l'attestation d'assurance (f)
to insure assurer
insured assuré(e)
to intend to avoir l'intention
  de
interesting intéressant(e)
international international(e)
internet l'internet (m)
  internet café le cybercafé
interpreter l'interprète (m/f)
interval (theatre) l'entracte (m)
interview l'entrevue (f)
  (TV, etc) l'interview (f)
into dans ; en
  into town en ville
to introduce présenter
invitation l'invitation (f)
to invite inviter
invoice la facture
Ireland l'Irlande (f)
Irish irlandais(e)
iron (for clothes) le fer à
  repasser
  (metal) le fer
to iron repasser
ironing board la planche à
  repasser
ironmonger's la quincaillerie
is est
island l'île (f)
it il ; elle
Italian italien(ne)

Italy l'Italie (f)
to itch démanger
  it itches ça me démange
item l'article (m)
itemized bill la facture
  détaillée

J

jack (for car) le cric
jacket la veste
  waterproof jacket l'anorak
  (m)
jam (food) la confiture
jammed (stuck) coincé(e)
January janvier
jar (honey, jam, etc) le pot
jaundice la jaunisse
jaw la mâchoire
jealous jaloux(-ouse)
jeans le jean
jellyfish la méduse
jet ski le jet-ski
jetty (landing pier)
  l'embarcadère (m)
Jew le Juif/la Juive
jeweller's la bijouterie
jewellery les bijoux
Jewish juif (juive)
job le travail ; l'emploi
to jog faire du jogging
to join (become member)
  s'inscrire
to join in participer
joint (body) l'articulation (f)
to joke plaisanter

K

joke la plaisanterie
journalist le/la journaliste
journey le voyage
judge le juge
jug le pichet
juice le jus
    fruit juice le jus de fruit
    orange juice le jus
    d'orange
    a carton of juice un brick
    de jus
July juillet
to jump sauter
jumper le pull
jump leads les câbles de
    raccordement pour
    batterie
junction (road) le
    croisement ; le carrefour
June juin
just: just two deux seulement
    I've just arrived je viens
    d'arriver

K

to keep (retain) garder
kennel la niche
kettle la bouilloire
key la clé
    the car key la clé de la
    voiture
keyboard le clavier
keyring le porte-clés
to kick donner un coup de
    pied à

kid (child) le gosse
kidneys (in body) les reins
kill tuer
kilo(gram) le kilo
kilometre le kilomètre
kind (person) gentil(-ille)
kind (sort) la sorte
kiosk (newsstand) le kiosque
    (phone box) la cabine
kiss le baiser
to kiss embrasser
kitchen la cuisine
kitchen paper l'essuie-tout
    (m)
kite (toy) le cerf-volant
knee le genou
knickers la culotte
knife le couteau
to knit tricoter
to knock (on door) frapper
to knock down (in car)
    renverser
to knock over (vase, glass,
    etc) faire tomber
knot le nœud
to know (be aware of) savoir
    (person, place) connaître
    I don't know je ne sais pas
    I don't know Paris je ne
    connais pas Paris
to know how to do sth
    savoir faire quelque chose
    to know how to swim
    savoir nager
kosher kascher

label l'étiquette (f)

lace la dentelle

laces (for shoes) les lacets

ladder l'échelle (f)

ladies (toilet) les toilettes pour dames

lady la dame

lager la bière
  bottled lager la bière en bouteille
  draught lager la bière pression

lake le lac

lamb l'agneau (m)

lamp la lampe

lamppost le réverbère

lampshade l'abat-jour (m)

to land atterrir

land la terre

landlady la propriétaire

landlord le propriétaire

landslide le glissement de terrain

lane la ruelle
  (of motorway) la voie

language la langue

language school l'école de langues (f)

laptop le portable

large grand(e)

last dernier(-ière)
  last month le mois dernier
  last night (evening/night-time) hier soir ; la nuit dernière

last time la dernière fois

last week la semaine dernière

last year l'année dernière
  the last bus le dernier bus
  the last train le dernier train

late tard
  the train is late le train a du retard
  sorry we are late excusez-nous d'arriver en retard

later plus tard

to laugh rire

launderette la laverie automatique

laundry service le service de blanchisserie

lavatory les toilettes

lavender la lavande

law la loi

lawn la pelouse

lawyer m/f l'avocat(e)

laxative le laxatif

layby l'aire de stationnement (f)

lead (electric) le fil

lead (metal) le plomb

lead-free petrol l'essence sans plomb (f)

leaf la feuille

leak la fuite

to leak: it's leaking il y a une fuite

to learn apprendre

lease (rental) le bail

leather le cuir

L

to leave (depart for) partir
(depart from) quitter
(to leave behind) laisser
to leave for Paris partir
pour Paris
to leave London quitter
Londres

left: on/to the left à gauche

left-handed (person)
gaucher(-ère)

left-luggage (office)
la consigne

left-luggage locker
la consigne automatique

leg la jambe

legal légal(e)

leisure centre le centre
de loisirs

lemon le citron

lemonade la limonade

to lend prêter

length la longueur

lens (of camera, etc)
l'objectif (m)
(contact lens) la lentille

lesbian la lesbienne

less moins
less than moins de

lesson la leçon

to let (allow) permettre
(to hire out) louer

letter la lettre

letterbox la boîte aux
lettres

lettuce la laitue

level crossing le passage
à niveau

library la bibliothèque

licence le permis

lid le couvercle

to lie down s'allonger

life belt la bouée de
sauvetage

lifeboat le canot de
sauvetage

lifeguard le maître nageur

life insurance l'assurance-
vie (f)

life jacket le gilet de
sauvetage

life raft le radeau de
sauvetage

lift (elevator) l'ascenseur (m)

lift pass (on ski slopes) le
forfait

light (not heavy) léger(-ère)

light la lumière
have you got a light?
avez-vous du feu?

light bulb l'ampoule (f)

lighter le briquet

lighthouse le phare

lightning les éclairs

like (preposition) comme
like this comme ça

to like aimer
I like coffee j'aime le café
I don't like coffee je
n'aime pas le café
I'd like... je voudrais...
we'd like... nous
voudrions...

lilo® le matelas pneumatique

lime (fruit) le citron vert

line (mark) la ligne
  (row) la file
  (telephone) la ligne
linen le lin
lingerie la lingerie
lip la lèvre
lip-reading lire sur les lèvres
lip salve le baume pour les lèvres
lipstick le rouge à lèvres
liqueur la liqueur
list la liste
to listen to écouter
litre le litre
litter (rubbish) les ordures
little petit(e)
  a little... un peu de...
to live (in a place) vivre ; habiter
  I live in London j'habite à Londres
  he lives in a flat il habite dans un appartement
liver le foie
living room le salon
loaf le pain
local local(e)
lock la serrure
  the lock is broken la serrure est cassée
to lock fermer à clé
locker (for luggage) le casier
locksmith le serrurier
log (for fire) la bûche
logbook (of car) la carte grise
lollipop la sucette

London Londres
  to/in London à Londres
long long(ue)
  for a long time longtemps
long-sighted hypermétrope
to look after garder
to look at regarder
to look for chercher
loose (not fastened) desserré(e)
  it's come loose (unscrewed) ça s'est desserré
  (detached) ça s'est détaché
lorry le camion
to lose perdre
lost (object) perdu(e)
  I've lost... j'ai perdu...
  I'm lost je suis perdu(e)
lost property office le bureau des objets trouvés
lot: *a lot of* beaucoup de
lotion la lotion
lottery le loto
loud fort(e)
lounge (in hotel, airport) le salon
love l'amour
to love (person) aimer
  I love you je t'aime
  (food, activity, etc) adorer
  I love swimming j'adore nager
lovely beau (belle)
low bas (basse)
low-alcohol peu alcoolisé(e)
to lower baisser
low-fat allégé(e)

M

low tide la marée basse
luck la chance
lucky chanceux(-euse)
luggage les bagages
luggage allowance le poids maximum autorisé
luggage rack le porte-bagages
luggage tag l'étiquette à bagages (f)
luggage trolley le chariot (à bagages)
lump (swelling) la bosse
lunch le déjeuner
lunchbreak la pause de midi
lung le poumon
luxury le luxe

M

machine la machine
mad fou (folle)
magazine la revue
maggot l'asticot (m)
magnet l'aimant (m)
magnifying glass la loupe
maid la domestique
maiden name le nom de jeune fille
mail le courrier
  by mail par la poste
main principal(e)
mains (electricity, water) le secteur
main course (of meal) le plat principal

main road la route principale
to make faire
make-up le maquillage
male (person) masculin
mallet le maillet
man l'homme (m)
to manage (to be in charge of) gérer
manager le/la directeur(-trice)
manual (car) manuel(le)
many beaucoup de
map la carte
  road map la carte routière
  street map le plan de la ville
March mars
margarine la margarine
marina la marina
mark (stain) la tache
market le marché
  where is the market? où est le marché?
  when is the market? le marché, c'est quel jour?
market place le marché
marmalade la marmelade d'oranges
married marié(e)
  I'm married je suis marié(e)
  are you married? vous êtes marié(e)?
marsh le marais
mascara le mascara
mass (in church) la messe

mast le mât

masterpiece le chef-d'œuvre

match *(game)* la partie

matches les allumettes

material *(cloth)* le tissu

to matter: it doesn't matter ça ne fait rien
what's the matter? qu'est-ce qu'il y a?

mattress le matelas

May mai

mayonnaise la mayonnaise

mayor le maire

maximum le maximum

me moi

meal le repas

to mean vouloir dire
what does this mean? qu'est-ce que ça veut dire?

measles la rougeole

to measure mesurer

meat la viande

mechanic le mécanicien

medical insurance l'assurance maladie *(f)*

medical treatment les soins médicaux

medicine le médicament

Mediterranean Sea la Méditerranée

medium rare *(meat)* à point

to meet rencontrer

meeting la réunion

meeting point le point de rencontre

to melt fondre

member *(of club, etc)* le membre

membership card la carte de membre

memory la mémoire

men les hommes

to mend réparer

meningitis la méningite

menu *(choices)* le menu
(card) la carte

message le message

metal le métal

meter le compteur

metre le mètre

metro le métro

metro station la station de métro

microwave oven le four à micro-ondes

midday midi
at midday à midi

middle le milieu

middle-aged d'un certain âge

midge le moucheron

midnight minuit
at midnight à minuit

migraine la migraine
I have a migraine j'ai la migraine

mild *(weather, cheese)* doux (douce)
(curry) peu épicé(e)
(tobacco) léger(-ère)

milk le lait
  baby milk (formula) le lait maternisé
  fresh milk le lait frais
  full cream milk le lait entier
  hot milk le lait chaud
  long-life milk le lait longue conservation
  powdered milk le lait en poudre
  semi-skimmed milk le lait demi-écrémé
  skimmed milk le lait écrémé
  soya milk le lait de soja
  UHT milk le lait UHT
  with/without milk avec/sans lait

milkshake le milk-shake

millimetre le millimètre

mince *(meat)* la viande hachée

to mind: *do you mind if I...?* ça vous gêne si je...?
  I don't mind ça m'est égal
  do you mind? vous permettez?

mineral water l'eau minérale *(f)*

minibar le minibar

minimum le minimum

minister *(church)* le pasteur

minor road la route secondaire

mint *(herb)* la menthe
  (sweet) le bonbon à la menthe

minute la minute

mirror le miroir
  (in car) le rétroviseur

miscarriage la fausse couche

to miss *(train, flight, etc)* rater

Miss Mademoiselle

missing *(disappeared)* disparu(e)

mistake l'erreur *(f)*

misty brumeux(-euse)

misunderstanding le malentendu

to mix mélanger

mobile phone le portable

modem le modem

modern moderne

moisturizer la crème hydratante

mole *(on skin)* le grain de beauté

moment: *at the moment* en ce moment

monastery le monastère

Monday lundi

money l'argent *(m)*
  I have no money je n'ai pas d'argent

moneybelt la ceinture porte-monnaie

money order le mandat

month le mois
  this month ce mois-ci
  last month le mois dernier
  next month le mois prochain

monthly mensuel(-elle)

monument le monument

moon la lune

mooring *(place)* le mouillage

mop *(for floor)* le balai à franges

moped le vélomoteur

more encore
more wine plus de vin

more than plus de
more than three plus de trois

morning le matin
in the morning le matin
this morning ce matin
tomorrow morning demain matin

morning-after pill la pilule du lendemain

mosque la mosquée

mosquito le moustique

mosquito bite la piqûre de moustique

mosquito coil la spirale anti-moustiques

mosquito net la moustiquaire

mosquito repellent le produit antimoustiques

most (of the) la plupart (de)

moth *(clothes)* la mite

mother la mère

mother-in-law la belle-mère

motor le moteur

motorbike la moto

motorboat le bateau à moteur

motorway l'autoroute *(f)*

mountain la montagne

mountain bike le VTT (vélo tout-terrain)

mountain rescue le sauvetage en montagne

mountaineering l'alpinisme

mouse *(animal, computer)* la souris

moustache la moustache

mouth la bouche

mouthwash le bain de bouche

to move bouger
it's moving ça bouge

movie le film

Mr Monsieur

Mrs Madame

Ms Madame

much beaucoup
too much trop

muddy boueux(-euse)

mug: *I've been mugged* je me suis fait agresser

mugging l'agression *(f)*

mumps les oreillons

muscle le muscle

museum le musée

mushrooms les champignons

music la musique

musical *(show)* la comédie musicale

Muslim musulman(e)

mussels les moules

must devoir
I/we must go il faut que j'y aille/que nous y allions

you must be there il faut que vous y soyez

mustard la moutarde

my mon/ma/mes
  my passport mon passeport
  my room ma chambre
  my suitcases mes valises

N

nail (metal) le clou
  (finger) l'ongle (m)

nailbrush la brosse à ongles

nail clippers le coupe-ongles

nail file la lime à ongles

nail polish le vernis à ongles

nail polish remover le dissolvant

nail scissors les ciseaux à ongles

name le nom
  my name is... je m'appelle...
  what is your name? comment vous appelez-vous?

nanny le/la baby-sitter

napkin la serviette de table

nappy la couche

narrow étroit(e)

national national(e)

nationality la nationalité

national park le parc national

natural naturel(le)

nature reserve la réserve naturelle

nature trail le sentier de grande randonnée

navy blue bleu marine

near près de
  near the bank près de la banque
  is it near? c'est près d'ici?

necessary nécessaire

neck le cou

necklace le collier

nectarine le brugnon

to need (to) avoir besoin de
  I need... j'ai besoin de...
  we need... nous avons besoin de...
  I need to phone j'ai besoin de téléphoner

needle l'aiguille (f)
  a needle and thread du fil et une aiguille

negative (photography) le négatif

neighbour le/la voisin(e)

nephew le neveu

net le filet
  the Net le net ; l'internet (m)

never jamais
  I never drink wine je ne bois jamais de vin

new nouveau(-elle)

news (TV, radio, etc) les informations

newsagent's le magasin de journaux

newspaper le journal

news stand le kiosque

New Year le Nouvel An
happy New Year! bonne
année!

New Year's Eve la Saint-
Sylvestre

New Zealand la Nouvelle-
Zélande

next prochain(e)
(after) ensuite
the next train le prochain
train
next month le mois
prochain
next week la semaine
prochaine
next Monday lundi prochain
next to à côté de
we're going to Paris next
ensuite nous allons à Paris

nice beau (belle)
(enjoyable) bon (bonne)
(person) sympathique

niece la nièce

night *(night-time)* la nuit
(evening) le soir
at night la nuit/le soir
last night hier soir
tomorrow night (evening)
demain soir
tonight ce soir

nightclub la boîte de nuit

nightdress la chemise de nuit

night porter le gardien de
nuit

no non
(without) sans
no problem pas de
problème
no thanks non merci

no ice sans glaçons
no sugar sans sucre

nobody personne

noise le bruit
it's very noisy il y a
beaucoup de bruit

non-alcoholic sans alcool

none aucun(e)

**non-smoker: I'm a non-
smoker** je ne fume pas

non-smoking *(seat, compartment)* non-fumeurs

north le nord

Northern Ireland l'Irlande
du Nord *(f)*

North Sea la mer du Nord

nose le nez

not ne ... pas
I am not... je ne suis pas...

note *(banknote)* le billet
(letter) le mot

note pad le bloc-notes

nothing rien
nothing else rien d'autre

notice *(warning)* l'avis *(m)*
(sign) le panneau

notice board le panneau
d'affichage

novel le roman

November novembre

now maintenant

nowhere nulle part

nuclear nucléaire

number *(quantity)* le nombre
(of room, house) le numéro
phone number le numéro
de téléphone

numberplate (of car) la plaque d'immatriculation

nurse m/f l'infirmier/l'infirmière

nursery la garderie

nursery slope la piste pour débutants

nut (to eat) la noix (for bolt) l'écrou (m)

O

oar l'aviron (m) ; la rame

oats l'avoine (f)

to obtain obtenir

occupation (work) l'emploi (m)

ocean l'océan (m)

October octobre

odd (strange) bizarre

of de
a glass of... un verre de...
made of... en...

off (light) éteint(e)
(rotten) mauvais(e) ; pourri(e)

office le bureau

often souvent

oil (for car, food) l'huile (f)

oil filter le filtre à huile

oil gauge la jauge de niveau d'huile

ointment la pommade

OK! (agreed) d'accord!

old vieux (vieille)
how old are you? quel âge avez-vous?
I'm... years old j'ai... ans

old-age pensioner le/la retraité(e)

olive l'olive (f)

olive oil l'huile d'olive (f)

on (light) allumé(e)
(engine, etc) en marche
on the table sur la table
on time à l'heure

once une fois
at once tout de suite

one-way (street) à sens unique

onion l'oignon (m)

only seulement

open ouvert(e)

to open ouvrir

opera l'opéra (m)

operation (surgical) l'opération (f)

operator (phone) le/la standardiste

opposite en face de
opposite the bank en face de la banque
quite the opposite bien au contraire

optician m/f l'opticien/l'opticienne

or ou

orange (fruit) l'orange
(colour) orange

orange juice le jus d'orange

orchestra l'orchestre (m)

order (in restaurant) la commande
out of order en panne

to order (in restaurant) commander

organic biologique

to organize organiser

ornament le bibelot

other autre
  have you any others? vous en avez d'autres?

our *(sing)* notre
  (plural) nos
  our room notre chambre
  our passports nos passeports
  our baggage nos bagages

out *(light)* éteint(e)
  he's/she's out il/elle est sorti(e)

outdoor *(pool, etc)* en plein air

outside dehors

oven le four

ovenproof dish le plat qui va au four

over *(on top of)* au-dessus de

to overbook faire du surbooking

to overcharge faire payer trop cher

overdone *(food)* trop cuit(e)

overdose la surdose

to overheat surchauffer

to overload surcharger

to oversleep se réveiller en retard

to overtake *(in car)* doubler ; dépasser

to owe devoir
  you owe me... vous me devez...

to own posséder

owner le/la propriétaire

oyster l'huître *(f)*

P

pace le pas

pacemaker le stimulateur (cardiaque)

to pack *(luggage)* faire les bagages

package le paquet

package tour le voyage organisé

packet le paquet

padded envelope l'enveloppe matelassée

paddling pool la pataugeoire

padlock le cadenas

page la page

paid payé(e)
  I've paid j'ai payé

pain la douleur

painful douloureux(-euse)

painkiller l'analgésique *(m)*

to paint peindre

painting *(picture)* le tableau

pair la paire

palace le palais

pale pâle

pan *(saucepan)* la casserole *(frying pan)* la poêle

pancake la crêpe

panniers *(for bike)* les sacoches

panties la culotte

pants *(underwear)* le slip
panty liner le protège-slip
paper le papier
paper hankies les mouchoirs en papier
paper napkins les serviettes en papier
paragliding le parapente
paralysed paralysé(e)
parcel le colis
pardon? comment?
  I beg your pardon! pardon!
parents les parents
Paris Paris
park le parc
to park garer (la voiture)
parking disk le disque de stationnement
parking meter le parcmètre
parking ticket le p.-v.
part: *spare parts* les pièces de rechange
partner *(business)* m/f l'associé(e)
  (boy/girlfriend) le compagnon/la compagne
party *(group)* le groupe
  (celebration) la fête ; la soirée
  (political) le parti
pass *(bus, train)* la carte
  (mountain) le col
passenger le passager/la passagère
passport le passeport
passport control le contrôle des passeports

pasta les pâtes
pastry la pâte
  (cake) la pâtisserie
path le chemin
patient *(in hospital)* le/la patient(e)
pavement le trottoir
to pay payer
  I'd like to pay je voudrais payer
  where do I pay? où est-ce qu'il faut payer?
payment le paiement
payphone le téléphone public
peace *(after war)* la paix
peach la pêche
peak rate le plein tarif
peanut allergy l'allergie aux cacahuètes (f)
pear la poire
peas les petits pois
pedal la pédale
pedalo le pédalo®
pedestrian le/la piéton(ne)
pedestrian crossing le passage clouté
to pee faire pipi
to peel *(fruit)* peler
peg *(for clothes)* la pince à linge
  (for tent) le piquet
pen le stylo
pencil le crayon
penfriend le/la correspondant(e)

penicillin la pénicilline

penis le pénis

penknife le canif

pensioner le/la retraité(e)

people les gens

pepper *(spice)* le poivre
(vegetable) le poivron

per par
  per day par jour
  per hour à l'heure
  per person par personne
  per week par semaine
  100 km per hour 100 km
  à l'heure

perfect parfait(e)

performance *(show)* le
spectacle

perfume le parfum

perhaps peut-être

period *(menstruation)* les règles

perm la permanente

permit le permis

person la personne

personal organizer l'agenda
(m)

personal stereo le baladeur

pet l'animal domestique *(m)*

pet food les aliments pour
animaux

pet shop la boutique
d'animaux

petrol l'essence *(f)*
  4-star le super
  unleaded l'essence sans
  plomb

petrol cap le bouchon de
réservoir

petrol pump la pompe à
essence

petrol station la station-
service

petrol tank le réservoir

pharmacy la pharmacie

phone le téléphone
  by phone par téléphone

to phone téléphoner

phonebook l'annuaire *(m)*

phonebox la cabine
(téléphonique)

phone call l'appel *(m)*

phonecard la télécarte

photocopy la photocopie

to photocopy photocopier

photograph la photo
  to take a photograph
  prendre une photo

phrase book le guide de
conversation

piano le piano

to pick *(choose)* choisir
(pluck) cueillir

pickpocket le pickpocket

picnic le pique-nique
  to have a picnic pique-
  niquer

picnic hamper le panier à
pique-nique

picnic rug la couverture

picture *(painting)* le tableau
(photo) la photo

pie *(savoury)* la tourte

piece le morceau

pier la jetée

P **pig** le cochon

pill la pilule
 I'm on the pill je prends
 la pilule

pillow l'oreiller (m)

pillowcase la taie d'oreiller

pilot le pilote

pin l'épingle (f)

pink rose

pint: *a pint of...* un demi-
 litre de...

pipe *(for water, gas)* le tuyau
 (smoking) la pipe

pity: *what a pity* quel
 dommage

pizza la pizza

place l'endroit (m)

place of birth le lieu de
 naissance

plain *(unflavoured)* ordinaire

plait la natte

to plan prévoir

plan *(map)* le plan

plane *(aircraft)* l'avion (m)

plant *(in garden)* la plante

plaster *(sticking plaster)*
 le sparadrap
 (for broken limb, on wall)
 le plâtre

plastic *(made of)*
 en plastique

plastic bag le sac en
 plastique

plate l'assiette (f)

platform *(railway)* le quai
 which platform? quel quai?

play *(at theatre)* la pièce

to play *(games)* jouer

play park l'aire de jeux (f)

playroom la salle de jeux

pleasant agréable

please s'il vous plaît

pleased content(e)
 pleased to meet you!
 enchanté(e)!

plenty of beaucoup de

pliers la pince

plug *(electrical)* la prise
 (for sink) la bonde

to plug in brancher

plum la prune

plumber le plombier

plumbing la tuyauterie

plunger *(to clear sink)* le
 débouchoir à ventouse

p.m. de l'après-midi

poached poché(e)

pocket la poche

points *(in car)* les vis
 platinées

poison le poison

poisonous vénéneux

police *(force)* la police

policeman le policier
 (police woman) la femme
 policier

police station
 le commissariat ;
 la gendarmerie

polish *(for shoes)* le cirage

pollen le pollen

polluted pollué(e)

pony le poney

pony-trekking la randonnée à cheval

pool *(swimming)* la piscine

pool attendant le/la surveillant(e) de baignade

poor pauvre

popcorn le pop-corn

pop socks les mi-bas

popular populaire

pork le porc

port *(seaport)* le port *(wine)* le porto

porter *(for luggage)* le porteur

portion la portion

Portugal le Portugal

possible possible

post *(letters)* le courrier *by post* par courrier

to post poster

postbox la boîte aux lettres

postcard la carte postale

postcode le code postal

poster l'affiche *(f)*

postman/woman le facteur/la factrice

post office la poste

to postpone remettre à plus tard

pot *(for cooking)* la casserole

potato la pomme de terre *baked potato* la pomme de terre cuite au four

boiled potatoes les pommes vapeur

fried potatoes les pommes de terres sautées

mashed potatoes la purée

roast potatoes les pommes de terre rôties

potato salad la salade de pommes de terre

pothole le nid de poule

pottery la poterie

pound *(money)* la livre

to pour verser

powder la poudre

powdered milk le lait en poudre

power *(electricity)* le courant

power cut la coupure de courant

pram le landau

to pray prier

to prefer préférer

pregnant enceinte *I'm pregnant* je suis enceinte

to prepare préparer

to prescribe prescrire

prescription l'ordonnance *(f)*

present *(gift)* le cadeau

preservative le conservateur

president le président

pressure la pression *tyre pressure* la pression des pneus

pretty joli(e)

P

price le prix
price list le tarif
priest le prêtre
print *(photo)* la photo
printer l'imprimante *(f)*
prison la prison
private privé(e)
prize le prix
probably probablement
problem le problème
professor le professeur
  d'université
programme *(TV, etc)*
  l'émission *(f)*
prohibited interdit(e)
promise la promesse
to promise promettre
to pronounce prononcer
  how's it pronounced?
  comment ça se prononce?
Protestant protestant(e)
to provide fournir
public public(-ique)
public holiday le jour férié
pudding le dessert
to pull tirer
  to pull a muscle se faire
  une élongation
to pull over *(car)* s'arrêter
pullover le pull
pump la pompe
puncture la crevaison
puncture repair kit la boîte
  de rustines®
puppet la marionnette

puppet show le spectacle
  de marionnettes
purple violet(-ette)
purpose le but
  on purpose exprès
purse le porte-monnaie
to push pousser
pushchair la poussette
to put *(place)* mettre
pyjamas le pyjama
Pyrenees les Pyrénées

Q

quality la qualité
quantity la quantité
quarantine la quarantaine
to quarrel se disputer
quarter le quart
quay le quai
queen la reine
query la question
question la question
queue la queue
to queue faire la queue
quick rapide
quickly vite
quiet *(place)* tranquille
quilt la couette
quite *(rather)* assez
  (completely) complètement
  quite good pas mal
  it's quite expensive c'est
  assez cher
quiz le jeu-concours

rabbit le lapin
rabies la rage
race *(people)* la race
(sport) la course
race course le champ de
courses
racket la raquette
radiator le radiateur
radio la radio
railcard la carte
d'abonnement (de chemin
de fer)
railway le chemin de fer
railway station la gare
rain la pluie
to rain: *it's raining* il pleut
raincoat l'imperméable *(m)*
rake le râteau
rape le viol
to rape violer
raped: *to be raped* être
violé(e)
rare *(uncommon)* rare
(steak) saignant(e)
rash *(skin)* la rougeur
rat le rat
rate *(price)* le tarif
rate of exchange le taux
de change
raw cru(e)
razor le rasoir
razor blades les lames de
rasoir
to read lire

ready prêt(e)
real vrai(e)
to realize (that ...) se rendre
compte (que ...)
rearview mirror le
rétroviseur
receipt le reçu
receiver *(of phone)* le
récepteur
reception *(desk)* la réception
receptionist le/la
réceptionniste
to recharge *(battery, etc)*
recharger
recipe la recette
to recognize reconnaître
to recommend
recommander
to record enregistrer
to recover *(from illness)*
se remettre
to recycle recycler
red rouge
to reduce réduire
reduction la réduction
to refer to parler de
refill la recharge
to refund rembourser
to refuse refuser
regarding concernant
region la région
register le registre
to register *(at hotel)* se
présenter
registered *(letter)*
recommandé(e)

R

registration form la fiche

to reimburse rembourser

relation *(family)* le/la parent(e)

relationship les rapports

to remain rester

remember se rappeler
I don't remember je ne m'en rappelle pas

remote control la télécommande

removal firm les déménageurs

to remove enlever

rent le loyer

to rent louer

rental la location

repair la réparation

to repair réparer

to repeat répéter

to reply répondre

report *(of theft, etc)* la déclaration

to report *(theft, etc)* déclarer

request la demande

to request demander

to require avoir besoin de

to rescue sauver

reservation la réservation

to reserve réserver

reserved réservé(e)

resident *m/f* l'habitant(e)

resort *(seaside)* la station balnéaire
ski resort la station de ski

rest *(relaxation)* le repos
(remainder) le reste

to rest se reposer

restaurant le restaurant

restaurant car le wagon-restaurant

retired retraité(e)

to return *(to a place)* retourner
(to return something) rendre

return ticket le billet aller-retour

to reverse faire marche arrière

to reverse the charges appeler en PCV

reverse-charge call l'appel en PCV *(m)*

reverse gear la marche arrière

rheumatism le rhumatisme

rib la côte

ribbon le ruban

rice le riz

rich *(person, food)* riche

to ride *(horse)* faire du cheval

right *(correct)* exact(e)

right la droite
on/to the right à droite

right of way la priorité

ring *(on finger)* la bague

to ring *(bell)* sonner
it's ringing (phone) ça sonne
to ring sb (phone) téléphoner à quelqu'un

ring road le périphérique

ripe mûr(e)

river la rivière

Riviera *(French)* la Côte d'Azur

road la route

road map la carte routière

road sign le panneau

roadworks les travaux

roast rôti(e)

roll *(bread)* le petit pain

roller blades les rollers

romantic romantique

roof le toit

roof-rack la galerie

room *(in house)* la pièce
(in hotel) la chambre
(space) la place
double room la chambre
pour deux personnes
family room la chambre
pour une famille
single room la chambre
pour une personne

room number le numéro de
chambre

room service le service des
chambres

root la racine

rope la corde

rose la rose

rosé wine le rosé

rotten *(fruit, etc)* pourri(e)

rough: *rough sea* la mer
agitée

round rond(e)

roundabout *(traffic)* le rond-
point

route la route ; l'itinéraire *(m)*

row *(theatre, etc)* la rangée

rowing *(sport)* l'aviron *(m)*

rowing boat la barque

rubber *(material)* le
caoutchouc
(eraser) la gomme

rubber band l'élastique *(m)*

rubber gloves les gants en
caoutchouc

rubbish les ordures

rubella la rubéole

rucksack le sac à dos

rug *(carpet)* le tapis

ruins les ruines

ruler *(for measuring)* la règle

to run courir

rush hour l'heure de pointe *(f)*

rusty rouillé(e)

S

sad triste

saddle la selle

safe *(for valuables)* le coffre-
fort

safe sûr ; sans danger
is it safe? ce n'est pas
dangereux?

safety belt la ceinture de
sécurité

safety pin l'épingle de
sûreté *(f)*

sail la voile

sailboard la planche à voile

sailing *(sport)* la voile

sailing boat le voilier
saint le/la saint(e)
salad la salade
  green salad la salade verte
  mixed salad la salade composée
  potato salad la salade de pommes de terre
  tomato salad la salade de tomates
salad dressing la vinaigrette
salami le salami
salary le salaire
sale la vente
sales *(reductions)* les soldes
salesman/woman le vendeur/la vendeuse
sales rep le/la représentant(e)
salt le sel
salt water l'eau salée
salty salé(e)
same même
sample l'échantillon *(m)*
sand le sable
sandals les sandales
sandwich le sandwich
  toasted sandwich le croque-monsieur
sanitary towel la serviette hygiénique
satellite dish l'antenne parabolique *(f)*
satellite TV la télévision par satellite
Saturday samedi
sauce la sauce

saucepan la casserole
saucer la soucoupe
sauna le sauna
sausage la saucisse
to save *(life)* sauver *(money)* épargner ; économiser
savoury salé(e)
saw la scie
to say dire
scales *(for weighing)* la balance
scarf *(headscarf)* le foulard *(woollen)* l'écharpe *(f)*
scenery le paysage
schedule le programme
school l'école *(f)*
  primary school l'école primaire
  secondary school (11-15) le collège
  (15-18) le lycée
scissors les ciseaux
score *(of match)* le score
to score *(goal, point)* marquer
Scot *m/f* l'Écossais(e)
Scotland l'Écosse *(f)*
Scottish écossais(e)
scouring pad le tampon à récurer
screen l'écran *(m)*
screen wash le lave-glace
screw la vis
screwdriver le tournevis
  phillips screwdriver le tournevis cruciforme

scuba diving la plongée
sous-marine

sculpture la sculpture

sea la mer

seafood les fruits de mer

seam *(of dress)* la couture

to search fouiller

seasickness le mal de mer

seaside le bord de la mer
  at the seaside au bord de
  la mer

season *(of year, holiday time)*
la saison
  in season de saison

seasonal saisonnier

season ticket la carte
d'abonnement

seat *(chair)* le siège
  (in train) la place
  (cinema, theatre) le fauteuil

seatbelt la ceinture de
sécurité

second second(e)

second *(time)* la seconde

second class seconde
classe

second-hand d'occasion

secretary le/la secrétaire

security guard le/la vigile

sedative le calmant

to see voir

to seize saisir

self-catering flat
l'appartement indépendant
(avec cuisine)

self-employed: *to be self*

employed travailler à son
compte

self-service le libre-service

to sell vendre
  do you sell…? vous
  vendez…?

sell-by date la date limite
de vente

Sellotape® le Scotch®

to send envoyer

senior citizen la personne
du troisième âge

sensible raisonnable

separated séparé(e)

separately: *to pay*
separately payer
séparément

September septembre

serious grave

to serve servir

service *(church)* l'office *(m)*
  (in restaurant, shop, etc)
  le service
  is service included?
  le service est compris?

service charge le service

service station la station-
service

set menu le menu à prix fixe

settee le canapé

several plusieurs

to sew coudre

sex le sexe

shade l'ombre *(f)*
  in the shade à l'ombre

to shake *(bottle, etc)* agiter

S

shallow peu profond(e)
shampoo le shampooing
shampoo and set le shampooing et la mise en plis
to share partager
sharp *(razor, knife)* tranchant
to shave se raser
shaving cream la crème à raser
shawl le châle
she elle
sheep le mouton
sheet *(for bed)* le drap
shelf le rayon
shell *(seashell)* le coquillage
sheltered abrité(e)
to shine briller
shingles *(illness)* le zona
ship le navire
shirt la chemise
shock le choc
shock absorber l'amortisseur *(m)*
shoe la chaussure
shoelaces les lacets
shoe polish le cirage
shoeshop le magasin de chaussures
shop le magasin
to shop faire du shopping
shop assistant le vendeur/ la vendeuse
shop window la vitrine
shopping centre le centre

commercial
shore le rivage
short court(e)
shortage le manque
short circuit le court-circuit
short cut le raccourci
shortly bientôt
shorts le short
short-sighted myope
shoulder l'épaule *(f)*
to shout crier
show le spectacle
to show montrer
shower *(wash)* la douche
  to take a shower prendre une douche
shower cap le bonnet de douche
shower gel le gel douche
to shrink *(clothes)* rétrécir
shut *(closed)* fermé(e)
to shut fermer
shutter *(on window)* le volet
shuttle service la navette
sick *(ill)* malade
  I feel sick j'ai envie de vomir
side le côté
side dish la garniture
sidelight le feu de position
sidewalk le trottoir
sieve la passoire
sightseeing le tourisme
  to go sightseeing faire du tourisme

sightseeing tour l'excursion touristique (f)

sign *(notice)* le panneau

to sign signer

signature la signature

signpost le poteau indicateur

silk la soie

silver l'argent (m)

similar (to) semblable (à)

since depuis

to sing chanter

single *(unmarried)* célibataire *(bed, room)* pour une personne

single ticket l'aller simple (m)

sink *(washbasin)* l'évier (m)

sir Monsieur

sister la sœur

sister-in-law la belle-sœur

to sit s'asseoir
 sit down! asseyez-vous!

size *(clothes)* la taille *(shoe)* la pointure

skates *(ice)* les patins à glace *(roller)* les patins à roulettes

to skate *(on ice)* patiner *(roller)* faire du patin à roulettes

skateboard le skate-board
 to go skateboarding faire du skate-board

ski le ski

to ski faire du ski

ski boots les chaussures de ski

skiing le ski

ski instructor le/la moniteur(-trice) de ski

ski jump *(place)* le tremplin de ski

ski lift le remonte-pente

ski pants le fuseau

ski pass le forfait

ski pole le bâton (de ski)

ski run la piste

ski suit la combinaison de ski

ski tow le remonte-pente

skilled adroit(e) ; qualifié(e)

skin la peau

skirt la jupe

sky le ciel

slate l'ardoise (f)

sledge la luge

to sleep dormir

sleeper la couchette *(carriage)* la voiture-lit *(train)* le train-couchettes

to sleep in faire la grasse matinée

sleeping bag le sac de couchage

sleeping car la voiture-lit

sleeping pill le somnifère

slice *(bread, cake, etc)* la tranche

sliced bread le pain de mie en tranches

slide *(photograph)* la diapositive

to slip glisser

S

slippers les pantoufles
slow lent(e)
to slow down ralentir
slowly lentement
small petit(e)
smaller than plus petit(e) que
smell l'odeur (f)
a bad smell une mauvaise odeur
smile le sourire
to smile sourire
smoke la fumée
to smoke fumer
I don't smoke je ne fume pas
can I smoke? on peut fumer?
smoke alarm le détecteur de fumée
smoked fumé(e)
smokers *(sign)* fumeurs
smooth lisse
snack le casse-croûte
to have a snack casser la croûte
snack bar le snack-bar
snail l'escargot (m)
snake le serpent
snake bite la morsure de serpent
to sneeze éternuer
snorkel le tuba
snow la neige
to snow: *it's snowing* il neige
snowboard le snowboard

snowboarding le surf des neiges
to go snowboarding faire du snowboard
snow chains les chaînes
snowed up enneigé(e)
snow tyres les pneus cloutés
soap le savon
soap powder *(detergent)* la lessive
sober: to be sober ne pas avoir bu
socket *(for plug)* la prise de courant
socks les chaussettes
soda water l'eau de Seltz (f)
sofa le canapé
sofa bed le canapé-lit
soft doux (douce)
soft drink le soda
software le logiciel
soldier le soldat
sole *(shoe)* la semelle
soluble soluble
some de (du/de la/des)
someone quelqu'un
something quelque chose
sometimes quelquefois
son le fils
son-in-law le gendre
song la chanson
soon bientôt
as soon as possible dès que possible
sore douloureux(-euse)

172

ENGLISH–FRENCH

sore throat: *to have a sore throat* avoir mal à la gorge

sorry: *I'm sorry!* excusez-moi!

sort la sorte
  what sort? de quelle sorte?

soup le potage ; la soupe

sour aigre

soured cream la crème fermentée

south le sud

souvenir le souvenir

spa la station thermale

space la place

spade la pelle

Spain l'Espagne *(f)*

Spanish espagnol(e)

spanner la clé plate

spare parts les pièces de rechange

spare room la chambre d'amis

spare tyre le pneu de rechange

spare wheel la roue de secours

sparkling *(wine)* mousseux(-euse)
  (water) gazeux(-euse)

spark plug la bougie

to speak parler
  do you speak English? vous parlez anglais?

special spécial(e)

specialist *(medical)* le/la spécialiste

speciality la spécialité

speeding l'excès de vitesse *(m)*
  a speeding ticket un p.-v. pour excès de vitesse

speed limit la limitation de vitesse
  to exceed speed limit dépasser la vitesse permise

speedboat le hors-bord

speedometer le compteur

to spell: *how is it spelt?* comment ça s'écrit?

to spend *(money)* dépenser *(time)* passer

spice l'épice *(f)*

spicy épicé(e)

spider l'araignée *(f)*

to spill renverser

spine la colonne vertébrale

spin dryer le sèche-linge

spirits *(alcohol)* les spiritueux

splinter *(in finger)* l'écharde *(f)*

spoke *(of wheel)* le rayon

sponge l'éponge *(f)*

spoon la cuiller

sport le sport

sports centre le centre sportif

sports shop le magasin de sports

spot *(pimple)* le bouton

sprain l'entorse *(f)*

S

spring (season) le printemps
(metal) le ressort
square (in town) la place
squeeze presser
squid le calmar
stadium le stade
stage la scène
staff le personnel
stain la tache
stained glass window
le vitrail
stairs l'escalier (m)
stale (bread) rassis(e)
stalls (in theatre) l'orchestre (m)
stamp le timbre
to stand (get up) se lever
(be standing) être debout
star l'étoile (f)
(celebrity) la vedette
to start commencer
starter (in meal) le hors
d'œuvre
(in car) le démarreur
station la gare
stationer's la papeterie
statue la statue
stay le séjour
enjoy your stay! bon séjour!
to stay (remain) rester
(reside for while) loger
I'm staying at... je loge à...
steak le bifteck
to steal voler
steam la vapeur
steamed cuit(e) à la vapeur
steel l'acier (m)

steep raide
steeple le clocher
steering wheel le volant
step le pas
stepdaughter la belle-fille
stepfather le beau-père
stepmother la belle-mère
stepson le beau-fils
stereo la chaîne (stéréo)
sterling la livre sterling
steward le steward
stewardess l'hôtesse (f)
sticking-plaster le
sparadrap
still: still water l'eau plate (f)
still (yet) encore
sting la piqûre
to sting piquer
stitches (surgical) les points
de suture
stockings les bas
stolen volé(e)
stomach l'estomac (m)
stomach ache: to have a
stomach ache avoir mal
au ventre
stomach upset l'estomac
dérangé
stone la pierre
to stop arrêter
store (shop) le magasin
storey l'étage (m)
storm l'orage (m)
story l'histoire (f)
straightaway tout de suite

straight on tout droit

strange bizarre

straw *(for drinking)* la paille

strawberries les fraises

stream le ruisseau

street la rue

street map le plan des rues

strength la force

stress le stress

strike *(of workers)* la grève

string la ficelle

striped rayé(e)

stroke *(haemorrhage)* l'attaque (d'apoplexie)
  to have a stroke avoir une attaque

strong fort(e)

stuck bloqué(e)

student *(male)* l'étudiant *(female)* l'étudiante

student discount le tarif étudiant

stuffed farci(e)

stung piqué(e)

stupid stupide

subscription l'abonnement *(m)*

subtitles les sous-titres

subway le passage souterrain

suddenly soudain

suede le daim

sugar le sucre

sugar-free sans sucre

to suggest suggérer

suit *(man's)* le costume *(woman's)* le tailleur

suitcase la valise

sum la somme

summer l'été *(m)*

summer holidays les vacances d'été

summit le sommet

sun le soleil

to sunbathe prendre un bain de soleil

sunblock l'écran total *(m)*

sunburn le coup de soleil

Sunday le dimanche

sunflower le tournesol

sunglasses les lunettes de soleil

sunny: *it's sunny* il fait beau

sunrise le lever du soleil

sunroof le toit ouvrant

sunscreen *(lotion)* l'écran solaire *(m)*

sunset le coucher de soleil

sunshade le parasol

sunstroke l'insolation *(f)*

suntan le bronzage

suntan lotion le lait solaire

supermarket le supermarché

supper *(dinner)* le souper

supplement le supplément

to supply fournir

to surf faire du surf
  to surf the Net surfer sur Internet

T

surfboard la planche de surf
surfing le surf
surgery (operation)
  l'opération chirurgicale (f)
surname le nom de famille
surprise la surprise
to survive survivre
to swallow avaler
to sweat transpirer
sweater le pull
sweatshirt le sweat-shirt
sweet sucré(e)
sweetener l'édulcorant (m)
sweets les bonbons
to swell enfler
to swim nager
swimming pool la piscine
swimsuit le maillot de bain
swing (for children) la
  balançoire
Swiss suisse
switch le bouton
to switch off éteindre
to switch on allumer
Switzerland la Suisse
swollen enflé(e)
synagogue la synagogue
syringe la seringue

T

table la table
tablecloth la nappe
table tennis le tennis
  de table

table wine le vin de table
tablet le comprimé
to take (something) prendre
to take away (something)
  emporter
to take off (clothes) enlever
talc le talc
to talk (to) parler (à)
tall grand(e)
tampons les tampons
  hygiéniques
tangerine la mandarine
tank (petrol) le réservoir
  (fish) l'aquarium (m)
tap le robinet
tap water l'eau du robinet (f)
tape le ruban
  (cassette) la cassette
  adhesive tape le Scotch®
  video tape la cassette
  vidéo
tape measure le mètre à
  ruban
tape recorder le
  magnétophone
tart la tarte
taste le goût
to taste goûter
  can I taste some? je peux
  goûter?
tax l'impôt (m)
taxi le taxi
taxi driver le chauffeur de
  taxi
taxi rank la station de taxis
tea le thé

herbal tea la tisane
lemon tea le thé au citron
tea with milk le thé au lait
teabag le sachet de thé
teapot la théière
teaspoon la cuiller à café
tea towel le torchon
to teach enseigner
teacher le professeur
team l'équipe (f)
tear (in material) la déchirure
teat (on bottle) la tétine
teenager l'adolescent(e)
teeth les dents
telegram le télégramme
telephone le téléphone
to telephone téléphoner
telephone box la cabine
téléphonique
telephone call le coup de
téléphone
telephone card la télécarte
telephone directory
l'annuaire (m)
telephone number le
numéro de téléphone
television la télévision
to tell dire
temperature la température
to have a temperature
avoir de la fièvre
temporary temporaire
tenant le/la locataire
tendon le tendon
tennis le tennis

tennis ball la balle de
tennis
tennis court le court de
tennis
tennis racket la raquette
de tennis
tent la tente
tent peg le piquet de tente
terminal (airport) l'aérogare (f)
terrace la terrasse
terracotta la terre cuite
to test (try out) tester
testicles les testicules
tetanus injection la piqûre
antitétanique
than que
to thank remercier
thank you merci
thank you very much
merci beaucoup
that cela
that one celui-là/celle-là
the le/la/l'/les
theatre le théâtre
theft le vol
their (sing) leur
(plural) leurs
them eux
there là
there is/are... il y a...
thermometer le
thermomètre
these ces
these ones ceux-ci/celles-ci
they ils/elles
thick (not thin) épais(se)

thief le voleur/la voleuse
thigh la cuisse
thin *(person)* mince
thing la chose
  my things mes affaires
to think penser
thirsty: I'm thirsty j'ai soif
this ceci
  this one celui-ci/celle-ci
thorn l'épine (f)
those ces
  those ones ceux-là/celles-là
thread le fil
throat la gorge
throat lozenges les pastilles
  pour la gorge
through à travers
thumb le pouce
thunder le tonnerre
thunderstorm l'orage (m)
Thursday jeudi
thyme le thym
ticket le billet ; le ticket
  a single ticket un aller
  simple
  a return ticket un aller-
  retour
  book of tickets le carnet
  de tickets
ticket inspector le
  contrôleur/la contrôleuse
ticket office le guichet
tide la marée
  low tide la marée basse
  high tide la marée haute
tidy bien rangé(e)

to tidy up tout ranger
tie la cravate
tight *(fitting)* serré(e)
tights le collant
tile *(on roof)* la tuile
  (on wall, floor) le carreau
till *(cash desk)* la caisse
till *(until)* jusqu'à
  till 2 o'clock jusqu'à deux
  heures
time le temps
  (of day) l'heure (f)
  this time cette fois
  what time is it? quelle
  heure est-il?
timer le minuteur
timetable l'horaire (m)
tin *(can)* la boîte
tinfoil le papier alu(minium)
tin-opener l'ouvre-boîtes
  (m)
tip *(to waiter, etc)*
  le pourboire
to tip *(waiter, etc)* donner
  un pourboire à
tipped *(cigarette)* à bout
  filtre
tired fatigué(e)
tissue *(Kleenex®)* le kleenex®
to à
  (with name of country) en/au
  to London à Londres
  to the airport à l'aéroport
  to France en France
  to Canada au Canada
toadstool le champignon
  vénéneux

toast *(to eat)* le pain grillé ;
le toast

tobacco le tabac

tobacconist's le bureau
de tabac

today aujourd'hui

toddler le bambin

toe le doigt de pied

together ensemble

toilet les toilettes
toilet for disabled les
toilettes pour handicapés

toilet brush la balayette
pour les WC

toilet paper le papier
hygiénique

toiletries les articles de
toilette

token le jeton

toll *(motorway)* le péage

tomato la tomate
tomato soup la soupe
de tomates
tinned tomatoes les
tomates en boîte

tomorrow demain
tomorrow morning
demain matin
tomorrow afternoon
demain après-midi
tomorrow evening demain
soir

tongue la langue

tonic water le tonic

tonight ce soir

tonsillitis l'angine *(f)*

too *(also)* aussi

it's too big c'est trop grand
it's too hot il fait trop chaud
it's too noisy il y a trop de
bruit

toolkit la trousse à outils

tools les outils

tooth la dent

toothache le mal de dents
I have toothache j'ai mal
aux dents

toothbrush la brosse à dents

toothpaste le dentifrice

toothpick le cure-dent

top: *the top floor* le dernier
étage

top *(of bottle)* le bouchon
(of pen) le capuchon
(of pyjamas, bikini, le haut
(of hill, mountain) le sommet
on top of sur

topless: *to go topless*
enlever le haut

torch la lampe de poche

torn déchiré(e)

total *(amount)* le total

to touch toucher

tough *(meat)* dur(e)

tour l'excursion *(f)*
guided tour la visite guidée

tour guide le/la guide

tour operator le tour-
opérateur ; le voyagiste

tourist le/la touriste

tourist (information) office
le syndicat d'initiative

tourist route l'itinéraire
touristique *(m)*

T

tourist ticket le billet touristique

to tow remorquer

towbar *(on car)* le crochet d'attelage

tow rope le câble de remorquage

towel la serviette

tower la tour

town la ville

town centre le centre-ville

town hall la mairie

town plan le plan de la ville

toxic toxique

toy le jouet

toyshop le magasin de jouets

tracksuit le survêtement

traditional traditionnel(-elle)

traffic la circulation

traffic jam l'embouteillage *(m)*

traffic lights les feux

traffic warden le/la contractuel(le)

trailer la remorque

train le train
  by train par le train
  the next train le prochain train
  the first train le premier train
  the last train le dernier train

trainers les baskets

tram le tramway

tranquillizer le tranquillisant

to translate traduire

translation la traduction

to travel voyager

travel agent's l'agence de voyages *(f)*

travel guide le guide

travel insurance l'assurance voyage *(f)*

travel pass la carte de transport

travel sickness le mal des transports

traveller's cheques les chèques de voyage

tray le plateau

tree l'arbre *(m)*

trip l'excursion *(f)*

trolley le chariot

trouble les ennuis
  to be in trouble avoir des ennuis

trousers le pantalon

truck le camion

true vrai(e)

trunk *(luggage)* la malle

trunks *(swimming)* le maillot (de bain)

to try essayer

to try on *(clothes, etc)* essayer

t-shirt le tee-shirt

Tuesday mardi

tumble dryer le sèche-linge

tunnel le tunnel

to turn tourner
  to turn round faire demi-tour

180

ENGLISH-FRENCH

to turn off *(light, etc)* éteindre *(engine)* couper le moteur

to turn on *(light, etc)* allumer *(engine)* mettre en marche

turquoise *(colour)* turquoise

tweezers la pince à épiler

twice deux fois

twin-bedded room la chambre à deux lits

twins *(male)* les jumeaux *(female)* les jumelles

to type taper à la machine

typical typique

tyre le pneu

tyre pressure la pression des pneus

U

ugly laid(e)

ulcer l'ulcère *(m)* **mouth ulcer** l'aphte *(m)*

umbrella le parapluie *(sunshade)* le parasol

uncle l'oncle *(m)*

uncomfortable inconfortable

unconscious sans connaissance

under sous

undercooked pas assez cuit(e)

underground le métro

underpants *(man's)* le caleçon

underpass le passage souterrain

to understand comprendre

I don't understand je ne comprends pas *do you understand?* vous comprenez?

underwear les sous-vêtements

to undress se déshabiller

unemployed au chômage

to unfasten *(seatbelt)* détacher

United Kingdom le Royaume-Uni

United States les États-Unis

university l'université *(f)*

unkind pas gentil(-ille)

unleaded petrol l'essence sans plomb *(f)*

unlikely peu probable

to unlock ouvrir

to unpack *(suitcase)* défaire

unpleasant désagréable

to unplug débrancher

to unscrew dévisser

up: to get up *(out of bed)* se lever

upside down à l'envers

upstairs en haut

urgent urgent(e)

urine l'urine *(f)*

us nous

to use utiliser

useful utile

usual habituel(-elle)

usually d'habitude

U-turn le demi-tour

vacancy *(in hotel)* la chambre

vacant libre

vacation les vacances

vaccination le vaccin

vacuum cleaner l'aspirateur *(m)*

vagina le vagin

valid *(ticket, driving licence, etc)* valable

valley la vallée

valuable d'une grande valeur

valuables les objets de valeur

value la valeur

valve la soupape

van la camionnette

vase le vase

VAT la TVA

vegan végétalien(ne)
I'm a vegan je suis végétalien(ne)

vegetables les légumes

vegetarian végétarien(ne)
I'm vegetarian je suis végétarien(ne)

vehicle le véhicule

vein la veine

velvet le velours

vending machine le distributeur automatique

venereal disease la maladie vénérienne

ventilator le ventilateur

very très

vest le maillot de corps

vet le/la vétérinaire

via par

to video *(from TV)* enregistrer

video *(machine)* le magnétoscope *(cassette)* la (cassette) vidéo

video camera la caméra vidéo

video cassette la cassette vidéo

video game le jeu vidéo

video recorder le magnétoscope

video tape la cassette vidéo

view la vue

villa la maison de campagne

village le village

vinegar le vinaigre

vineyard le vignoble

viper la vipère

virus le virus

visa le visa

visit le séjour

to visit visiter

visiting hours les heures de visite

visitor le/la visiteur(-euse)

vitamin la vitamine

voice la voix

volcano le volcan

volleyball le volley-ball

voltage le voltage

to vomit vomir
voucher le bon

W

wage le salaire
waist la taille
waistcoat le gilet
to wait for attendre
waiter le/la serveur(-euse)
waiting room la salle
  d'attente
waitress la serveuse
to wake up se réveiller
Wales le pays de Galles
walk la promenade
  to go for a walk faire
  une promenade
to walk aller à pied ;
  marcher
walking boots les
  chaussures de marche
walking stick la canne
wall le mur
wallet le portefeuille
to want vouloir
  I want... je veux...
  we want... nous voulons...
war la guerre
ward *(hospital)* la salle
wardrobe l'armoire *(f)*
warehouse l'entrepôt *(m)*
warm chaud(e)
  it's warm (weather) il fait
  bon
  it's too warm il fait trop
  chaud

to warm up *(milk, etc)* faire
  chauffer
warning triangle le triangle
  de présignalisation
to wash laver
  to wash oneself se laver
washbasin le lavabo
washing machine la machine
  à laver
washing powder la lessive
washing-up bowl la cuvette
washing-up liquid le produit
  pour la vaisselle
wasp la guêpe
wasp sting la piqûre de
  guêpe
waste bin la poubelle
watch la montre
to watch *(look at)* regarder
watchstrap le bracelet de
  montre
water l'eau *(f)*
  bottled water l'eau en
  bouteille
  cold water l'eau froide
  drinking water (fit to drink)
  l'eau potable
  hot water l'eau chaude
  sparkling mineral water
  l'eau minérale gazeuse
  still mineral water l'eau
  minérale plate
waterfall la cascade
water heater le chauffe-eau
watermelon la pastèque
waterproof imperméable
water-skiing le ski nautique

W

water sports les sports nautiques

waterwings les bracelets gonflables

waves *(on sea)* les vagues

waxing *(hair removal)* l'épilation à la cire *(f)*

way *(manner)* la manière *(route)* le chemin

way in *(entrance)* l'entrée *(f)*

way out *(exit)* la sortie

we nous

weak faible *(coffee, etc)* léger(-ère)

to wear porter

weather le temps

weather forecast la météo

web *(internet)* le Web

website le site web

wedding le mariage

wedding anniversary l'anniversaire de mariage *(m)*

wedding present le cadeau de mariage

Wednesday mercredi

week la semaine
last week la semaine dernière
next week la semaine prochaine
per week par semaine
this week cette semaine

weekday le jour de semaine

weekend le week-end
next weekend le week-end prochain
this weekend ce week-end

weekly par semaine ; hebdomadaire *(pass, ticket)* valable pendant une semaine

to weigh peser

weight le poids

welcome! bienvenu(e)!

well *(for water)* le puits

well *(healthy)* en bonne santé
I'm very well je vais très bien
he's not well il est souffrant

well done *(steak)* bien cuit(e)

wellingtons les bottes en caoutchouc

Welsh gallois(e)

west l'ouest *(m)*

wet mouillé(e)

wetsuit la combinaison de plongée

what que ; quel/quelle ; quoi
what is it? qu'est-ce que c'est?

wheel la roue

wheelchair le fauteuil roulant

wheel clamp le sabot

when quand
(at what time?) à quelle heure?
when is it? c'est quand? ; à quelle heure?

where où
where is it? c'est où?
where is the hotel? où est l'hôtel?

which quel/quelle
which (one)? lequel/laquelle?

which (ones)?
lesquels/lesquelles?

while pendant que
in a while bientôt ; tout à
l'heure

white blanc (blanche)

who qui
who is it? qui c'est?

whole entier(-ière)

wholemeal bread le pain
complet

whose: *whose is it?* c'est
à qui?

why pourquoi

wide large

widow la veuve

widower le veuf

width la largeur

wife la femme

wig la perruque

to win gagner

wind le vent

windbreak *(camping, etc)* le
pare-vent

windmill le moulin à vent

window la fenêtre
(shop) la vitrine

windscreen le pare-brise

windscreen wipers les
essuie-glaces

windsurfing la planche à voile
to go windsurfing faire de
la planche à voile

windy: *it's windy* il y a du
vent

wine le vin

dry wine le vin sec
house wine le vin en
pichet
red wine le vin rouge
rosé wine le rosé
sparkling wine le vin
mousseux
sweet wine le vin doux
white wine le vin blanc

wine list la carte des vins

wing *(bird, aircraft)* l'aile *(f)*

wing mirror le rétroviseur
latéral

winter l'hiver *(m)*

wire le fil

with avec
with ice avec des glaçons
with milk/sugar avec du
lait/sucre

without sans
without ice sans glaçons
without milk/sugar sans
lait/sucre

witness le témoin

woman la femme

wonderful merveilleux(-euse)

wood le bois

wooden en bois

wool la laine

word le mot

work le travail

to work *(person)* travailler
(machine, car) fonctionner ;
marcher
it doesn't work ça ne
marche pas

work permit le permis
de travail

Y

world le monde
worried inquiet(-iète)
worse pire
worth: *it's worth...* ça vaut...
to wrap (up) emballer
wrapping paper le papier d'emballage
wrinkles les rides
wrist le poignet
to write écrire
 please write it down vous me l'écrivez, s'il vous plaît?
writing paper le papier à lettres
wrong faux (fausse)
wrought iron le fer forgé

X

X-ray la radiographie
to x-ray radiographier

Y

yacht le yacht
year l'an *(m)* ; l'année *(f)*
 this year cette année
 next year l'année prochaine
 last year l'année dernière
yearly annuel(le)
yellow jaune
Yellow Pages les pages jaunes
yes oui
 yes please oui, merci
yesterday hier

yet: *not yet* pas encore
yoghurt le yaourt
 plain yoghurt le yaourt nature
yolk le jaune d'œuf
you *(familiar)* tu
 (polite) vous
young jeune
your *(familiar sing)* ton/ta
 (familiar plural) tes
 (polite singular) votre
 (polite plural) vos
youth hostel l'auberge de jeunesse *(f)*

Z

zebra crossing le passage pour piétons
zero le zéro
zip la fermeture éclair
zone la zone
zoo le zoo
zoom lens le zoom

A

à to ; at
abbaye f abbey
abcès m abscess
abeille f bee
abîmer to damage
abonné(e) m/f subscriber ;
season ticket holder
abonnement m subscription ;
season ticket
abri m shelter
abrité(e) sheltered
accélérateur m accelerator
accepter to accept
accès m access
accès aux trains to the
trains
accès interdit no entry
accès réservé authorized
entry only
accident m accident
accompagner to accompany
accord m agreement
accotement m verge
accueil m reception ;
information
accueillir to greet ;
to welcome
ACF m Automobile Club
de France
achat m purchase
acheter to buy
acier m steel
acte de naissance m birth
certificate
activité f activity

adaptateur m adaptor
(electrical)
addition f bill
adhérent(e) m/f member
adolescent(e) m/f teenager
adresse f address
adresse électronique e-mail
address
adresser to address
adressez-vous à enquire
at (office)
adroit(e) skilful
adulte m/f adult
aérogare f terminal
aéroglisseur m hovercraft
aéroport m airport
affaires fpl business ;
belongings
bonne affaire bargain
affiche f poster ; notice
affluence f crowd
affreux(-euse) awful
âge m age
d'un certain âge middle-
aged
du troisième âge senior
citizen
âgé(e) elderly
âgé de ... ans aged ... years
agence f agency ; branch
agence de voyages travel
agency
agence immobilière estate
agent's
agenda m diary
agenda électronique m
personal organizer)

A

agent m agent
  agent de police police officer
agiter to shake
  agiter avant emploi shake before use
agneau m lamb
agrandissement m enlargement
agréable pleasant ; nice
agréé(e) registered ; authorized
agression f attack (mugging)
aider to help
aigre sour
aiguille f needle
ail m garlic
aimer to enjoy ; to love (person)
air: *en plein air* in the open air
aire: *aire de jeux* play area
  aire de repos rest area
  aire de service service area
  aire de stationnement layby
airelles fpl bilberries ; cranberries
alarme f alarm
alcool m alcohol ; fruit brandy
alcoolisé(e) alcoholic
alentours mpl surroundings
algues fpl seaweed
alimentation f food
allée f driveway ; path

allégé(e) low-fat
Allemagne f Germany
allemand(e) German
aller to go
aller (simple) m single ticket
aller-retour m return ticket
allergie f allergy
allô? hello? (on telephone)
allumage m ignition
allumé(e) on (light)
allume-feu m fire lighter
allumer to turn on ; to light
  allumez vos phares switch on headlights
allumette f match
alpinisme m mountaineering
alsacien(ne) Alsatian
ambassade f embassy
ambulance f ambulance
améliorer to improve
amende f fine
amer(-ère) bitter
américain(e) American
Amérique f America
ameublement m furniture
ami(e) m/f friend
  petit(e) ami(e) boyfriend/girlfriend
amortisseur m shock absorber
amour m love
  faire l'amour to make love
ampoule f blister ; light bulb
amusant(e) funny (amusing)

amuser to entertain
(bien) s'amuser to enjoy
oneself

an *m* year
Nouvel An m New Year

analgésique *m* painkiller

ananas *m* pineapple

ancien(ne) old ; former

ancre *f* anchor

anesthésique *m* anaesthetic

ange *m* angel

angine *f* tonsillitis
angine de poitrine angina

Anglais *m* Englishman

anglais *m* English *(language)*

anglais(e) English

Angleterre *f* England

animal *m* animal
animal domestique pet

animations *fpl* entertainment ;
activities

anis *m* aniseed

anisette *f* aniseed liqueur

année *f* year ; vintage
bonne année! happy New
Year!

anniversaire *m* anniversary ;
birthday

annonce *f* advertisement

annuaire *m* directory

annulation *f* cancellation

annuler to cancel

antenne *f* aerial
antenne parabolique f
satellite dish

anti-insecte *m* insect
repellent

antibiotique *m* antibiotic

antigel *m* antifreeze

antihistaminique *m* antihistamine

antimoustique *m* mosquito
repellent

antiquaire *m/f* antique
dealer

antiquités *fpl* antiques

antiseptique *m* antiseptic

antivol *m* bike lock

août August

apéritif *m* apéritif

aphte *m* mouth ulcer

appareil *m* appliance ;
camera
appareil acoustique
hearing aid
appareil photo camera

appartement *m* apartment

appât *m* bait *(for fishing)*

appel *m* phone call

appeler to call *(speak, phone)*
appeler en PCV to reverse
the charges

appendicite *f* appendicitis

apporter to bring

apprendre to learn

appuyer to press

après after

après-midi *m* afternoon

après-rasage *m* after-shave

après-shampooing *m*
conditioner

aquarium *m* fish tank

arachide *f* groundnut

araignée f spider
arbre m tree
arête f fishbone
argent m money ; silver
  argent de poche pocket money
  argent liquide cash
argot m slang
armoire f wardrobe
arranger to arrange
arrêt m stop
  arrêt d'autobus bus stop
  arrêt facultatif request stop
arrêter to arrest ; to stop
  arrêter le moteur to turn off the engine
arrêtez! stop!
arrhes fpl deposit *(part payment)*
arrière m rear ; back
arrivées fpl arrivals
arriver to arrive ; to happen
arrobase @
arrondissement m district
art m art
arthrite f arthritis
article m item ; article
  articles de toilette toiletries
articulation f joint *(body)*
artisan(e) craftsman/woman
artisanat m arts and crafts
artiste m/f artist
ascenseur m lift
aspirateur m vacuum cleaner

aspirine f aspirin
assaisonnement m seasoning ; dressing
asseoir to sit (someone) down
  s'asseoir to sit down
assez enough ; quite *(rather)*
assiette f plate
associé(e) m/f partner *(business)*
assorti(e) assorted ; matching
assurance f insurance
assuré(e) insured
assurer to assure ; to insure
asthme m asthma
atelier m workshop ; artist's studio
attaque f fit *(medical)*
  attaque (d'apoplexie) stroke
attendre to wait (for)
attention! look out!
  attention au feu danger of fire
  faire attention to be careful
attestation f certificate
  l'attestation d'assurance green card
attrayant(e) attractive
au-delà de beyond
au-dessus de above ; on top of
au lieu de instead of
au revoir goodbye

au secours! help!
aube f dawn
auberge f inn
  auberge de jeunesse
  youth hostel
aubergine f aubergine
aucun(e) none ; no ; not any
audiophone m hearing aid
augmenter to increase
aujourd'hui today
aussi also
aussitôt immediately
  aussitôt que possible as
  soon as possible
Australie f Australia
australien(ne) Australian
autel m altar
auteur m author
auto-école f driving school
auto-stop m hitch-hiking
autobus m bus
autocar m coach
automatique automatic
automne m autumn
automobiliste m/f motorist
autoradio m car radio
autorisé(e) permitted ;
  authorized
autoroute f motorway
autre other
  autres directions other
  routes
avalanche f avalanche
avaler to swallow
  ne pas avaler not to be
  taken internally

avance f advance
  à l'avance in advance
avant before ; front
  à l'avant at the front
  en avant forward
avec with
avenir m future
avenue f avenue
avertir to inform ; to warn
avion m aeroplane
aviron m oar ; rowing *(sport)*
avis m notice ; warning
aviser to advise
avocat m avocado ; lawyer
avoine f oats
avoir to have
avortement m abortion
avril April

B

bacon m bacon
bagages mpl luggage
  bagages à main hand
  luggage
  faire les bagages to pack
bague f ring *(on finger)*
baguette f stick of French
  bread
baie f bay *(along coast)*
baignade f bathing
  baignade interdite no
  bathing
baignoire f bath *(tub)*
bain m bath
  bain de bouche mouthwash
  bain moussant bubble bath

B

baiser kiss

baisser to lower

bal m ball ; dance

balade f walk ; drive ; trek

balai m broom (brush)
  balai à franges mop

balance f weighing scales

balançoire f swing

balcon m circle (theatre) ;
  balcony

ball-trap m clay pigeon
  shooting

balle f ball (small: golf, tennis)

ballet m ballet

ballon m balloon ; ball (large) ;
  brandy glass

bambin m toddler

banane f banana ; bumbag

banc m seat ; bench

banlieue f suburbs

banque f bank

bar m bar

barbe f beard
  barbe à papa candy floss

barque f rowing boat

barrage m dam
  barrage routier road block

barré: *route barrée* road
  closed

barrer to cross out

barrière f barrier

bas m bottom (of page, etc) ;
  stocking
  en bas below ; downstairs

bas(se) low

baskets fpl trainers

bassin m pond ; washing-up
  bowl

bateau m boat ; ship
  bateau à rames row boat
  bateau-mouche river boat

bâtiment m building

bâton (de ski) m ski pole

batte f bat (baseball, cricket)

batterie f battery (for car)
  batterie à plat flat battery

baume pour les lèvres m lip
  salve

bavoir m bib (baby's)

beau (belle) lovely ;
  handsome ; beautiful ; nice
  (enjoyable)

beau-frère m brother-in-law

beau-père m father-in-law ;
  stepfather

beaucoup (de) much/many ;
  a lot of

bébé m baby

beignet m fritter ; doughnut

belge Belgian

Belgique f Belgium

belle-fille f daughter-in-law

belle-mère f mother-in-law ;
  step-mother

béquilles fpl crutches

berger m shepherd

berlingots mpl boiled sweets

besoin: *avoir besoin de* to
  need

beurre m butter
  beurre doux unsalted
  butter

biberon m baby's bottle
bibliothèque f library
bicyclette f bicycle
bien well ; right ; good
  bien cuit(e) well done (steak)
bientôt soon ; shortly
bienvenu(e) welcome!
bière f beer
  bière (à la) pression
  draught beer
  bière blonde lager
  bière bouteille bottled
  lager
  bière brune bitter
bifteck m steak
bijouterie f jeweller's ;
  jewellery
bijoux mpl jewellery
bikini m bikini
billet m note ; ticket
  billet aller-retour return
  ticket
  billet d'avion plane ticket
  billet de banque banknote
  billet simple one-way
  ticket
biologique organic
biscotte f breakfast biscuit ;
  rusk
biscuit m biscuit
bisque f thick seafood soup
blanc (blanche) white ; blank
  en blanc blank (on form)
blanc d'œuf m egg white
blanchisserie f laundry
blé m wheat
blessé(e) injured

blesser to injure
bleu m bruise
bleu(e) blue ; very rare
  (steak)
  bleu marine navy blue
bloc-notes m note pad
blond(e) fair (hair)
bloqué(e) stuck
body m body (clothing)
bœuf m beef
boire to drink
bois m wood
boisson f drink
  boisson non alcoolisée
  soft drink
boîte f can ; box
  boîte à fusibles fuse box
  boîte à lettres post box
  boîte de conserve tin (of
  food)
  boîte de nuit night club
  boîte de vitesses gearbox
bol m bowl (for soup, etc)
bombe f aerosol ; bomb
bon m token ; voucher
bon (bonne) good ; right ;
  nice
  bon anniversaire happy
  birthday
  bon marché inexpensive
bonbon m sweet
bondé(e) crowded
bonhomme m chap
  bonhomme de neige
  snowman
bonjour hello ; good
  morning/afternoon

B

bonnet *m* hat
  bonnet de bain bathing cap
bonneterie *f* hosiery
bonsoir good evening
bord *m* border ; edge ; verge
  à bord on board
  au bord de la mer at the seaside
bosse *f* lump (swelling)
botte *f* boot ; bunch
bottillons *mpl* ankle boots
bouche *f* mouth
  bouche d'incendie fire hydrant
bouché(e) blocked
bouchée *f* mouthful ; chocolate
  bouchée à la reine vol-au-vent
boucherie *f* butcher's shop
bouchon *m* cork ; plug (for sink) ; top (of bottle)
boucle d'oreille *f* earring
bouée de sauvetage *f* life belt
bougie *f* candle ; spark plug
bouillabaisse *f* rich fish soup/stew
bouilli(e) boiled
bouillir to boil
bouilloire *f* kettle
bouillon *m* stock

bouillotte *f* hot-water bottle
boulangerie *f* bakery
boule *f* ball
boules *fpl* game similar to bowls
bouquet *m* bunch (of flowers)
Bourgogne Burgundy
boussole *f* compass
bout *m* end
  à bout filtre filter-tipped
bouteille *f* bottle
boutique *f* shop
bouton *m* button ; switch ; spot
  bouton de fièvre cold sore
  boutons de manchette cufflinks
boxe *f* boxing
bracelet *m* bracelet
  bracelet de montre watch-strap
braisé(e) braised
bras *m* arm
brasserie *f* café ; brewery
Bretagne *f* Brittany
breton(ne) from Brittany
bricolage *m* do-it-yourself
briquet *m* cigarette lighter
briser to break ; to smash
britannique British
brocante *f* second-hand goods ; flea market
broche *f* brooch ; spit
brochette *f* skewer ; kebab

brocoli *m* broccoli

brodé main hand-embroidered

bronzage *m* suntan

bronze *m* bronze

brosse *f* brush
brosse à cheveux hairbrush
brosse à dents toothbrush

brouillard *m* fog

bru *f* daughter-in-law

bruit *m* noise

brûlé(e) burnt

brûler to burn

brûlures d'estomac *fpl* heartburn

brun(e) brown ; dark

brushing *m* blow-dry

brut(e) gross ; raw

Bruxelles Brussels

bûche *f* log *(for fire)*

buisson *m* bush

bulletin de consigne *m* left-luggage ticket

bureau *m* desk ; office
bureau de change foreign exchange office
bureau de location booking office
bureau de poste post office
bureau de renseignements information office
bureau des objets trouvés lost-property

bus *m* bus

butane *m* camping gas

C

ça va it's OK ; I'm OK
ça va? are you OK?

cabaret *m* cabaret

cabine *f* beach hut ; cubicle
cabine d'essayage changing room

cabinet *m* office

câble de remorquage *m* tow rope

cacahuète *f* peanut

cacao *m* cocoa

cacher to hide

cadeau *m* gift

cadenas *m* padlock

cadre *m* picture frame

cafard *m* cockroach

café *m* coffee ; café
café au lait white coffee
café crème white coffee
café décaféiné decaff coffee
café instantané instant coffee
café noir black coffee

cafetière *f* coffee pot

cahier *m* exercise book

caisse *f* cash desk ; case
caisse d'épargne savings bank

caissier(-ière) *m/f* cashier ; teller

calculatrice *f* calculator

caleçon *m* boxer shorts

calendrier *m* calendar ; timetable

calmant m sedative
cambriolage m break-in
cambrioleur(-euse) m/f burglar
caméra vidéo f video camera
caméscope m camcorder
camion m lorry ; truck
camionnette f van
camomille f camomile
campagne f countryside ; campaign
camper to camp
camping m camping ; camp-site
  camping sauvage camping on unofficial sites
  camping-gaz® camping stove
Canada m Canada
canadien(ne) Canadian
canal m canal
canapé m sofa ; open sandwich
  canapé-lit sofa bed
canard m duck
canif m penknife
canne f walking stick
  canne à pêche fishing rod
cannelle f cinnamon
canoë m canoe
canot m boat
  canot de sauvetage lifeboat
canotage m boating
caoutchouc m rubber

capable efficient
capitale f capital (city)
capot m bonnet ; hood (of car)
câpres fpl capers
capuchon m hood ; top (of pen)
car m coach
carabine de chasse f hunting rifle
carafe f carafe ; decanter
caravane f caravan
carburateur m carburettor
Carême m Lent
carnet m notebook ; book
  carnet de billets book of tickets
  carnet de chèques cheque book
carotte f carrot
carré m square
carreau m tile (on wall, floor)
carrefour m crossroads
carte f map ; card ; menu ; pass (bus, train)
  carte bleue credit card
  carte d'abonnement season ticket
  carte d'embarquement boarding card/pass
  carte d'identité identity card
  carte de crédit credit card
  carte des vins wine list
  carte grise log book (car)
  carte orange monthly or yearly season ticket (for Paris transport system)
  carte postale postcard

carte routière road map
carte vermeille senior citizen's rail pass
cartes (à jouer) fpl playing cards
carton m cardboard
cartouche f carton (of cigarettes)
cas m case
cascade f waterfall
caserne f barracks
casier m rack ; locker
casino m casino
casque m helmet
  casque (à écouteurs) headphones
casquette f cap (hat)
cassé(e) broken
casse-croûte m snacks
casser to break
  casser la croûte to have a snack
casserole f saucepan
cassette f cassette
catch m wrestling
cathédrale f cathedral
catholique Catholic
cause f cause
  pour cause de on account of
caution f security (for loan) ; deposit
  caution à verser deposit required
cave f cellar
caveau m cellar

caviar m caviar(e)
CD m CD
ceci this
cédez le passage give way
CE f EC (European Community)
ceinture f belt
  ceinture de sécurité seatbelt
  ceinture porte-monnaie moneybelt
cela that
célèbre famous
célibataire single (unmarried)
cendrier m ashtray
cent m hundred
centimètre m centimetre
central(e) central
centre m centre
  centre commercial shopping centre
  centre de loisirs leisure centre
  centre équestre riding school
  centre-ville city centre
céramique f ceramics
cercle m circle ; ring
céréales fpl cereal (for breakfast)
cerise f cherry
certain(e) certain (sure)
certificat m certificate
cerveau m brain
cervelle f brains (as food)
cesser to stop

C

cette this ; that

ceux-ci/celles-ci these ones

ceux-là/celles-là those ones

CFF *mpl* Swiss Railways

chacun/chacune each

chaîne *f* chain ; channel ;
  (mountain) range
  chaîne (stéréo) stereo
  chaînes obligatoires snow
  chains compulsory

chair *f* flesh

chaise *f* chair
  chaise de bébé high chair
  chaise longue deckchair

châle *m* shawl

chalet *m* chalet

chambre *f* bedroom ; room
  chambre à air inner tube
  chambre à coucher
  bedroom
  chambre à deux lits twin-
  bedded room
  chambre d'hôte bed and
  breakfast
  chambre individuelle
  single room
  *chambre pour deux
  personnes* double room
  chambres rooms to let

champ *m* field
  champ de courses
  racecourse

champagne *m* champagne

champignon *m* mushroom
  champignon vénéneux
  toadstool

chance *f* luck

change *m* exchange

changement *m* change

changer to change
  changer de l'argent to
  change money
  changer de train to change
  train
  se changer to change
  clothes

chanson *f* song

chanter to sing

chanterelle *f* chanterelle

chantier *m* building site ;
  roadworks

chapeau *m* hat

chapelle *f* chapel

chaque each ; every

charbon *m* coal
  charbon de bois charcoal

charcuterie *f* pork butcher's ;
  delicatessen ; cooked meat

chariot *m* trolley

charter *m* charter flight

chasse *f* hunting ; shooting
  chasse gardée private
  hunting

chasse-neige *m* snowplough

chasser to hunt

chasseur *m* hunter

chat *m* cat

châtaigne *f* chestnut

château *m* castle ; mansion

chaud(e) hot

chauffage *m* heating

chauffer to heat up *(milk,
  water)*

chauffeur *m* driver

chaussée f carriageway
  chaussée déformée
  uneven road surface
  chaussée rétrécie road
  narrows
  chaussée verglacée icy
  road
chaussette f sock
chaussure f shoe ; boot
chauve bald *(person)*
chauve-souris f bat *(creature)*
chef m chef ; chief ; head ;
  leader
  chef de train train guard
chef-d'œuvre m masterpiece
chef-lieu m county town
chemin m path ; lane ; track ;
  way
  chemin de fer railway
cheminée f chimney ;
  fireplace
chemise f shirt
  chemise de nuit nightdress
chemisier m blouse
chèque m cheque
  chèque de voyage
  traveller's cheque
cher (chère) dear ;
  expensive
chercher to look for
  aller chercher to fetch ; to
  collect
cheval m horse
  faire du cheval to ride
cheveux mpl hair
cheville f ankle
chèvre f goat

chevreau m kid *(goat, leather)*
chevreuil m venison
chez at the house of
  chez moi at my home
chien m dog
chiffon m duster ; rag
chips fpl crisps
chirurgien m surgeon
chocolat m chocolate
  chocolat à croquer plain
  chocolate
  chocolat au lait milk
  chocolate
choisir to choose
choix m range ; choice ;
  selection
chômage: *au chômage*
  unemployed
chope f tankard
chorale f choir
chose f thing
chou m cabbage
chou-fleur m cauliflower
chute f fall
cidre m cider
ciel m sky
cigare m cigar
cigarette f cigarette
cil m eyelash
cimetière m cemetery ;
  graveyard
cinéma m cinema
cintre m coat hanger
cirage m shoe polish
circuit m round trip ; circuit

circulation f traffic
circuler to operate (train, bus, etc)
cire f wax ; polish
cirque m circus
ciseaux mpl scissors
cité f city ; housing estate
citron m lemon
  citron vert lime
citronnade f still lemonade
clair(e) clear ; light
classe f grade ; class
clavicule f collar bone
clavier m keyboard
clé f key ; spanner
  clé de contact ignition key
  clé minute keys cut while you wait
clef f key
client(e) m/f client ; customer
clignotant m indicator (on car)
climatisation f air-conditioning
climatisé(e) air-conditioned
clinique f clinic (private)
cloche f bell (church, school)
clocher m steeple
clou m nail (metal)
  clou de girofle clove
cocher to tick (on form)
cochon m pig
cocktail m cocktail
cocotte f casserole dish
cocotte-minute f pressure cooker

code m code
  code barres barcode
  code postal postcode
  code secret pin number
cœur m heart
coffre-fort m safe
cognac m brandy
coiffeur m hairdresser ; barber
coiffeuse f hairdresser
coin m corner
coincé(e) jammed ; stuck
col m collar ; pass (in mountains)
colis m parcel
collant m pair of tights
colle f glue
collège m secondary school
collègue m/f colleague
coller to stick ; to glue
collier m necklace ; dog collar
colline f hill
collision f crash (car)
colonne f column
  colonne vertébrale spine
combien how much/many
combinaison de plongée f wetsuit
combinaison de ski f ski suit
combustible m fuel
comédie f comedy
  comédie musicale musica)
commande f order (in restaurant)
commander to order
comme like

comme ça like this ; like that

commencer to begin

comment? pardon? ; how?

commerçant(e) *m/f* trader

commerce *m* commerce ; business ; trade

commissariat (de police) *m* police station

commode *f* chest of drawers

commotion *f* shock
commotion (cérébrale) concussion

communication *f* communication ; call *(on telephone)*

communion *f* communion

compagne *f* girlfriend

compagnie *f* firm ; company

compagnon *m* boyfriend

compartiment *m* compartment *(train)*

complet(-ète) full (up)

complètement completely

comporter to consist of
se comporter to behave

composer to dial *(a number)*

composter to date-stamp/punch *(ticket)*
composter votre billet validate your ticket

comprenant including

comprendre to understand

comprimé *m* tablet

compris(e) included
non compris not included

comptant *m* cash

compte *m* number ; account
compte en banque bank account

compter to count *(add up)*

compteur *m* speedometer ; meter

comptoir *m* counter *(in shop, bar, etc)*

comte *m* count ; earl

concert *m* concert

concierge *m/f* caretaker ; janitor

concours *m* contest ; aid

concurrent(e) *m/f* competitor

conducteur(-trice) *m/f* driver

conduire to drive

conduite *f* driving ; behaviour

confection *f* ready-to-wear clothes

conférence *f* conference

confession *f* confession

confirmer to confirm

confiserie *f* sweetshop

confiture *f* jam ; preserve

congélateur *m* freezer

congelé(e) frozen

connaître to know

conseil *m* advice ; council

conseiller to advise

conserver to keep ; to retain *(ticket, etc)*

consigne *f* deposit ; left luggage

consommation *f* drink

consommé *m* clear soup

constat m report

constipé(e) constipated

construire to build

consulat m consulate

contacter to contact

contenir to contain

content(e) pleased

contenu m contents

continuer to continue

contraceptif m contraceptive

contrat m contract
  contrat de location lease

contravention f fine *(penalty)*

contre against ; versus

contre-filet m sirloin

contrôle m check
  contrôle des passeports
  passport control
  contrôle radar speed trap

contrôler to check

contrôleur(-euse) m/f ticket
  inspector

convenu(e) agreed

convoi exceptionnel m large
  load

copie f copy *(duplicate)*

copier to copy

coque f shell ; cockle

coquelicot m poppy

coquet(te) pretty *(place, etc)*

coquillages mpl shellfish

coquille f shell
  coquille Saint-Jacques
  scallop

corail m coral ; type of train

corde f rope
  corde à linge clothes line

cordonnerie f shoe repairer's

cornet m cone

corniche f coast road

cornichon m gherkin

corps m body

correspondance f
  connection *(transport)*

correspondant(e) m/f
  penfriend

corrida f bull-fight

Corse f Corsica

costume m suit *(man's)*

côte f coast ; hill ; rib
  Côte d'Azur French Riviera

côté m side
  à côté de beside ; next to

côtelette f cutlet

coton m cotton
  coton hydrophile cotton
  wool
  coton-tige® cotton bud

cou m neck

couche (de bébé) f nappy

coucher de soleil m sunset

couchette f bunk ; berth

coude m elbow

coudre to sew

couette f continental quilt ;
  duvet

couler to run *(water)*

couleur f colour

coulis m purée

couloir m corridor ; aisle

coup m stroke ; shot ; blow

coup de pied kick
coup de soleil sunburn
coup de téléphone phone call

coupe f goblet *(ice cream)*
coupe (de cheveux) haircut

coupe-ongles m nail clippers

couper to cut

couple m couple *(two people)*

coupure f cut
coupure de courant power cut

cour f court ; courtyard

courant m power ; current

courant(e) common ; current

courir to run

couronne f crown

courrier m mail ; post
courrier électronique e-mail

courroie de ventilateur f fan belt

cours m lesson ; course ; rate

course f race *(sport)* ; errand
course hippique horse race
faire des courses to go shopping

court de tennis m tennis court

court(e) short

cousin(e) m/f cousin

coussin m cushion

coût m cost

couteau m knife

coûter to cost

coûteux(-euse) expensive

couture f sewing ; seam

couvent m convent ; monastery

couvercle m lid

couvert m cover charge ; place setting
couverts cutlery

couvert(e) covered

couverture f blanket ; cover

crabe m crab

crapaud m toad

cravate f tie

crayon m pencil

crème f cream *(food, lotion)*
crème à raser shaving cream
crème anglaise custard
crème Chantilly whipped cream
crème fermentée soured cream
crème hydratante moisturizer
crème pâtissière confectioner's custard

crémerie f dairy

crêpe f pancake

crêperie f pancake shop/restaurant

cresson m watercress

crevaison f puncture

crevette f shrimp ; prawn

cric m jack *(for car)*

crier to shout

crime m crime ; offence ; murder

crise f crisis ; attack *(medical)*
crise cardiaque heart attack

cristal m crystal

crochet d'attelage m towbar

croire to believe

croisement m junction *(road)*

croisière f cruise

croix f cross

croquant(e) crisp ; crunchy

croque-madame m toasted cheese sandwich with ham and fried egg

croque-monsieur m toasted ham and cheese sandwich

croûte f crust

cru(e) raw

crudités fpl raw vegetables

crue subite f flash flood

crustacés mpl shellfish

cube de bouillon m stock cube

cuiller f spoon
  cuiller à café teaspoon

cuir m leather

cuisiné(e) cooked

cuisine f cooking ; cuisine ; kitchen
  cuisine familiale home cooking
  faire la cuisine to cook

cuisiner to cook

cuisinier m cook

cuisinière f cook ; cooker

cuisse f thigh
  cuisses de grenouille frogs' legs

cuit(e) cooked
  bien cuit well done *(steak)*

cuivre m copper
  cuivre jaune brass

culotte f panties

curieux(-euse) strange

curseur m cursor *(computer)*

cuvée f vintage

cuvette f washing up bowl

cyclisme m cycling

cystite f cystitis

D

daltonien(ne) colour-blind

dame f lady
  dames ladies

danger m danger

dangereux(-euse) dangerous

dans into ; in ; on

danser to dance

date f date *(day)*
  date de naissance date of birth
  date limite de vente sell-by date

daube f stew

de from ; of ; some

dé m dice

début m beginning

débutant(e) m/f beginner

décaféiné(e) decaffeinated

décembre December

décès m death

décharge f electric shock
  décharge publique rubbish dump

déchargement m unloading

déchirer to rip

déclaration f statement ; report
déclaration de douane customs declaration

décollage m takeoff

décoller to take off (plane)

décolleté m low neck

décongeler to defrost

découvrir to discover

décrire to describe

décrocher to lift the receiver

dedans inside

défaire to unfasten ; to unpack

défaut m fault ; defect

défectueux(-euse) faulty

défense de... no.../ ... forbidden
défense de fumer no smoking
défense de stationner no parking

dégâts mpl damage

dégeler to thaw

dégivrer to de-ice (

dégustation f tasting
dégustation de vins wine tasting

dehors outside ; outdoors

déjeuner m lunch

délicieux(-euse) delicious

délit m offence

deltaplane m hang-glider

demain tomorrow

demande f application ; request
demandes d'emploi situations wanted

demander to ask (for)

demandeur d'emploi m job seeker

démaquillant m make-up remover

démarqué(e) reduced (goods)

démarreur m starter (in car)

demi(e) half

demi-pension f half board

demi-sec medium-dry

demi-tarif m half fare

demi-tour m U-turn

dent f tooth

dentelle f lace

dentier m dentures

dentifrice m toothpaste

dentiste m/f dentist

déodorant m deodorant

dépannage m breakdown service

dépanneuse f breakdown van

départ m departure

département m county

dépasser to exceed ; to overtake

dépenses fpl expenditure

dépliant m brochure

dépôt m deposit ; depot
dépôt d'ordures rubbish dump

dépression f depression ;
nervous breakdown
depuis since
déranger to disturb
dernier(-ère) last ; latest
derrière at the back ; behind
derrière m bottom *(buttocks)*
dès from ; since
  dès votre arrivée as soon
  as you arrive
désagréable unpleasant
descendre to go down ; to
  get off
description f description
déshabiller to undress
  se déshabiller to get
  undressed
désirer to want
désodorisant m air
  freshener
désolé(e) sorry
dessein m design ; plan
desserré(e) loose *(not
  fastened)*
dessert m pudding
dessous (de) underneath)
dessus (de) on top (of)
destinataire m/f addressee
destination f destination
  à destination de bound
  for
détail m detail
  au détail retail
détergent m detergent
détourner to divert

deux two
  deux fois twice
  les deux both
deuxième second
devant in front (of)
développer to develop
devenir to become
déviation f diversion
devis m quotation *(price)*
devises fpl currency
dévisser to unscrew
devoir to have to ; to owe
diabète m diabetes
diabétique diabetic
diamant m diamond
diaphragme m cap
  (contraceptive)
diapositive f slide
  (photograph)
diarrhée f diarrhoea
dictionnaire m dictionary
diététique f dietary ; health
  foods
différent(e) different
difficile difficult
digue f dyke ; jetty
dimanche m Sunday
dinde f turkey
dîner to have dinner
dîner m dinner
  dîner spectacle cabaret
  dinner
dire to say ; to tell
direct: *train direct* through
  train

directeur m manager ;
headmaster

direction f management ;
direction

directrice f manageress ;
headmistress

discothèque f disco ;
nightclub

discussion f argument

disjoncteur m circuit breaker

disloquer to dislocate

disparaître to disappear

disparu(e) missing
(disappeared)

disponible available

disque m record ; disk
disque de stationnement
parking disk
disque dur hard disk

disquette f floppy disk

dissolvant m nail polish
remover

distractions fpl entertainment

distributeur m dispenser
distributeur automatique
vending machine ; cash
machine

divers(e) various

divertissements mpl
entertainment

divorcé(e) divorced

docteur m doctor

doigt m finger
doigt de pied toe

domestique m/f servant ;
maid

domicile m home ; address

donner to give ; to give
away

doré(e) golden

dormir to sleep

dos m back *(of body)*

dossier m file
dossier attaché
attachment

douane f customs

double double

doubler to overtake

douche f shower

douleur f pain

douloureux(-euse) painful

doux (douce) mild ; gentle ;
soft ; sweet

douzaine f dozen

dragée f sugared almond

drap m sheet

drapeau m flag

drogue f drug

droguerie f hardware shop

droit m right *(entitlement)*

droit(e) right *(not left)* ;
straight

droite f right-hand side
à droite on/to the right
tenez votre droite keep
to right

dur(e) hard ; hard-boiled ;
tough

durée f duration

eau f water
eau de Javel bleach
eau douce fresh water (not salt)
eau du robinet tap-water
eau minérale mineral water
eau potable drinking water
eau salée salt water
eau-de-vie brandy
ébène f ebony
échanger to exchange
échantillon m sample
échapper to escape
écharpe f scarf (woollen)
échelle f ladder
échelle de secours fire escape
éclairage m lighting
éclairs mpl lightning
écluse f lock (in canal)
école f school
école maternelle nursery school
écorce f peel (of fruit)
écossais(e) Scottish
Écosse f Scotland
écouter to listen to
écran m screen
écran solaire sunscreen lotion
écran total sunblock
écrire to write
écrivain m author
écrou m nut (for bolt)

écurie f stable
édulcorant m sweetener
église f church
élastique m elastic band
électricien m electrician
électricité f electricity
électrique electric
élément m unit ; element
emballer to wrap (up)
embarcadère m jetty
embarquement m boarding
embouteillage m traffic jam
embrayage m clutch (in car)
émission f programme ; broadcast
emplacement m parking space ; pitch
emploi m use ; job
emporter to take away
à emporter take-away
emprunter to borrow
en some ; any ; in ; to ; made of
en cas de in case of
en face de opposite
en gros in bulk ; wholesale
en panne out of order
en retard late
en train by train
encaisser to cash (cheque)
enceinte pregnant
enchanté(e)! pleased to meet you!
encore still ; yet ; again
encre f ink

endommager to damage

endroit m place ; spot

enfant m/f child

enfler to swel

enlever to take away ; to take off *(clothes)*
enlever le haut to go topless

enneigé(e) snowed up

ennui m boredom ; nuisance ; trouble

ennuyeux boring

enregistrement m check-in desk

enregistrer to record ; to check in ; to video

enseignement m education

enseigner to teach

ensemble together

ensuite next ; after that

entendre to hear

entier(-ière) whole

entorse f sprain

entracte m interval

entre between

entrecôte f rib steak

entrée f entrance ; admission ; starter *(food)*
entrée gratuite admission free
entrée interdite no entry

entreprise f firm ; company

entrer to come in ; to go in

entretien m maintenance ; interview

entrez! come in!

enveloppe f envelope
enveloppe matelassée padded envelope

envers: *l'envers* wrong side
à l'envers upside down ; back to front

environ around ; about

environs mpl surroundings

envoyer to send

épais(se) thick

épargner to save *(money)*

épaule f shoulder

épi m ear (of corn)
épi de maïs corn-on-the-cob

épice f spice

épicerie f grocer's shop
épicerie fine delicatessen

épilation f hair removal
épilation à la cire f waxing

épileptique epileptic

épinards mpl spinach

épine f thorn

épingle f pin
épingle de sûreté safety pin

éponge f sponge

époque f age
d'époque period *(furniture)*

épuisé(e) sold out ; used up

épuiser to use up ; to run out of

équipage m crew

équipe f team ; shift

équipement m equipment

équitation f horse-riding

erreur f mistake

escalade f climbing

escalator m escalator

escalier m stairs
  escalier de secours
  fire escape
  escalier mécanique
  escalator

escargot m snail

escarpement m cliff

Espagne f Spain

espagnol(e) Spanish

espèce f sort

espérer to hope

esquimau m ice lolly

essai m trial ; test

essayer to try ; to try on

essence f petrol
  essence sans plomb
  unleaded petrol

essorer to spin(-dry) ; to wring

essoreuse f spin dryer

essuie-glace m windscreen
  wipers

essuie-tout m kitchen paper

esthéticienne f beautician

estivants mpl summer
  holiday-makers

estomac m stomach

estragon m tarragon

et and

étage m storey
  le dernier étage the top
  floor

étain m tin ; pewter

étang m pond

étape f stage

état m state
  États-Unis United States

été m summer

éteindre to turn off

éteint(e) out *(light)*

étiquette f label
  étiquette à bagages
  luggage tag

étoile f star

étranger(-ère) m/f foreigner
  à l'étranger overseas ;
  abroad

être to be

étroit(e) narrow ; tight

étudiant(e) m/f student

étudier to study

étui m case *(camera, glasses)*

étuvée: à l'étuvée braised

eurochèque m eurocheque

Europe f Europe

européen(ne) European

eux them

évanoui(e) fainted

événement m occasion ;
  event

éventail m fan *(handheld)*

éventé(e) flat *(beer)*

évêque m bishop

évier m sink *(washbasin)*

éviter to avoid

exact(e) right *(correct)*

examen m examination

excédent de bagages m
  excess baggage

excellent(e) excellent
excès de vitesse m speeding
exclu(e) excluded
exclure to expel
exclusif (-ive) exclusive
excursion f trip ; outing ;
  excursion
excuses fpl apologies
excusez-moi! excuse me!
exemplaire m copy
exercice m exercise
expéditeur m sender
expert(e) m/f expert
expirer to expire
expliquer to explain
exporter to export
exposition f exhibition
exprès on purpose ;
  deliberately
  en exprès express (parcel,
  etc)
extérieur(e) outside
extincteur m
  fire extinguisher
extra top-quality ; first-rate

F

fabrication f manufacturing
fabriquer to manufacture
  fabriqué en... made in...
face: en face (de) opposite
fâché(e) angry
facile easy
façon f way ; manner
facteur(-trice) m/f postman

facture f invoice
  facture détaillée itemized
  bill
faible weak
faïence f earthenware
faim f hunger
  avoir faim to be hungry
faire to make ; to do
  faire du stop to hitchhike
faisan m pheasant
fait main handmade
falaise f cliff
famille f family
farci(e) stuffed
farine f flour
fatigue f tiredness
fatigué(e) tired
fausse couche f miscarriage
faute f mistake ; foul
  (football)
fauteuil m armchair ; seat
  fauteuil roulant wheelchair
faux (fausse) fake ; false ;
  wrong
fax m fax
faxer to fax
félicitations fpl congratulations
femme f woman ; wife
  femme au foyer housewife
  femme d'affaires business-
  woman
  femme de chambre
  chambermaid
  femme de ménage
  cleaner
  femme policier
  policewoman

F

fenêtre f window

fenouil m fennel

fente f crack ; slot

fer m iron (material, golf club)
  fer à repasser iron (for clothes)

férié(e): jour férié public holiday

ferme f farmhouse ; farm

fermé(e) closed

fermer to close/shut ; to turn off
  fermer à clé to lock

fermeture f closing
  fermeture Éclair® zip

ferroviaire railway ; rail

ferry m car ferry

fête f holiday ; fête ; party
  fête des rois Epiphany
  fête foraine funfair

feu m fire ; traffic lights
  feu (de joie) bonfire (celebration)
  feu d'artifice fireworks
  feu de position sidelight
  feu rouge red light

feuille f leaf ; sheet (of paper)

feuilleton m soap opera

feutre m felt ; felt-tip pen

février February

fiancé(e) engaged (to marry)

ficelle f string ; thin French stick

fiche f token ; form ; slip (of paper)

fichier m file (computer)

fièvre f fever

avoir de la fièvre to have a temperature

figue f fig

fil m thread ; lead (electrical)
  fil dentaire dental floss

file f lane ; row

filet m net ; fillet (of meat, fish)
  filet à bagages luggage rack

fille f daughter ; girl

film m film

fils m son

filtre m filter (on cigarette)
  filtre à huile oil filter

fin f end

fin(e) thin (material) ; fine (delicate)

fini(e) finished

finir to end ; to finish

fixer to fix

flacon m bottle (small)

flamand(e) Flemish

flan m custard tart

flash m flash (for camera)

fleur f flower

fleuriste m/f florist

fleuve m river

flipper m pinball

flûte f long, thin loaf

foie m liver
  foie gras goose liver

foire f fair
  foire à/aux... special offer on...

fois f time
  cette fois this time

une fois once
folle mad
foncé(e) dark (colour)
fonctionner to work (machine)
fond m back (of hall, room) ; bottom
fondre to melt
force f strength
forêt f forest
forfait m fixed price ; ski pass
forme f shape ; style
formidable great (wonderful)
formulaire m form (document)
fort(e) loud; strong
forteresse f fort
fosse f pit ; grave
    fosse septique septic tank
fou (folle) mad
fouetté(e) whipped (cream, eggs)
foulard m scarf (headscarf)
foule f crowd
four m oven
    four à micro-ondes microwave
fourchette f fork
fournir to supply
fourré(e) filled ; fur-lined
fourrure f fur
fraîche fresh ; cool ; wet (paint)
frais fresh ; cool
frais mpl costs ; expenses
fraise f strawberry

framboise f raspberry
français(e) French
Français(e) Frenchman/woman
frapper to hit; to knock (on door)
frein m brake
freiner to brake
fréquent(e) frequent
frère m brother
fret m freight (goods)
frigo m fridge
frit(e) fried
friterie f chip shop
frites fpl french fries ; chips
friture f small fried fish
froid(e) cold
fromage m cheese
froment m wheat
front m forehead
frontière f border ; boundary
frotter to rub
fruit m fruit
    fruits de mer seafood
    fruits secs dried fruit
fuite f leak
fumé(e) smoked
fumée f smoke
fumer to smoke
fumeurs smokers
fumier m manure
funiculaire m funicular railway
fuseau m ski pants
fusible m fuse
fusil m gun

G

gagner to earn ; to win

galerie *f* art gallery ; arcade ; roof-rack

gallois(e) Welsh

gambas *fpl* large prawns

gant *m* glove
 gant de toilette face cloth
 gants de ménage rubber gloves

garage *m* garage

garantie *f* guarantee

garçon *m* boy ; waiter

garde *f* custody ; guard
 garde-côte coastguard

garder to keep ; to look after

gardien(ne) *m/f* caretaker ; warden

gare *f* railway station
 gare routière bus terminal

garer to park

garni(e) served with vegetables or chips

gas-oil *m* diesel fuel

gâteau *m* cake ; gateau

gauche left
 à gauche to/on the left

gâteau *m* cake

gaufre *f* waffle

gaz *m* gas
 gaz d'échappement exhaust fumes

gaz-oil *m* diesel fuel

gazeux(-euse) fizzy

gel *m* frost
 gel pour cheveux hair gel

214

gelé(e) frozen

gelée *f* jelly ; aspic

gênant inconvenient

gendarme *m* policeman *(in rural areas)*

gendarmerie *f* police station

gendre *m* son-in-law

généreux(-euse) generous

genou *m* knee

gentil(-ille) kind *(person)*

gérant(e) *m/f* manager/manageress

gérer to manage *(be in charge of)*

gibier *m* game *(hunting)*

gilet *m* waistcoat
 gilet de sauvetage life jacket

gingembre *m* ginger

gîte *m* self-catering house/flat

glace *f* ice ; ice cream ; mirror

glacé(e) chilled ; iced

glacier *m* glacier ; ice-cream maker

glacière *f* cool-box *(for picnic)*

glaçon *m* ice cube

glissant(e) slippery

glisser to slip

gomme *f* rubber *(eraser)*

gorge *f* throat ; gorge

gosse *m/f* kid *(child)*

gothique Gothic

goût *m* flavour ; taste
goûter to taste
graine *f* seed
gramme *m* gram
grand(e) great ; high *(speed, number)* ; big ; tall
grand-mère *f* grandmother
grand-père *m* grandfather
Grande-Bretagne *f* Great Britain
grands-parents *mpl* grandparents
grange *f* barn
granité *m* flavoured crushed ice
grappe *f* bunch *(of grapes)*
gras(se) *f* at ; greasy
gratis for free
gratuit(e) free of charge
grave serious
gravure *f* print *(picture)*
grêle *f* hail
grenier *m* attic
grenouille *f* frog
grève *f* strike
grillé(e) grilled
grille-pain *m* toaster
Grèce *f* Greece
grippe *f* flu
gris(e) grey
gros(se) big ; large ; fat
gros lot *m* jackpot
grotte *f* cave
groupe *m* group ; party ; band

groupe sanguin blood group
guêpe *f* wasp
guerre *f* war
gueule de bois *f* hangover
guichet *m* ticket office ; counter
guide *m* guide ; guidebook
 guide de conversation phrase book
guidon *m* handlebars
guitare *f* guitar

H

habillé(e) dressed
habiller to dress
 s'habiller to get dressed
habitant(e) *m/f* inhabitant
habiter to live (in)
habituel(le) usual ; regular
haché(e) minced
 steak haché m hamburger
hachis *m* minced meat
halles *fpl* central food market
hamburger *m* burger
hameçon *m* hook *(fishing)*
hanche *f* hip
handicapé(e) disabled *(person)*
haricot *m* bean
haut *m* top *(of ladder, bikini)*
 en haut upstairs
haut(e) high ; tall
hauteur *f* height

hebdomadaire weekly
hébergement m lodging
hépatite f hepatitis
herbe f grass
  fines herbes herbs
hernie f hernia
heure f hour ; time of day
  à l'heure on time
  heure de pointe rush hour
heureux(-euse) happy
hibou m owl
hier yesterday
hippisme m horse riding
hippodrome m racecourse
historique historic
hiver m winter
hollandais(e) Dutch
homard m lobster
homéopathie f homeopathy
homme m man
  homme au foyer house-
  husband
  homme d'affaires
  businessman
  hommes gents
homo m gay (person)
honnête honest
honoraires mpl fee
hôpital m hospital
horaire m timetable ;
  schedule
horloge f clock
hors: *hors de* out of
  hors service out of order
  hors-taxe duty-free
  hors-saison off-season

hôte m host ; guest
hôtel m hotel
  hôtel de ville town hall
hôtesse f stewardess
huile f oil
  huile d'olive olive oil
  huile d'arachide peanut oil
  huile de tournesol
  sunflower oil
huître f oyster
hypermarché m
  hypermarket
hypermétrope long-sighted
hypertension f high blood
  pressure

I

ici here
idée f idea
il y a... there is/are...
  il y a un défaut there's a
  fault
  il y a une semaine a week
  ago
île f island
illimité(e) unlimited
immédiatement immediately
immeuble m building (offices,
  flats)
immunisation f immunisation
impair(e) odd (number)
impasse f dead end
imperméable waterproof
important(e) important
importer to import

impossible impossible
impôt m tax
imprimer to print
incendie m fire
inclus(e) included ; inclusive
inconfortable uncomfortable
incorrect(e) wrong
indicateur m guide ;
timetable
indicatif m dialling code
indications fpl instructions ;
directions
indigestion f indigestion
indispensable essential
infectieux(-euse) infectious
infection f infection
inférieur(e) inferior ; lower
infirmerie f infirmary
infirmier(-ière) m/f nurse
informations fpl news ;
information
infusion f herbal tea
ingénieur m/f engineer
ingrédient m ingredient
inhalateur m inhaler
inondation f flood
inquiet(-iète) worried
inscrire to write (down) ;
to enrol
insecte m insect
insolation f sunstroke
installations fpl facilities
instant m moment
un instant! just a minute!

institut m institute
institut de beauté beauty
salon
insuline f insulin
intelligent(e) intelligent
interdit forbidden
intéressant(e) interesting
intérieur: à l'intérieur
indoors
international(e) international
interprète m/f interpreter
intervention f operation
(surgical)
intoxication alimentaire f
food poisoning
introduire to introduce ;
to insert
inutile useless ; unnecessary
invalide m/f disabled person
invité(e) m/f guest
inviter to invite
irlandais(e) Irish
Irlande f Ireland
Irlande du Nord f Northern
Ireland
issue de secours f emergency
exit
Italie f Italy
italien(ne) Italian
itinéraire m route
itinéraire touristique scenic
route
ivoire m ivory
ivre drunk

jaloux(-ouse) jealous
jamais never
jambe f leg
jambon m ham
janvier January
Japon m Japan
jardin m garden
jauge (de niveau d'huile) f dipstick
jaune yellow
jaune d'œuf m egg yolk
jaunisse f jaundice
jetable disposable
jetée f pier
jeter to throw
jeton m token
jeu m game ; set (of tools, etc) ; gambling
  jeu électronique computer game
  jeu vidéo video game
  jeu-concours quiz
jeudi m Thursday
jeune young
jeunesse f youth
joindre to join ; to enclose
joli(e) pretty
jonquille f daffodil
joue f cheek
jouer to play (games)
jouet m toy
jour m day
  jour férié public holiday
journal m newspaper

journaliste m/f journalist
journée f day (length of time)
juge m/f judge
juif (juive) Jewish
juillet July
juin June
jumeaux mpl twins
jumelles fpl twins ; binoculars
jupe f skirt
jus m juice
  jus d'orange orange juice
  jus de fruit fruit juice
  jus de viande gravy
jusqu'à (au) until ; till
juste fair ; reasonable

K

kart m go-cart
kas(c)her kosher
kayak m canoe
kilo m kilo
kilométrage m mileage
  kilométrage illimité unlimited mileage
kilomètre m kilometre
kiosque m kiosk ; newsstand
klaxonner to sound one's horn
kyste m cyst

L

là there
lac m lake
lacets mpl shoelaces

laid(e) ugly
laine f wool
  laine polaire fleece (top/jacket)
laisse f leash
laisser to leave
  laissez en blanc leave blank
lait m milk
  lait cru unpasteurised milk
  lait démaquillant cleansing milk
  lait demi-écrémé semi-skimmed milk
  lait écrémé skim(med) milk
  lait entier full-cream milk
  lait longue conservation long-life milk
  lait maternisé baby milk (formula)
  lait solaire suntan lotion
laiterie f dairy
laitue f lettuce
lame f blade
  lames de rasoir razor blades
lampe f light ; lamp
  lampe de poche torch
landau m pram ; baby carriage
langue f tongue ; language
lapin m rabbit
laque f hair spray
lard m fat ; (streaky) bacon
lardons mpl diced bacon
large wide ; broad
largeur f width

laurier m sweet bay ; bay leaves
lavable washable
lavabo m washbasin
  lavabos toilets
lavage m washing
lavande f lavender
lave-auto m car wash
lave-glace m screen wash
lave-linge m washing machine
laver to wash
  se laver to wash oneself
laverie automatique f launderette
lave-vaisselle m dishwasher
laxatif m laxative
layette f baby clothes
leçon f lesson
  leçons particulières private lessons
lecture f reading
légal(e) legal
léger(-ère) light ; weak (tea, etc)
légume m vegetable
lendemain m next day
lent(e) slow
lentement slowly
lentille f lentil ; lens (of glasses)
  lentille de contact contact lens
lesbienne f lesbian
lessive f soap powder ; washing

lettre f letter
lettre recommandée registered letter
leur(s) their
levée f collection (of mail)
lever to lift
se lever to get up (out of bed)
lever de soleil m sunrise
lèvre f lip
levure f yeast
libellule f dragonfly
librairie f bookshop
libre free ; vacant
libre-service self-service
lieu m place (location)
lièvre m hare
ligne f line ; service ; route
lime à ongles f nail file
limitation de vitesse f speed limit
limonade f lemonade
lin m linen (cloth)
linge m linen (bed, table) ; laundry
lingerie f lingerie
lingettes fpl baby wipes
lion m lion
liquide f liquid
liquide de freins brake fluid
lire to read
liste f list
lit m bed
lit d'enfant cot
lit simple single bed

lits jumeaux twin beds
grand lit double bed
litre m litre
livraison f delivery (of goods)
livraison des bagages baggage reclaim
livre f pound
livre m book
local(e) local
locataire m/f tenant ; lodger
location f hiring (out) ; letting
logement m accommodation
loger to stay (reside for while)
logiciel m computer software
loi f law
loin far
lointain(e) distant
loisir m leisure
Londres London
long(ue) long
le long de along
longe f loin (of meat)
longtemps for a long time
longueur f length
lot m prize ; lot (at auction)
loterie f lottery
lotion f lotion
loto m numerical lottery
lotte f monkfish ; angler fish
louer to let ; to hire ; to rent
à louer for hire/to rent
loup m wolf ; sea perch
loupe f magnifying glass
lourd(e) heavy

loyer m rent

luge f sledge ; toboggan

lumière f light

lundi m Monday

lune f moon
  lune de miel honeymoon

lunettes fpl glasses
  lunettes de soleil
  sunglasses
  lunettes protectrices
  goggles

luxe m luxury

lycée m secondary school

M

M sign for the Paris metro

machine f machine
  machine à laver washing
  machine

mâchoire f jaw

Madame f Mrs ; Ms ; Madam

madeleine f small sponge
cake

Mademoiselle f Miss

madère m Madeira *(wine)*

magasin m shop
  grand magasin department
  store

magnétophone m tape
recorder

magnétoscope m video-
cassette recorder

magret de canard m breast
· fillet of duck

mai May

maigre lean *(meat)*

maigrir to slim

maillet m mallet

maillot m vest
  maillot de bain swimsuit

main f hand

maintenant now

maire m mayor

mairie f town hall

mais but

maison f house ; home
  maison de campagne villa

maître d'hôtel m head
waiter

majuscule f capital letter

mal badly

mal m harm ; pain
  mal de dents toothache
  mal de mer seasickness
  mal de tête headache
  faire du mal à quelqu'un
  to harm someone

malade sick *(ill)*

malade m/f sick person ;
patient

maladie f disease

malentendu m misunderstanding

malle f trunk *(luggage)*

maman f mummy

manche m sleeve

Manche f the Channel

mandat m money order

manger to eat

manière f way *(manner)*

manifestation f
demonstration

manque m shortage ; lack
manteau m coat
maquereau m mackerel
maquillage m make-up
marais m marsh
marbre m marble (material)
marc m white grape spirit
marchand m dealer ;
merchant
marchand de poisson
fishmonger
marchand de vin wine
merchant
marche f step ; march;
walking
marche arrière reverse
gear
marché m market
marché aux puces flea
market
marcher to walk; to work
(machine, car)
en marche on (machine)
mardi m Tuesday
mardi gras Shrove Tuesday
marée f tide
marée basse low tide
marée haute high tide
margarine f margarine
mari m husband
mariage m wedding
marié m bridegroom
marié(e) married
mariée f bride
marier to marry
se marier to get married
mariné(e) marinated

marionnette f puppet
marque f make ; brand
marquer to score (goal, point)
marron brown
marron m chestnut
mars March
marteau m hammer
masculin(e) male (person, on
forms)
mât m mast
match de football m football
match
match en nocturne m floodlit
fixture
matelas m mattress
matelas pneumatique lilo®
matériel m equipment ; kit
matin m morning
mauvais(e) bad ; wrong ;
off (food)
maximum m maximum
mazout m oil (for heating)
mécanicien m mechanic
méchant(e) naughty ; wicked
médecin m doctor
médicament m medicine ;
drug ; medication
médiéval(e) medieval
Méditerranée f
Mediterranean Sea
méduse f jellyfish
meilleur(e) best ; better
meilleurs vœux best wishes
mél m e-mail address
membre m member (of club,
etc)

même same
mémoire f memory
ménage m housework
méningite f meningitis
mensuel(le) monthly
menthe f mint ; mint tea
menu m menu (set)
  menu à prix fixe set price menu
  menu du jour today's menu
mer f sea
  mer du Nord North Sea
mercerie f haberdasher's
merci thank you
mercredi m Wednesday
mère f mother
merlan m whiting
merlu m hake
mérou m grouper
merveilleux(-euse) wonderful
message m message
messe f mass (church)
messieurs mpl men
  Messieurs gentlemen
messieurs gents
mesure f measurement
mesurer to measure
métal m metal
météo f weather forecast
métier m trade ; occupation
mètre m metre
  mètre à ruban tape measure
métro m underground
mettre to put ; to put on

mettre au point focus (camera)
mettre en marche to turn on
meublé(e) furnished
meubles mpl furniture
  meubles de style period furniture
mi-bas mpl pop-socks ; knee-highs
midi m midday ; noon
Midi m the south of France
miel m honey
mieux better ; best
migraine f headache ; migraine
milieu m middle
mille m thousand
millimètre m millimetre
million m million
mince slim ; thin
mine f expression ; mine (coal, etc)
mineur m miner
mineur(e) under age ; minor
minimum m minimum
minuit m midnight
minuscule tiny
minute f minute
minuteur m timer
mirabelle f plum ; plum brandy
miroir m mirror
mise en plis f set (for hair)
mistral m strong cold dry wind

M

mite f moth (clothes)

mixte mixed

mobilier m furniture

mode f fashion
à la mode fashionable
mode d'emploi
instructions for use

modem m modem

moderne modern

moelle f marrow (beef, etc)

moi me

moineau m sparrow

moins less ; minus
moins (de) less (than)
moins cher cheaper

moins the least

mois m month

moisissure f mould (fungus)

moitié f half
à moitié prix half-price

moka m coffee cream cake ;
mocha coffee

molle soft

moment m moment
en ce moment at the
moment

mon/ma/mes my

monastère m monastery

monde m world
il y a du monde there's a
lot of people

moniteur m instructor ;
coach

monitrice f instructress ;
coach

monnaie f currency ; change

monnayeur m automatic
change machine

monsieur m gentleman

Monsieur m Mr ; Sir

montagne f mountain

montant m amount (total)

monter to take up ; to go
up ; to rise ; to get in (car)
monter à cheval to horse-
ride

montre f watch

montrer to show

monument m monument

moquette f fitted carpet

morceau m piece ; bit ; cut
(of meat)

mordu(e) bitten

morsure f bite
morsure de serpent snake
bite

mort(e) dead

mosquée f mosque

mot m word ; note (letter)
mot de passe password
mots croisés crossword
puzzle

motel m motel

moteur m engine ; motor

motif m pattern

moto f motorbike

mou (molle) soft

mouche f fly

moucheron m midge

mouchoir m handkerchief

mouette f seagull

mouillé(e) wet

moule f mussel

moulin m mill
  moulin à vent windmill

moulinet m reel (fishing)

mourir to die

mousse f foam ; mousse
  mousse à raser shaving
  foam
  mousse coiffante hair
  mousse

mousseux(-euse) sparkling
  (wine)

moustache f moustache

moustique m mosquito

moutarde f mustard

mouton m sheep ; lamb ;
  mutton

moyen(ne) average

moyenne f average

muguet m lily of the valley ;
  thrush
  (candida)

muni(e) de supplied with ;
  in possession of

mur m wall

mûr(e) mature ; ripe

mûre f blackberry

muscade f nutmeg

musée m museum
  musée d'art art gallery

musique f music

Musulman(e) Muslim

myope short-sighted

nager to swim

naissance f birth

nappe f tablecloth

nappé(e) coated (with
  chocolate, etc)

natation f swimming

national(e) national

nationalité f nationality

natte f plait

nature f wildlife

naturel(le) natural

nautique nautical ; water

navette f shuttle (bus service)

navigation f sailing

navire m ship

né(e) born

négatif m negative
  (photography)

neige f snow

neiger to snow

nettoyage m cleaning
  nettoyage à sec dry-
  cleaning

nettoyer to clean

neuf (neuve) new

neveu m nephew

névralgie f headache

nez m nose

niche f kennel

nid m nest
  nid de poule pothole

nièce f niece

niveau m level ; standard

noce f wedding

nocturne m late opening

Noël m Christmas
joyeux Noël! merry
Christmas!

noir(e) black

noisette f hazelnut

noix f nut ; walnut

nom m name ; noun
nom de famille family
name
nom de jeune fille maiden
name

nombre m number

nombreux(-euse) numerous

non no ; not

non alcoolisé(e)
non-alcoholic

non-fumeur non-smoking

nord m north

normal(e) normal ; standard
(size)

nos our

notaire m solicitor

note f note ; bill ; memo

notre our

nœud m knot

nourrir to feed

nourriture f food

nouveau (nouvelle) new
de nouveau again

nouvelles fpl news

novembre November

nu(e) naked ; bare

nuage m cloud

nuageux(-euse) cloudy

nucléaire nuclear

nuit f night
bonne nuit good night

numéro m number ; act ;
issue

O

objectif m objective ; lens
(of camera)

objet m object
objets de valeur valuable
items
objets trouvés lost
property

obligatoire compulsory

oblitérer to stamp (ticket,
stamp)

obsèques fpl funeral

obtenir to get ; to obtain

occasion f occasion ; bargain

occupé(e) busy ; hired (taxi)

occupé(e) engaged

océan m ocean

octobre October

odeur f smell

œuf m egg
œuf de Pâques Easter
egg

office m service (church) ;
office
office du tourisme tourist
office

offre f offer

oie f goose

oignon m onion

œil m eye

œillet m carnation
oiseau m bird
olive f olive
ombre f shade/shadow
  à l'ombre in the shade
oncle m uncle
onde f wave
ongle m nail (finger)
opéra m opera
or m gold
orage m storm
orange orange ; amber
  (traffic light)
orange f orange
orangeade f orange squash
orchestre m orchestra ; stalls
  (in theatre)
ordinaire ordinary
ordinateur m computer
ordonnance f prescription
ordre m order
  à l'ordre de payable to
ordures fpl litter (rubbish)
oreille f ear
oreiller m pillow
oreillons mpl mumps
organiser to organize
orge f barley
origan m oregano
os m bone
oseille f sorrel
osier m wicker
ou or
où where
oublier to forget

ouest m west
oui yes
ours(e) m/f bear (animal)
oursin m sea urchin
outils mpl tools
ouvert(e) open ; on (tap,
  gas, etc)
ouvert(e) open
ouverture f overture ;
  opening
ouvrable working (day)
ouvre-boîtes m tin-opener
ouvre-bouteilles m bottle-
  opener
ouvrir to open

P

page f page
  pages jaunes Yellow
  Pages
paiement m payment
paille f straw
pain m bread ; loaf of bread
  pain bis brown bread
  pain complet wholemeal
  bread
  pain grillé toast
pair(e) even
paire f pair
paix f peace
palais m palace
pâle pale
palmes fpl flippers
palourde f clam
pamplemousse m grapefruit

P

panaché m shandy
pané(e) in breadcrumbs
panier m basket
  panier repas packed lunch
panne f breakdown
panneau m sign
pansement m bandage
pantalon m trousers
pantoufles fpl slippers
pape m pope
papeterie f stationer's shop
papier m paper
  papier à lettres writing paper
  papier alu(minium) foil
  papier cadeau gift-wrap
  papier hygiénique toilet paper
  papiers identity papers ; driving licence
papillon m butterfly
pâquerette f daisy
Pâques m or fpl Easter
paquet m package ; packet
par by ; through ; per
  par example for example
  par jour per day
  par téléphone by phone
  par voie orale take by mouth *(medicine)*
paradis m heaven
paralysé(e) paralysed
parapluie m umbrella
parasol m sunshade
parc m park
  parc d'attractions funfair

parce que because
parcmètre m parking meter
parcours m route
pardon! sorry! ; excuse me!
parer to ward off
pare-brise m windscreen
pare-chocs m bumper
parent(e) m/f relative
parents mpl parents
paresseux(-euse) lazy
parfait(e) perfect
parfum m perfume ; flavour
parfumerie f perfume shop
pari m bet
parier sur to bet on
parking m car park
  parking assuré parking facilities
  parking souterrain underground car park
  parking surveillé attended car park
parler (à) to speak (to) ; to talk (to)
paroisse f parish
partager to share
parterre m flowerbed
parti m political party
partie f part ; match *(game)*
partir to leave ; to go
  à partir de from
partout everywhere
pas not
  pas encore not yet
pas m step ; pace

passage m passage
  passage à niveau level crossing
  passage clouté pedestrian crossing
  passage interdit no through way
  passage souterrain underpass

passager(-ère) m/f passenger

passé(e) past

passe-temps m hobby

passeport m passport

passer to pass ; to spend *(time)*
  se passer to happen

passerelle f gangway *(bridge)*

passionnant(e) exciting

passoire f sieve ; colander

pastèque f watermelon

pasteur m minister *(of religion)*

pastille f lozenge

pastis m aniseed-flavoured apéritif

pataugeoire f paddling pool

pâte f pastry ; dough ; paste

pâté m pâté

pâtes fpl pasta

patient(e) m/f patient *(in hospital)*

patin m skate
  patins à glace ice skates
  patins à roulettes roller skates

patinoire f skating rink

pâtisserie f cake shop ; little cake

patron m boss ; pattern *(knitting, dress, etc)*

patronne f boss

pauvre poor

payer to pay (for)
  payé(e) paid
  payé(e) d'avance prepaid

pays m land ; country
  du pays local

Pays-Bas mpl Netherlands

paysage countryside ; scenery

péage m toll *(motorway, etc)*

peau f hide *(leather)* ; skin

pêche f peach ; fishing

pêcher to fish

pêcheur m angler

pédale f pedal

pédalo m pedal boat/pedalo

pédicure m/f chiropodist

peigne m comb

peignoir m dressing gown ; bath-robe

peindre to paint ; to decorate

peinture f painting ; paintwork

peler to peel *(fruit)*

pèlerinage m pilgrimage

pelle f spade
  pelle à poussière dustpan

pellicule f film *(for camera)*
  pellicule couleur colour film

pellicule noir et blanc black and white film

pelote f ball (of string, wool)
pelote basque pelota (ball game for 2 players)

pelouse f lawn

pencher to lean

pendant during

pendant que while

pénicilline f penicillin

péninsule f peninsula

pénis m penis

penser to think

pension f guesthouse
pension complète full board

pente f slope

Pentecôte f Whitsun

pépin m pip

perceuse électrique f electric drill

perdre to lose

perdu(e) lost (object)

père m father

périmé(e) out of date

périphérique m ring road

perle f bead ; pearl

permanente f perm

permettre to permit

permis m permit ; licence
permis de chasse hunting permit
permis de conduire driving licence
permis de pêche fishing permit

perruque f wig

persil m parsley

personne f person

peser to weigh

pétanque f type of bowls

pétillant(e) fizzy

petit(e) small ; slight
petit déjeuner breakfast
petit pain roll

petit-fils m grandson

petite-fille f granddaughter

pétrole m oil (petroleum) ; paraffin

peu little ; few
à peu près approximately
un peu (de) a bit (of)

peur f fear
avoir peur (de) to be afraid (of)

peut-être perhaps

phare m headlight ; lighthouse

pharmacie f chemist's ; pharmacy

phoque m seal (animal)

photo f photograph

photocopie f photocopy

photocopier to photocopy

piano m piano

pichet m jug ; carafe

pie f magpie

pièce f room (in house) ; play (theatre) ; coin
pièce d'identité means of identification
pièce de rechange spare part

pied m foot

à *pied* on foot
pierre f stone
piéton m pedestrian
pignon m pine kernel
pile f pile ; battery pilon m drumstick *(of chicken)*
pilote m/f pilot
pilule f pill
pin m pine
pince f pliers
 pince à cheveux hairgrip
 pince à épiler tweezers
 pince à linge clothes peg
pipe f pipe *(smoking)*
piquant(e) spicy ; hot
pique-nique m picnic
piquer to sting
piquet m peg *(for tent)*
piqûre f insect bite ; injection ; sting
pire worse
piscine f swimming pool
pissenlit m dandelion
pistache f pistachio *(nut)*
piste f ski-run ; runway
 piste cyclable cycle track
 piste de luge toboggan run
 piste pour débutants nursery slope
 pistes tous niveaux slopes for all levels of skiers
pistolet m pistol
placard m cupboard
place f square *(in town)* ; seat ; space *(room)*
 places debout standing room

plafond m ceiling
plage f beach
 plage seins nus topless beach
plainte f complaint
plaisanterie f joke
plaisir m enjoyment ; pleasure
plaît: *s'il vous/te plaît* please
plan m map *(of town)*
 plan de la ville street map
planche f plank
 planche à découper chopping board
 planche à repasser ironing board
 planche à voile sailboard ; wind-surfing
 planche de surf surfboard
plancher m floor *(of room)*
plante f plant ; sole
plaque f sheet ; plate
 plaque d'immatriculation f numberplate
plat m dish ; course *(of meal)*
 plat de résistance main course
 plat principal main course
 plat à emporter take-away meal
plat(e) level *(surface)* ; flat
 à *plat* flat *(battery)*
platane m plane tree
plateau m tray
plâtre m plaster
plein(e) (de) full (of)
 le plein! fill it up! *(car)*
 plein sud facing south

P

plein tarif peak rate

pleurer to cry *(weep)*

pleuvoir to rain
il pleut it's raining

plier to fold

plomb m lead ; fuse

plombage m filling *(in tooth)*

plombier m plumber

plonger to dive

pluie f rain

plume f feather

plus more ; most
plus grand(e) (que) bigger (than)
plus tard later

plusieurs several

pneu m tyre
pneu de rechange spare tyre
pneu dégonflé flat tyre
pneus cloutés snow tyres

poche f pocket

poché(e) poached

poêle f frying-pan

poème m poem

poids m weight
poids lourd heavy goods vehicle

poignée f handle

poignet m wrist

poil m hair ; coat *(of animal)*

poinçonner to punch *(ticket, etc)*

point m place ; point ; stitch ; dot
à point medium rare *(meat)*

pointure f size *(of shoes)*

poire f pear ; pear brandy

poireau m leek

pois m pea ; spot *(dot)*
petits pois peas

poison m poison

poisson m fish

poissonnerie f fishmonger's shop

poitrine f breast ; chest

poivre m pepper

poivron m pepper *(capsicum)*

police f policy *(insurance)* ; police

policier m policeman ; detective film/novel

pollué(e) polluted

pommade f ointment

pomme f apple ; potato

pomme de terre f potato

pompe f pump

pompes funèbres fpl undertaker's

pompier m fireman
pompiers fire brigade

poney m pony

pont m bridge ; deck *(of ship)*
faire le pont to have a long weekend

populaire popular

porc m pork ; pig

port m harbour ; port

portable m mobile phone ; laptop

portatif portable

porte *f* door ; gate

portefeuille *m* wallet

porter to wear; to carry

porte-bagages *m* luggage rack

porte-clefs *m* keyring

porte-monnaie *m* purse

porteur *m* porter

portier *m* doorman

portion *f* helping ; portion

porto *m* port *(wine)*

poser to put ; to lay down

posologie *f* dosage

posséder to own

poste *f* post ; post office
  poste de contrôle check-point
  poste de secours first-aid post

poste *m* radio/television set ; extension *(phone)*

poster *m* poster *(decorative)*

poster to post

pot *m* pot ; carton
  pot d'échappement exhaust pipe

potable ok to drink

potage *m* soup

poteau *m* post *(pole)*
  poteau indicateur signpost

poterie *f* pottery

poubelle *f* dustbin

pouce *m* thumb

poudre *f* powder

poule *f* hen

poulet *m* chicken

poumon *m* lung

poupée *f* doll

pour for

pourboire *m* tip

pourquoi why

pourri(e) rotten *(fruit, etc)*

pousser to push

poussette *f* push chair

pousser to push

poussière *f* dust

pouvoir to be able to

pré *m* meadow

préfecture de police *f* police headquarters

préféré(e) favourite

préférer to prefer

premier(-ière) first
  premier cru first-class wine
  premiers secours first aid

prendre to take ; to get ; to catch

prénom *m* first name

préparer to prepare ; to cook

près de near (to)

présenter to present ; to introduce

préservatif *m* condom

pressé(e) squeezed ; pressed

pressing *m* dry cleaner's

pression *f* pressure
  pression des pneus tyre pressure

prêt(e) ready
  prêt à cuire ready to cook
prêt-à-porter m ready-to-wear
prêter to lend
prêtre m priest
prévision f forecast
prier to pray
prière de... please...
prince m prince
princesse f princess
principal(e) main
printemps m spring
priorité f right of way
  priorité à droite give way to traffic from right
prise f plug ; socket
privé(e) private
prix m price ; prize
  à prix réduit cut-price
  prix d'entrée admission fee
  prix de détail retail price
probablement probably
problème m problem
prochain(e) next
proche close *(near)*
produits mpl produce ; product
professeur m teacher
profiter de to take advantage of
profond(e) deep
programme m schedule ; programme *(list of performers, etc)*
  programme informatique computer program

promenade f walk ; promenade ; ride *(in vehicle)*
  faire une promenade to go for a walk
promettre to promise
promotionnel(le) special low-price
prononcer to pronounce
propre clean ; own
propriétaire m/f owner
propriété f property
protège-slip m panty-liner
protestant(e) Protestant
provenance f origin ; source
provisions fpl groceries
province f province
provisoire temporary
provisoirement for the time being
proximité: à proximité nearby
prune f plum ; plum brandy
pruneau m prune
public m audience
public(-ique) public
publicité f advert *(on TV)*
puce f flea
puissance f power
puits m well *(for water)*
pull m sweater
pullover m sweater
purée f purée ; mashed
PV m parking ticket
pyjama m pyjamas

Q

quai m platform

qualifié(e) skilled

qualité f quality

quand when

quantité f quantity

quarantaine f quarantine

quart m quarter

quartier m neighbourhood ; district

que that ; than ; whom ; what
qu'est-ce que c'est? what is it?

quel(le) which ; what

quelqu'un someone

quelque some

quelque chose something

quelquefois sometimes

question f question

queue f queue ; tail
faire la queue to queue (up)

qui who ; which

quincaillerie f hardware ; hardware shop

quinzaine f fortnight

quitter to leave a place

quoi what

quotidien(ne) daily

R

rabais m reduction

raccourci m short cut

raccrocher to hang up (phone)

race f race (people)

racine f root

radiateur m radiator

radio f radio

radiographie f X-ray

radis m radish

rafraîchissements mpl refreshments

rage f rabies

ragoût m stew ; casserole

raide steep

raie f skate (fish)

raifort m horseradish

raisin m grapes
raisins secs sultanas ; raisins ; currants
raisin blanc green grapes
raisin noir black grapes

raison f reason

ralentir to slow down

ralentissement m tailback

rallonge f extension (electrical)

randonnée f hike
randonnée à cheval pony-trekking

râpe f grater

râpé(e) grated

rappel m reminder (on signs)

rappeler to remind
se rappeler to remember

rapide quick ; fast

rapide m express train

raquette f racket ; bat ; snowshoe

R

rare rare ; unusual

raser to shave off
se raser to shave

rasoir *m* razor

rater to miss *(train, flight etc)*

RATP *f* Paris transport
authority

rayé(e) striped

rayon *m* shelf ; department
(in store) ; spoke *(of wheel)*
rayon hommes menswear

RC ground floor

reboucher to recork

récemment recently

récepteur *m* receiver
(of phone)

réception *f* reception ;
check-in

réceptionniste *m/f*
receptionist

recette *f* recipe

recharge *f* refill

rechargeable refillable
(lighter, pen)

recharger to recharge
(battery, etc)

réchaud de camping *m*
camping stove

réclamation *f* complaint

réclame *f* advertisement

recommandé(e) registered
(mail)

recommander to
recommend

récompense *f* reward

reconnaître to recognize

reçu *m* receipt

réduction *f* reduction ;
discount; concession

réduire to reduce

refuge *m* mountain hut

refuser to reject ; to refuse

regarder to look at

régime *m* diet *(slimming)*

région *f* region

règle *f* rule ; ruler *(for
measuring)*

règles *fpl* period
(menstruation)
règles douloureuses
cramps

règlement *m* regulation ;
payment

régler to pay ; to settle

réglisse *f* liquorice

reine *f* queen

relais routier *m* roadside
restaurant

rembourser to refund

remède *m* remedy

remercier to thank

remettre to put back
remettre à plus tard
to postpone
se remettre to recover
(from illness)

remonte-pente *m* ski tow

remorque *f* trailer

remorquer to tow

remplir to fill ; to fill
in/out/up

renard *m* fox

rencontrer to meet

rendez-vous m date ; appointment

rendre to give back

renouveler to renew

renseignements mpl information

rentrée f return to work after break
rentrée (des classes) start of the new school year

renverser to knock down (in car)

réparations fpl repairs

réparer to fix (repair)

repas m meal

repasser to iron

répondeur automatique m answer-phone

répondre (à) to reply ; to answer

réponse f answer ; reply

repos m rest
se reposer to rest

représentation f performance

requis(e) required

RER m Paris high-speed commuter train

réseau m network

réservation f reservation ; booking

réserve naturelle f nature reserve

réservé(e) reserved

réserver to book (reserve)

réservoir m tank
réservoir d'essence fuel tank

respirer to breathe

ressort m spring (metal)

restaurant m restaurant

reste m rest (remainder)

rester to remain ; to stay

restoroute m roadside or motorway restaurant

retard m delay

retirer to withdraw ; to collect (tickets)

retour m return

retourner to go back

retrait m withdrawal ; collection
retrait d'espèces cash withdrawal

retraité(e) retired

retraité(e) m/f old-age pensioner

rétrécir to shrink (clothes)

rétroviseur m rearview mirror
rétroviseur latéral wing mirror

réunion f meeting

réussir (à) to succeed

réussite f success ; patience (game)

réveil m alarm clock

réveiller to wake (someone)
se réveiller to wake up

réveillon m Christmas/New Year's Eve

revenir to come back

réverbère m lamppost

revue f review ; magazine

rez-de-chaussée m ground floor

rhum m rum

rhumatisme m rheumatism

rhume m cold *(illness)*
  rhume des foins hay fever

riche rich

rideau m curtain

rides fpl wrinkles

rien nothing ; anything
  rien à déclarer nothing to declare

rire to laugh

rivage m shore

rive f river bank

rivière f river

riz m rice

RN trunk road

robe f gown ; dress

robinet m tap

rocade f ringroad

rocher m rock *(boulder)*

rognon m kidney *(to eat)*

roi m king

roman m novel

roman(e) Romanesque

romantique romantic

romarin m rosemary

rond(e) round

rond-point m roundabout

rose pink

rose f rose

rossignol m nightingale

rôti(e) roast

rôtisserie f steakhouse ; roast meat counter

roue f wheel
  roue de secours spare wheel

rouge red

rouge à lèvres m lipstick

rouge-gorge m robin

rougeole f measles

rougeur f rash *(skin)*

rouillé(e) rusty

rouleau à pâtisserie m rolling pin

rouler to roll ; to go *(by car)*

route f road ; route
  route barrée road closed
  route nationale trunk road
  route principale major road
  route secondaire minor road

routier m lorry driver

Royaume-Uni m United Kingdom

ruban m ribbon ; tape

rubéole f rubella

rue f street
  rue sans issue no through road

ruelle f lane ; alley

ruisseau m stream

russe Russian

S

SA Ltd ; plc
sable *m* sand
  sables mouvants quicksand
sabot *m* wheel clamp
sac *m* sack ; bag
  sac à dos backpack
  sac à main handbag
  sac de couchage sleeping bag
  sac poubelle bin liner
sachet de thé *m* tea bag
sacoche *f* panniers (for bike)
safran *m* saffron
sage good (well-behaved) ; wise
saignant(e) rare (steak)
saigner to bleed
saint(e) *m/f* saint
Saint-Sylvestre *f* New Year's Eve
saisir to seize
saison *f* season
  basse saison low season
  de saison in season
  haute saison high season
saisonnier seasonal
salade *f* lettuce ; salad
  salade de fruits fruit salad
salaire *m* salary ; wage
sale dirty
salé(e) salty ; savoury
salle *f* lounge (airport) ; hall ; ward (hospital)
  salle à manger dining room

  salle d'attente waiting room
  salle de bains bathroom
salon *m* sitting room ; lounge
  salon de beauté beauty salon
salut! hi!
samedi *m* Saturday
SAMU *m* emergency services
sandales *fpl* sandals
sandwich *m* sandwich
sang *m* blood
sanglier *m* wild boar
sans without
  sans alcool alcohol-free
  sans connaissance unconscious
  sans issue no through road
santé *f* health
  santé! cheers!
  en bonne santé well
sapeurs-pompiers *mpl* fire brigade
SARL *f* Ltd ; plc
sauce *f* sauce
sauf except (for)
saumon *m* salmon
sauter to jump
sauvegarder to back up (computer)
sauver to rescue
savoir to know (be aware of)
  savoir faire quelque chose to know how to do sth
savon *m* soap

S

Scellofrais® m Clingfilm®

scène f stage

scie f saw

score m score (of match)

scotch m whisky

séance f meeting ; performance

seau bucket

sec (sèche) dried (fruit, beans)

sèche-cheveux m hairdryer

sèche-linge m tumble dryer

sécher to dry

seconde f second (in time)
en seconde second class

secouer to shake

secours m help

secrétaire m/f secretary

secrétariat m office

secteur m sector ; mains

sécurité f security ; safety

séjour m stay ; visit

sel m salt

self m self-service restaurant

selle f saddle

semaine f week

sens m meaning ; direction
sens interdit no entry
sens unique one-way street

sentier m footpath
sentier écologique nature trail

sentir to feel

septembre September

séparément separately

série f series ; set

seringue f syringe

serré(e) tight (fitting)

serrer to grip ; to squeeze
serrez à droite keep to the right

serrure f lock

serrurerie f locksmith's

serveur m waiter

serveuse f waitress

servez-vous help yourself

service m service ; service charge ; favour
service compris service included
service d'urgences A & E

serviette f towel ; briefcase
serviette hygiénique sanitary towel

servir to dish up ; to serve

seul(e) alone ; lonely

seulement only

sexe m sex

shampooing m shampoo
shampooing antipelliculaire anti-dandruff shampoo

short m shorts

si if ; yes (to negative question)

SIDA m AIDS

siècle m century

siège m seat ; head office
siège pour bébés/enfants car seat (for children)

signaler to report

signer to sign

simple simple ; single ; plain

site m site

site web web site
situé(e) located
ski m ski ; skiing
  ski de piste downhill skiing
  ski de randonnée/fond
  cross-country skiing
  ski nautique water-skiing
slip m underpants ; panties
  slip (de bain) swimming
  trunks
snack m snack bar
SNCB f Belgian Railways
SNCF f French Railways
société f company ; society
sœur f sister
soie f silk
soif f thirst
  avoir soif to be thirsty
soin m care
  soins du visage facial
soir m evening
soirée f evening ; party
soja m soya ; soya bean
sol m ground ; soil
soldat m soldier
solde m balance (remainder
  owed)
soldes mpl sales
  soldes permanents sale
  prices all year round
sole f sole (fish)
soleil m sun ; sunshine
somme f sum
sommelier m wine waiter
sommet m top (of hill,
  mountain)

somnifère m sleeping pill
sonner to ring ; to strike
sonnette f doorbell
sonner to ring bell
sorbet m water ice
sorte f kind (sort, type)
sortie f exit
  sortie de secours
  emergency exit
  sortie interdite no exit
sortir to go out (leave)
soucoupe f saucer
soudain suddenly
souhaiter to wish
soûl(e) drunk
soulever to lift
soupape f valve
soupe f soup
souper m supper
sourcils mpl eyebrows
sourd(e) deaf
sourire to smile
souris f mouse (also for
  computer)
sous underneath ; under
sous-sol m basement
sous-titres mpl subtitles
sous-vêtements mpl
  underwear
souterrain(e) underground
soutien-gorge m bra
souvenir m memory ;
  souvenir
souvent often

S

sparadrap *m* sticking plaster
spécial(e) special
spécialité *f* speciality
spectacle *m* show *(in theatre)* ;
  entertainment
spectateurs *mpl* audience
spiritueux *mpl* spirits
sport *m* sport
  sports nautiques water
  sports
sportif(-ive) sports ; athletic
stade *m* stadium
stage *m* course
standard *m* switchboard
station *f* station *(metro)* ;
  resort
  station balnéaire seaside
  resort
  station de taxis taxi rank
  station thermale spa
  station-service service
  station
stationnement *m* parking
stérilet *m* coil *(IUD)*
stimulateur (cardiaque) *m*
  pacemaker
store *m* blind ; awning
stylo *m* pen
sucette *f* lollipop ; dummy
sucre *m* sugar
sucré(e) sweet
sud *m* south
suisse Swiss
Suisse *f* Switzerland
suite *f* series ; continuation ;
  sequel

suivant(e) following
suivre to follow
  faire suivre please forward
super *m* four-star petrol
supermarché *m* super-
  market
supplément *m* extra charge
supplémentaire extra
sur on ; onto ; on top of ;
  upon
  sur place on the spot
sûr safe ; sure
surcharger to overload
surchauffer to overheat
surf *m* surfing
  faire du surf to surf
  surf des neiges snowboard
  surf sur neige snow-
  boarding
surgelés *mpl* frozen foods
surveillé(e) supervised
survêtement *m* tracksuit
sympa(thique) nice ;
  pleasant
synagogue *f* synagogue
syndicat d'initiative *m*
  tourist office

T

tabac *m* tobacco ;
  tobacconist's
table *f* table
tableau *m* painting ; picture ;
  board
  tableau de bord dashboard
tablier *m* apron

tache f stain

taie d'oreiller f pillowcase

taille f size (of clothes) ; waist
taille unique one size
grande taille outsize
(clothes)

tailleur m tailor ; suit

talc m talc

talon m heel ; stub
(counterfoil)
talon minute shoes
reheeled while you wait

tampon m tampon
tampon Jex® scouring pad

tante f aunt

taper to strike ; to type

tapis m carpet
tapis de sol groundsheet

tard late
au plus tard at the latest

tarif m price-list ; rate ; tarif

tarte f flan ; tart

tartine f slice of bread and
butter (or jam)

tartiner: *à tartiner* for
spreading

tasse f cup ; mug

taureau m bull

tauromachie f bull-fighting

taux m rate
taux de change exchange
rate
taux fixe flat rate

taxe f duty ; tax (on goods)

taxi m cab (taxi)

TCF m Touring Club de
France (AA)

teinture f dye

teinturerie f dry cleaner's

télé f TV

télébenne f gondola lift

télécabine f gondola lift

télécarte f phonecard

télécommande f remote
control

téléphérique m cable-car

téléphone m telephone
téléphone portable
mobile phone

téléphoner (à) to phone

téléphoniste m/f operator

télésiège m chair-lift

téléviseur m television (set)

télévision f television

température f temperature

tempête f storm

temple m temple ;
synagogue ;
protestant church

temps m weather ; time

tendon m tendon

tenir to hold ; to keep

tennis m tennis

tension f voltage ; blood
pressure

tente f tent

tenue f clothes ; dress
tenue de soirée evening
dress

terrain m ground ; land ;
pitch ; course

terrasse f terrace

terre f land ; earth ; ground
  terre cuite terracotta

tête f head

tétine f dummy *(for baby)* ;
  teat *(for bottle)*

TGV m high-speed train

thé m tea
  thé au lait tea with milk
  thé nature black tea

théâtre m theatre

théière f teapot

thermomètre m
  thermometer

ticket m ticket *(bus, cinema, museum)*
  ticket de caisse receipt

tiède lukewarm

tiers m third ; third party

timbre m stamp

tirage m printing ; print
  (photo)
  tirage le mercredi lottery
  draw on Wednesdays

tire-bouchon m corkscrew

tire-fesses m ski tow

tirer to pull
  tirez pull

tiroir m drawer

tisane f herbal tea

tissu m material ; fabric

titre m title
  à titre indicatif for info
  only
  à titre provisoire
  provisionally

titulaire m/f holder of

toile f canvas ; web *(spider)*

Toile World Wide Web

toilettes fpl toilet ; powder
  room

toit m roof
  toit ouvrant sunroof

tomate f tomato

tomber to fall

tonalité f dialling tone

tongs fpl flip flops

tonneau m barrel
  (wine/beer)

tonnerre m thunder

torchon m tea towel

tordre to twist

tôt early

total m total *(amount)*

toucher to touch

toujours always ; still ;
  forever

tour f tower

tour m trip ; walk ; ride

tourisme m sightseeing

touriste m/f tourist

touristique tourist *(route, resort, etc)*

tourner to turn

tournesol m sunflower

tournevis m screwdriver
  tournevis cruciforme
  phillips screwdriver

tourte f pie

tous all *(plural)*
  tous les jours daily

Toussaint f All Saints' Day

tousser to cough

tout(e) all ; everything
tout à l'heure in a while
tout compris all inclusive
tout de suite straight away
tout droit straight ahead
tout le monde everyone
toutes all (plural)
toutes directions all routes
toux f cough
tradition f custom (tradition)
traditionnel(-elle) traditional
traduction f translation
traduire to translate
train m train
trajet m journey
tramway m tram
tranchant sharp (razor, knife)
tranche f slice
tranquille quiet (place)
transférer to transfer
transpirer to sweat
travail m work
travailler to work (person)
travailler à son compte to be self employed
travaux mpl road works ; alterations
travers: *à travers* through
traversée f crossing (voyage)
traverser to cross (road, sea)
tremplin m diving-board
tremplin de ski ski jump
très very ; much
triangle de présignalisation m warning triangle

tricot m knitting ; sweater
tricoter to knit
trimestre m term
triste sad
trop too ; too much
trottoir m pavement ; sidewalk
trou m hole
trousse f pencil case
trousse de premiers secours first aid kit
trouver to find
se trouver to be (situated)
tuer kill
tunnel m tunnel
tuyau m pipe (for water, gas)
tuyau d'arrosage hosepipe
TVA f VAT
typique typical

U

UE f EU
ulcère m ulcer
ultérieur(e) later (date, etc)
un(e) one ; a ; an
l'un ou l'autre either one
uni(e) plain (not patterned)
Union européenne f European Union
université f university
urgence f urgency ; emergency
Urgences A & E
urine f urine
usage m use

245

usine f factory
utile useful
utiliser to use

V

vacances fpl holiday(s)
  en vacances on holiday
  grandes vacances summer
  holiday
vaccin m vaccination
vache f cow
vagin m vagina
vague f wave (on sea)
vaisselle f crockery
valable valid (ticket, licence, etc)
valeur f value
valider to validate
valise f suitcase
vallée f valley
valoir to be worth
  ça vaut... it's worth...
vanille f vanilla
vapeur f steam
varicelle f chickenpox
varié(e) varied ; various
vase m vase
veau m calf ; veal
vedette f speedboat ; star (film)
végétal(e) vegetable
végétarien(ne) vegetarian
véhicule m vehicle
  véhicules lents slow-
  moving vehicles

veille f the day before ; eve
  veille de Noël Christmas
  Eve
veine f vein
vélo m bike
  vélo tout terrain (VTT)
  mountain bike
velours m velvet
venaison f venison
vendange(s) fpl harvest
  (of grapes)
vendeur(-euse) m/f sales
  assistant
vendre to sell
  à vendre for sale
vendredi m Friday
  vendredi saint Good
  Friday
vénéneux poisonous
venir to come
vent m wind
vente f sale
  vente aux enchères
  auction
ventilateur m ventilator ; fan
verglas m black ice
vérifier to check ; to audit
vernis m varnish
  vernis à ongles nail varnish
verre m glass
  verres de contact contact
  lenses
verrouillage central m
  central locking
vers toward(s) ; about
versement m payment ;
  instalment

verser to pour ; to pay

vert(e) green

veste f jacket

vestiaire m cloakroom

vêtements mpl clothes

vétérinaire m/f vet

veuf m widower

veuillez... please...

veuve f widow

via by (via)

viande f meat
viande hachée mince (meat)

vidange f oil change (car)

vide empty

videoclub m video shop

vie f life

vieux (vieille) old

vigile m security guard

vigne f vine ; vineyard

vignoble m vineyard

VIH m HIV

village m village

ville f town ; city

vin m wine
vin en pichet house wine
vin pétillant sparkling wine

vinaigre m vinegar

violer to rape

violet(-ette) purple

vipère f adder ; viper

virage m bend ; curve ; corner

vis f screw
vis platinées points (in car)

visage m face

visite f visit ; consultation (of doctor)
visite guidée guided tour

visiter to visit (a place)

visiteur(-euse) m/f visitor

visser to screw on

vite quickly ; fast

vitesse f gear (of car) ; speed
vitesse limitée à... speed limit...

vitrail m stained-glass window

vitrine f shop window

vivre to live

VO: *en VO* with subtitles (film)

vœu m wish

voici here is/are

voie f lane (of road) ; line ; track

voilà there is/are

voile f sail ; sailing

voilier m sailing boat

voir to see

voisin(e) m/f neighbour

voiture f car ; coach (of train)

vol m flight ; theft
vol intérieur domestic flight

volaille f poultry

volant m steering wheel

voler to fly (bird) ; to steal

volet m shutter (on window)

voleur(-euse) m/f thief

W

volonté *f* will
  à *volonté* as much as you like
vomir to vomit
v.o.s.t. original version with subtitles *(film)*
vouloir to want
voyage *m* journey
  voyage d'affaires business trip
  voyage organisé package holiday
voyager to travel
voyageur(-euse) *m/f* traveller
vrai(e) real ; true
VTT *m* mountain bike
vue *f* view ; sight

W

w-c *mpl* toilet
wagon *m* carriage ; waggon
wagon-couchettes *m* sleeping car
wagon-restaurant *m* dining car
web *m* internet

X

xérès *m* sherry

Y

yacht *m* yacht
yaourt *m* yoghurt
  yaourt nature plain yoghurt
yeux *mpl* eyes
youyou *m* dinghy

Z

zéro *m* zero
zona *m* shingles *(illness)*
zone *f* zone
  zone piétonne pedestrian area
zoo *m* zoo

GRAMMAR

NOUNS

Unlike English, French nouns have a gender: they are either masculine (**le**) or feminine (**la**). Therefore words for **the** and **a(n)** must agree with the noun they accompany – whether *masculine*, *feminine* or *plural*:

	masc.	*fem.*	*plural*
the	le chat	la rue	les chats, les rues
a, an	un chat	une rue	des chats, des rues

If the noun begins with a vowel (**a, e, i, o** or **u**) or an unsounded **h**, le and la shorten to l', i.e. **l'avion** (*m*), **l'école** (*f*), **l'hôtel** (*m*).

NOTE: le and les used after the prepositions à (**to, at**) and de (**any, some, of**) contract as follows:

à	+ **le**	= au (au cinéma but à <u>la</u> gare)
à	+ **les**	= aux (aux magasins – applies to both (*m*) and (*f*))
de	+ **le**	= du (du pain but de <u>la</u> confiture)
de	+ **les**	= des (<u>des</u> pommes – applies to both (*m*) and (*f*))

There are some broad rules as to noun endings which indicate whether they are *masculine* or *feminine*:

Generally *masculine* endings: -er, -ier, -eau, -t, -c, -ail, -oir, -é, -on, -acle, -ège, -ème, -o, -ou.

Generally *feminine* endings: -euse, -trice, -ère, -ière, -elle, -te, -tte, -de, -che, -age, -aille, -oire, -ée, -té, -tié, -onne, -aison, -ion, -esse, -ie, -ine, -une, -ure, -ance, -anse, -ence, -ense.

PLURALS

The general rule is to add an **s** to the singular:

> le chat → les chats

Exceptions occur with the following noun endings: **-eau, -eu, -al**

> le bat<u>eau</u> → les bat<u>eaux</u>
> le nev<u>eu</u> → les nev<u>eux</u>
> le chev<u>al</u> → les chev<u>aux</u>

Nouns ending in **s**, **x**, or **z** do not change in the plural.

> le dos → les dos
> le prix → les prix
> le nez → les nez

ADJECTIVES

Adjectives normally follow the noun they describe in French,

e.g.   **la pomme verte** (**the green apple**)

Some common exceptions which go infront of the noun are:

**beau beautiful, bon good, grand big, haut high, jeune
young, long long, joli pretty, mauvais bad, nouveau new,
petit small, vieux old,**

e.g.   **un bon livre** (**a good book**)

French adjectives have to reflect the gender of the noun they
describe. To make an adjective feminine, an **e** is added to the
masculine form (where this does not already end in an **e**,
i.e. **jeune**). A final consonant, which is usually silent in the
masculine form, is pronounced in the *feminine*:

masc. le livre vert	*fem.* la pomme verte
luh leevr vehr	la pom vehrt
(**the green book**)	(**the green apple**)

To make an adjective plural, an **s** is added to the singular form:
masculine plural – **verts** (remember – the ending is still silent:
vehr) or feminine plural – **vertes** (because of the **e**, the **t** ending
is sounded: *vehrt*).

MY, YOUR, HIS, HER

These words also depend on the gender and number of the
noun they accompany and not on the sex of the 'owner'.

	with masc. sing. noun	with fem. sing. noun	with plural nouns
my	mon	ma	mes
your (familiar, singular)	ton	ta	tes
his/her	son	sa	ses
our	notre	notre	nos
your (polite, plural)	votre	votre	vos
their	leur	leur	leurs

e.g. la clé (**key**)   sa clé (**his/her key**)

le passeport (**passport**) son passeport (**his/her passport**)

les billets (**tickets**)   ses billets (**his/her tickets**)

PRONOUNS

subject		object	
I	je, j'	me	me
you *(familiar)*	tu	you	te
you *(polite, plural)*	vous	you	vous
he/it	il	him/it	le, l'
she/it	elle	her/it	la, l'
we	nous	us	nous
they *(masc.)*	ils	them	les
they *(fem.)*	elles	them	les

In French there are two forms of **you** – tu and vous Tu is the familiar form which is used with people you know well (friends and family). **Vous**, as well as being the plural form for **you**, is also the polite form of addressing someone. You should take care to use this form until the other person invites you to use the more familiar **tu**

Object pronouns are placed before the verb,

e.g.   **il vous aime (he loves you)**

         nous la connaissons (we know her)

However, in commands or requests, object pronouns follow the verb,

e.g.   **écoutez-le (listen to him)**

         aidez-moi (help me)

NOTE: this does not apply to negative commands or requests,

e.g.   **ne le faites pas (don't do it)**

The object pronouns shown above are also used to mean **to me**, **to us**, etc. except:

         le and **la** become **lui (to him, to her)**

         les becomes **leur (to them)**,

e.g.   **il le lui donne (he gives it to** him)

VERBS

There are three main patterns of endings for verbs in French –
those ending -er, -ir and -re in the dictionary.

DONNER

je donne	I give
tu donnes	you give
il/elle donne	he/she gives
nous donnons	we give
vous donnez	you give
ils/elles donnent	they give

TO GIVE

FINIR

je finis	I finish
tu finis	you finish
il/elle finit	he/she finishes
nous finissons	we finish
vous finissez	you finish
ils/elles finissent	they finish

TO FINISH

RÉPONDRE

je réponds	I reply
tu réponds	you reply
il/elle répond	he/she replies
nous répondons	we reply
vous répondez	you reply
ils/elles répondent	they reply

TO REPLY

IRREGULAR VERBS

Among the most important irregular verbs are the following:

ÊTRE	TO BE
je suis	I am
tu es	you are
il/elle est	he/she is
nous sommes	we are
vous êtes	you are
ils/elles sont	they are

AVOIR	TO HAVE
j'ai	I have
tu as	you have
il/elle a	he/she has
nous avons	we have
vous avez	you have
ils/elles ont	they have

ALLER	TO GO
je vais	I go
tu vas	you go
il/elle va	he/she goes
nous allons	we go
vous allez	you go
ils/elles vont	they go

POUVOIR	TO BE ABLE
je peux	I can
tu peux	you can
il/elle peut	he/she can
nous pouvons	we can
vous pouvez	you can
ils/elles peuvent	they can

GRAMMAR

To form the simple past tense, **I gave/I have given**, **I finished/ I have finished**, combine the present tense of the verb **avoir – to have** with the past participle of the verb (**donné**, **fini**, **répondu**),

e.g.

j'ai donné	**I gave/I have given**
j'ai fini	**I finished/I have finished**
j'ai répondu	**I replied/I have replied**

Not all verbs take **avoir** (**j'ai...**, **il a...**) as their auxiliary verb; some verbs take **être** (**je suis...**, **il est...**). These are intransitive verbs (which have no object),

e.g.

je suis allé	**I went**
je suis né	**I was born**

When the auxiliary verb **être** is used, the past participle (**allé**, **né**, etc.) becomes adjectival and agrees with the subject of the verb,

e.g.

nous sommes allés	**we went** (plural)
je suis née	**I was born** (female)